In his phenomenal best-seller, **The Battle for the Mind**, Tim LaHaye awakened America to the stranglehold of secular humanism upon our culture. Then, in **The Battle for the Family**, he identified humanism's threat to the home. Now, in the third book of this series, Dr. LaHaye provides the most shocking and significant exposé of all. **The Battle for the Public Schools** reveals how our system of "free" education actually costs you what you value most—the mind and faith of your children. The facts may alarm you — until you discover what you can do to counteract humanism's tyranny in your local school system. If you're a parent, a pastor, an educator, or a concerned taxpayer, this book will show you how to win **The Battle for the Public Schools**.

The Battle for the Public Schools

Tim LaHaye

FLEMING H. REVELL COMPANY
OLD TAPPAN, NEW JERSEY

Scripture quotations are from the King James Version of the Bible.

"How I Slid Into Education's Permissive Pit and Climbed Out Again," by Bill Freeman, copyright 1981, Christianity Today. Used by permission.

Quotations and charts from THE LITERACY HOAX by Paul Copperman. Copyright © 1978 by, Paul Copperman. By permission of William Morrow & Company.

"Field Trip Gives 6th–7th Graders Facts on Death" from *Longview* (Tex.) *Morning Journal.*

"An Interview With Marva Collins," conducted by Allan Brownfeld and Solveig Eggerz, reprinted by permission of Human Events, Inc., copyright 1981.

"Result of Sex Education Programs" © FAMILY REVIEW; 1981; Vol. #2. Publisher: American Life Lobby.

Quotations from DAN SMOOT REPORT used by permission of Dan Smoot, Route One, Box 765, Big Sandy, Texas 75755.

"Death Education—Emotional Manipulation" used by permission of Dr. Murray Norris, J.D., Ph.D. Valley Christian University.

Quotations from IS PUBLIC EDUCATION NECESSARY, by Samuel L. Blumenfeld used by permission of the Devin Adair Company, Old Greenwich Ct. Copyright © 1981 by Samuel Blumenfeld.

Quotations from "The Grave National Decline in Education," and "Sex Study," by Gary Allen, from *American Opinion,* used by permission of *American Opinion.*

Quotations from VALUES CLARIFICATION: A HANDBOOK OF PRACTICAL STRATEGIES FOR TEACHERS AND STUDENTS, reprinted by permission of A & W Publishers, Inc. from VALUES CLARIFICATION: A HANDBOOK OF PRACTICAL STRATEGIES FOR TEACHERS AND STUDENTS New Revised Edition by Sidney B. Simon, Leland W. Howe and Howard Kirschenbaum. Copyright © 1972; Copyright © 1978. Hart Publishing Company, Inc.

Quotations from *Humanist Manifesto I & II* reprinted from Humanist Manifesto I & II, Paul Kurtz, ed. Buffalo, New York: Prometheus Books, 1973, with permission of the publisher and the author.

Library of Congress Cataloging in Publication Data

LaHaye, Tim F.
   The battle for the public schools.

   Bibliography: p.
   1. Public schools—United States.
2. Sex instruction for children.   3. Moral
education—United States.   4. Christian
education of children.   I. Title.
LA217.L33   1983   371'.01'0973   82-13257
ISBN 0-8007-1320-6
ISBN 0-8007-5091-8 (pbk.)

To the millions of concerned parents, educators, taxpayers, and fellow Americans who have watched our once-great school system deteriorate academically, morally, and socially—and don't understand why.

To the growing army within that group who realize that secular humanism, the religious doctrine of our public schools, has brought on this decline.

To the millions of children, soon to be young people, who are functionally illiterate or who, in spite of regular attendance in our "progressive" public schools, cannot read well enough to hold a job worthy of their talents.

To those courageous educators, parents, and taxpayers willing to pay the price to warn our nation that a handful of secular humanists are destroying our once-great school system and robbing millions of children of the great American dream.

To those informed parents and educators who, out of their concern, are using their sphere of influence to call their community educators back to teaching basic skills and character building based on traditional moral values, without which no young person is truly equipped to face life in the future.

Contents

Introduction

For twenty-five years I have watched secular humanism take over the most influential institutions in our nation: government, education, media, and a network of organizations. At first I contented myself with speaking out against it in my church or wherever I could get a hearing. In 1965 I founded Christian High School of San Diego, now the largest Protestant Christian high school in the country. In 1975 it became a school system, offering to 2,500 kindergarten through twelfth-grade students in ten different locations a Christian alternative to the public schools' indoctrination in atheistic humanism. In 1970 I founded Christian Heritage College, with Dr. Henry M. Morris and the current president of the institution, Dr. Arthur L. Peters, to help train elementary and secondary teachers who are not afflicted with humanistic philosophy, for the growing Christian-school movement. (We also train ministers, counselors, scientists, home-economics students, and others.) In 1972 Dr. Peters and I helped in a small way as Dr. Henry M. Morris, one of the most outstanding Christian scholars of our generation, launched the Institute for Creation Research to combat the evolution-only style of teaching and give scientific creationism a chance for consideration. Under his leadership and together with his outstanding array of Christian scholars, ICR has become the most powerful force in getting some state legislatures to require that the scientific theory of creationism be taught alongside the theory of evolution in public schools—usually against the will of our humanistically controlled school leadership.

In 1971 I founded Family Life Seminars to provide married couples with training in biblical principles for family living as a means of counteracting the harmful influence of humanistic education on their interpersonal relationships. In 1981 FLS launched a national TV program to provide this training to families in their own homes.

During those same years I wrote sixteen books on family living, interpersonal relationships, and Bible prophecy, which provided me with a readership of over 6 million people. By this time humanism had such a stranglehold on our government that it not only dominated our courts and our state and national legislatures, but even permeated the president's cabinet. That was when I felt led to write a series of books on humanism, to expose its incredible power over our citizens—far out of proportion to the number of humanists in our population. When the Gallup poll and subsequent studies clearly indicated that the vast majority of American citizens (at least 84 percent) "still believed the Ten Commandments were valid for today," I felt it was time for the silent moral majority to awaken to the fact that they were being led into Sodom and Gomorrah by a few thousand committed humanists who had worked their way into key areas of government, education, and media, forcing us to confine our traditional moral values to the church and home, while their antimoral values dominated everything else, including the schoolhouse, TV, newspapers, and government itself.

Realizing that secular humanists fully intended to use their influence to so weaken our national character that we would lose our American identity and merge with the other countries of the world in the creation of their carefully planned new world order—by the year 2000—I was compelled to do whatever I could to thwart their efforts. Remembering, "The pen is mightier than the sword," I began this series of books in an attempt to awaken and mobilize a sufficient number of citizens to this assault on our nation's destiny.

This third book in my *Battle* series is sent forth with the prayers that it will ignite in the taxpayers' hearts a fire to reclaim control of public education and that it will inspire thousands of parents to protect the minds of their children by providing them with a Christian alternative.

THE BATTLE FOR THE PUBLIC SCHOOLS

Public Education
Is in Trouble

According to the secretary of the Department of Education, this year Americans will spend $198.3 billion on 57.6 million students from kindergarten through college.[1] Most taxpayers, though frustrated by burgeoning educational costs, reluctantly concede, "Even though it's expensive, I guess the dollars needed to train the younger generation in the skills required to make it in life can be justified."

Wrong!

Secular educators no longer make learning their primary objective. Instead our public schools have become conduits to the minds of our youth, training them to be anti-God, antimoral, antifamily, anti-free enterprise and anti-American.

Some of us who have been announcing this for over twenty years are gratified that many taxpayers are finally beginning to pay attention. During those years our educators have demanded more money, more school bonds, more buildings, higher wages, and so on—but school grades have dropped to an all-time low. In August of 1981 only 34 percent of the American parents scored the public schools an A or B rating.[2]

Think of it! The second-largest industry in America, with 2.3 million classroom teachers; the largest union in the world; the second-largest budget in government (second only to the welfare department); and it is doing a second-rate job.

If parents and taxpayers were really aware of our schools' incredibly poor performance, we would experience the greatest taxpayers' revolt in the history of our country. If tax money were allocated on the basis of quality of education, many public schools would be closed down.

Public education today is a self-serving institution controlled by elitists of an atheistic, humanist viewpoint; they are more interested in indoctrinating their charges against the recognition of God, absolute moral values, and a belief in the American dream than they are in teaching them to read, write, and do arithmetic. I call these people humanist educrats.

The only good sign I see in public education today is that its intellectual poverty is being exposed so widely that the public is beginning to demand reforms of these "public servants" who would be our masters if we remain silent.

What's Wrong With Our Schools?

The American honeymoon with public education is almost over. Unless educational leaders heed the spontaneous outcries of parents and citizen groups throughout the land, we are headed for the biggest divorce in American history.

All parents expect their children to at least learn reading, writing, arithmetic, geography, and history. Our children spend over 16,000 hours in the finest educational buildings known to man, taught by the highest-paid teachers in history, under the supervision of the most educated and well-qualified administrators in the world. Thus parents cannot understand why education is getting worse instead of better.

Thomas Jefferson said, "If a nation expects to be ignorant and free, in a state of civilization, it expects what never was and never will be."[3] Every parent agrees! It only takes common sense to know you *must* agree. Yet education is not taking place, and our public-school educators refuse to face the fact that they are responsible.

I definitely am *not* saying that all teachers are inept or slothful. Thousands of well-trained and very dedicated teachers still strive valiantly to give their charges the best education they can within a deficient educational system. Others, equally dedicated, were corrupted at our teachers colleges—with liberal humanist theories of education best described as "progressive education." Such brainwashed victims of our "higher educational system"—a system controlled by secular humanist thinkers for over one hundred years—are really dangerous to the mental health of our children. In addition, many young teachers who were radical activists in the sixties and seventies realized that "Revolution now!" was not possible in America until the proper mental climate was created for the overthrow of our American system. So they carted their radical views into the public-school classrooms, where, under the guise of academic freedom, they can corrupt an entire generation of youthful minds.

Lack of money is not the problem in the public school. It has been said that we spend more on education each year in America than all the rest of the countries in the world combined!

The problem is philosophy. As I shall prove, our public schools are committed to the philosophy of atheistic humanism—the most harmful thought process in the history of mankind. Given enough time, it will destroy everything it touches—as the academic level of our schools testify. We once boasted the highest literacy level in the world. But that was before humanism took over the schoolhouse.

The Grave National Decline in Education

Gary Allen was for many years a junior-high-school teacher. Today he is contributing editor to *American Opinion* magazine and author of several best-selling books. I particularly enjoy his careful research. In a March 1979 issue of *American Opinion,* he reported:

> "American education is a sorry mess because of permissive schools, incompetent teachers, irresponsible parents and the lower learning standards brought about by integration, top experts charge. Johnny can't read, Susie can't spell, and Willie can't write because an ineffectual school system has failed them, the experts agree . . ." [*National Enquirer* 26 September 1978].
>
> The national press is full of horror stories about the schools. One poll reveals that only three percent of the nation's high-school seniors can correctly identify Alaska and Hawaii as the last two states admitted to the Union; only thirty-eight percent are aware a voter can split his ballot between the Presidential nominee of one party and lesser office-seekers of another; a miniscule four percent can name the three Presidents immediately preceding Gerald Ford; a quarter of those polled don't even realize that New Jersey is on the east coast and Oregon is on the west coast; and, fifty-six percent cannot identify the nation's most populous state.

A "citizenship test" conducted with a grant from the Scherman Foundation revealed that only sixty percent of teenagers about to become eligible to vote could name the war in which states' rights was an issue; only fifty-seven percent knew Russia fought on our side in World War II; and, only fifty-five percent knew the nationality of Josef Stalin.

In geography, ninety-three percent did manage to identify the capital of their own state. But only twenty-three percent had any idea of the distance between New York and San Francisco and a bare twenty-eight percent came anywhere near guessing the population of the United States. Forty-one percent of these high-school worthies did not know that Red China is the world's most populous nation, and sixty-one percent did not know that Mexico has more people than Canada.

The results on foreign-policy questions shocked even us. Just forty percent could identify the North Atlantic Treaty Organization; only eighteen percent had any notion of what "détente" means; and, a scant fifteen percent were able to identify Ottawa as the capital of Canada. Eighty-seven percent did identify Adolph Hitler with Germany, but only fifty-three percent matched Golda Meir with Israel while only twenty percent associated Josíp Broz Tito with Yugoslavia.

The National Assessment of Educational Progress tested seventeen-year-olds on their knowledge of our government. Barely half knew that each state has two U.S. Senators and that the number of Representatives is based on population. Half thought that the President can appoint people to Congress; less than half knew the Senate must confirm Supreme Court appointments; and, a third of those high-school seniors said they did not believe that newspapers or magazines should be allowed to publish articles critical of government officials. So much for the First Amendment.[4]

It is no wonder quality teachers are leaving the public schools embittered, disillusioned, and depressed. As one former teacher, now an executive secretary, told me, "The very thought of signing my teaching contract made me think I was signing on the *Titanic.*" Our schools are no longer educational institutions, but experimental laboratories whose frequently changing policies have produced educational chaos.

Those Pesky SAT Scores

Nothing has angered the taxpayers like the declining Scholastic Aptitude Test scores. The nation was shocked in 1976 to find that

SATs, used for years to determine the success or failure of our public schools, were consistently declining at an alarming rate. Verbal skills had dropped thirty points in nine years!

The following chart, based on the National Assessment of Educational Progress Report, tells the sad tale of a fifty-one point decline in twenty years.

Some educators are beginning to hear the clamor of parents and taxpayers. According to Michael Kirst, formerly the head of the California State Board of Education, " 'Schools realize that the public is demanding a cutback in flaky electives and a return to more rigorous, challenging academic courses.' "[5]

The present condition of education in America (except in those few schools and districts where administrators have refused to adopt the humanistically inspired fads that have proved so disastrous to the learning level) is much worse than the SAT scores indicate. One courageous educator, Dr. Paul Copperman, a Phi Beta Kappa graduate of Berkeley, wrote a best-selling book in 1978 that hit public education like a bombshell. I recommend *The Literacy Hoax* to anyone interested in knowing what is really going on in our so-called public schools. Copperman is no stranger to education. He has not only taught in the public sector, but in recent years has run private reading schools for the benefit of the victims of public miseducation.

In 1974 Copperman became so burdened over the inadequate skills of public-school students who came to his institutes that he began a special research project on reading achievement since 1960. He discovered before the 1976 SAT scores hit the press that education had declined significantly after the mid-1960s. His studies were confirmed by an unpublished Harcourt report that verified a sharp ten-year decline in basic academic skills.

To our dismay, this reading decline comes at a time when reading readiness skills of preschool children have reached an all-time high. Many children know their ABCs before they arrive at kindergarten, and not a few are already readers. No wonder an increasing number of parents believe it is better to teach their children at home or send them to private schools than to let them learn bad habits in our public schools.

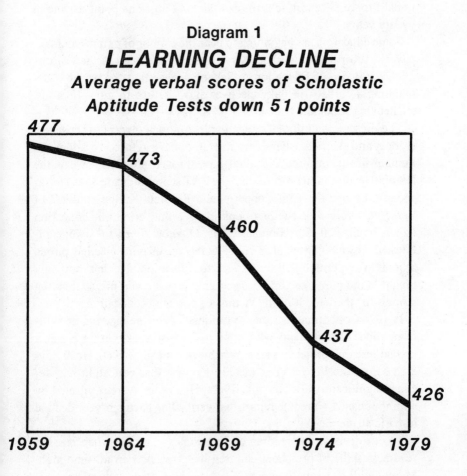

Diagram 1
LEARNING DECLINE
Average verbal scores of Scholastic
Aptitude Tests down 51 points

When Eighth Grade Equals Twelfth Grade

My father only had an eighth-grade education, yet I always remembered him as a very intelligent man. He was extremely well-informed and articulate; above all, he was an avid reader. Dr. Copperman's research provides some interesting insight into this disparity.

He discovered that educators from 1850 to the early 1900s established the goal of providing a maximum number of students with an eighth-grade education. By 1950, "The goal of America's educational system became the high school graduation of as high a percentage of the population as possible."[6] Careful studies indicated very little difference in academic achievement scores in 1950 over those of 1850—and the 1980 scores registered 51 points below the 1964 level. Could it be that today's twelfth-grade graduates have the same skills as the past generation's eighth graders?

As incredible as that possibility may seem, reading ability, according to SAT scores, tends to confirm it. Evidence for that came to light when investigation revealed that the SAT tests had been altered, making them eight to twelve points easier than those taken before 1963. This prompted Copperman to comment:

> Thus, the real drop in verbal aptitude between 1963 and 1977 was not 49 points, it was approximately 59 points, and the real drop in math aptitude was not the indicated 32 points, but 42 points. The 59-point drop in verbal aptitude means that 75 percent of the high-school seniors taking the test in 1977 scored below the average recorded in 1963.[7]

In addition, the number of students scoring above 600 (generally considered an indication of academic excellence) declined 48 percent during the same period.[8] Obviously our present educational system is not harmful only to average students, but retards the learning of many superior students.

Before Christian Heritage College was five years old (in 1975), we detected that, comparing public-school and Christian-school graduates, more public-school graduates had to take remedial English. In talking to registrars and deans of other Christian colleges, I found that to be generally true. When, during a TV documentary on education, I heard the dean of Stanford University say, "Over fifty percent of our incoming freshmen have to take remedial English—and we only matriculate the upper twelve percent of the nation's high-school seniors," I realized the severity of the problem.

Now Johnny Can't Count

In a recent *U.S. News & World Report* article entitled "Johnny Can't Count—The Dangers for U.S.," we were appraised of the serious "math gap" that is growing in today's schools.

"The Science Race," a new study by SRI International, finds American high schoolers far behind their Soviet counterparts as the result of a "carefully articulated" strategy initiated in Russia more than a decade ago.

All Soviet students study algebra, for example, compared with only half of American students. Calculus is taken by all Russian high-school students, but by only 3 percent of students in U.S. schools. Seven states require no high-school math at all. . . .

"Technological illiteracy" poses a major threat to American economic security and national defense. Fears are growing that too few mathematically adept graduates are coming out of schools to develop technologies that hold the key to national well being. . . .[9]

The sharp decline of math scores reflected in the following chart has been confirmed by the National Assessment of Educational Progress in its latest survey of math skills, indicating that students are having a difficult time applying the theories of the classroom to the everyday numerical problems of life.

One test question: Mr. Baker has between $8,000 and $8,500 in his savings account. He wants to buy a car that costs between $5,300 and $5,400. After he buys the car how much money will he have left? Only 27 percent of high-school seniors gave the correct answer: Between $2,600 and $3,200.[10]

If classroom teachers and school administrators had been held accountable for reasonable student progress per grade level, this "math gap" would never have happened. Instead, the very notion of teachers' accountability for learning makes one vulnerable to attack or ridicule

Skidding Scores[11]
Average Math Scores on SAT's

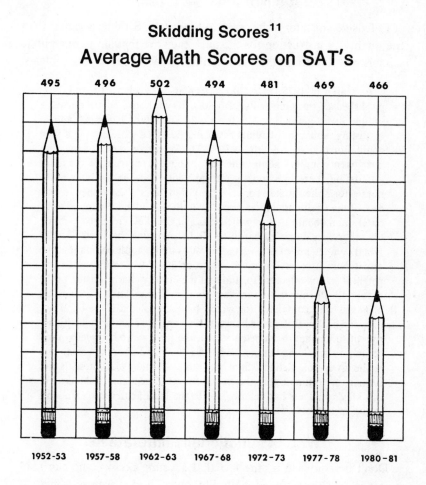

| 495 | 496 | 502 | 494 | 481 | 469 | 466 |

| 1952-53 | 1957-58 | 1962-63 | 1967-68 | 1972-73 | 1977-78 | 1980-81 |

from the NEA, AFT, and many professional educrats. As long as they remain in their ivory-tower dream world of no accountability, scores will continue to plummet, unless they tamper with the tests.

It's Not Just SAT Tests

Defensive educators who want to blame the SAT tests rather than the quality of instruction for the mess they are making in our public schools will find that other tests confirm some of the same problems.

In March of 1975 the Adult Performance Level (APL) study was published at the University of Texas. Its authors had conducted a unique investigation into the functional literacy of American adults, by testing thousands of adults with tasks designed to determine if they could function in modern society. The researchers discovered that over twenty million adult Americans, about 20 percent of the adult population, were functionally incompetent. These individuals could not perform the simplest societally required tasks. . . . Another 34 percent of the adult population, about 39 million adults, were found to be barely functional in these basic skills. . . . One key fact uncovered by the report was discussed hardly at all. In analyzing the levels of functional competence of different age groups in the adult population, the researchers discovered that the age group 30–39 was much more competent than any other group, and that the literacy characteristics of the groups 18–29 and 40–49 were very similar. This means that the group of adults who completed (or would have completed if they had not dropped out) twelfth grade between 1964 and 1975 had a much higher rate of functional incompetency than the group who completed their secondary schooling between 1954 and 1963, and about the same rate as the group completing school between 1944 and 1953. These figures support my estimate that the average level of academic achievement of today's students has deteriorated to the level achieved by students in the early 1950's.[12]

Who Is Functionally Illiterate?

Don't be confused by the fact that a young person who can read words is considered functionally illiterate. The look-and-say method of reading instruction that is so popular with humanistic educators and greedy book publishers (it takes more textbooks to teach look-and-say than phonics) but is distrusted by parents (see chapter 3) is really the problem. Look-and-say may teach a child to recognize words—but whether he can link them together with others and make sense out of a sentence is another matter.

A literacy test really measures understanding. For example, here is one question given to students: "If a doctor's prescription advises that you take one capsule every twelve hours, how many capsules should you take a day?" Twenty-five percent did not know! That is functional illiteracy. Another test revealed that a large number of students "would rather earn $155 a week than $4 an hour."

Textbooks Tell the Story

More informative than the deterioration in Scholastic Aptitude Test scores is the alarming decline in the reading level of our student's textbooks. According to Dr. Copperman:

> Over the past ten years, most of the major textbook publishers have instituted a conscious policy of rewriting their textbooks in order to reduce their readability to a level two years below the grade for which they are intended. Thus, eleventh-grade American government texts are being rewritten to a tenth-grade level. This movement to reduce the readability levels of textbooks is widely known and accepted among secondary-school teachers and administrators, yet most parents have not been informed of it.[13]

You may wonder why textbook publishers are lowering the reading level of their material. Quite simply, if a student can't read a textbook, the schools won't buy it, and the companies are in business to make money. They know that to sell books, they must lower the grade level of their texts at least two years and, in some instances, even more.

There is little question that for the most part, many of our schools are doing a poor job of teaching our children to read. When I told that to a local educator, he responded, "But we are teaching more students than ever before." "Yes," I replied, "you are doing a bad job of teaching more students at a higher cost." Something is drastically wrong at the schoolhouse!

The Great Literacy Hoax

Are you ready for this? Poor reading, writing, and math scores are only part of the problem. The unpublicized story of the decade is the educators' cover-up of their academic failure to teach Johnny and Jane to learn.

As a result of Sputnik being launched ahead of our NASA project, educators cried, "Give us more money, and we will catch up with the Russians in education and technology." We have shoveled billions of dollars into their coffers, but are further behind educationally than we were in 1957. But why weren't parents suspicious until the 1976 SAT scores came out? Because Johnny and Jane's grades were going *up* during that period, while their actual learning ability was going down.

The following graph, based on the College Entrance Examination Board Annual Reports for 1972–1977, tells it like it is.[14]

Unsuspecting parents think Johnny is doing well in school; after all, he's getting A's and Bs. They fail to realize that his grades may be rising, but his knowledge is declining. Educators have a name for it: *grade inflation.*

Newsweek carried a pathetic story of a Washington, D.C., valedictorian, from Western High School, who was refused admission to George Washington University. Because of his excellent grades, he understandably considered himself a superior student, but he faced academic rejection because he only scored 280 on the math and 320 on the verbal SAT scores. In other words, the honor student tested out on the bottom 2 percent of high-school seniors in math and the lowest 13 percent in verbal competence.[15]

Whom do you blame, the boy or his parents? They trusted the educators who deliberately deceived him. According to the dean of admissions at George Washington University, "My feeling is that a kid like this has been conned.... He's been deluded into thinking he's gotten an education."[16]

Copperman believes grade inflation can be attributed to the younger faculty "with their more liberal educational philosophy." Many of them think it is more important to "feel good" or "have a good time in school" than to learn something. When teachers alone set grading levels, the stringent teachers become "unpopular ogres" and may cave in to the pressure. Thus grades become artificially inflated. As Dr. Copperman states, "Grade inflation is teaching America's young people that good work and hard work are almost pointless. Throughout their secondary schooling they are learning that there is only a very

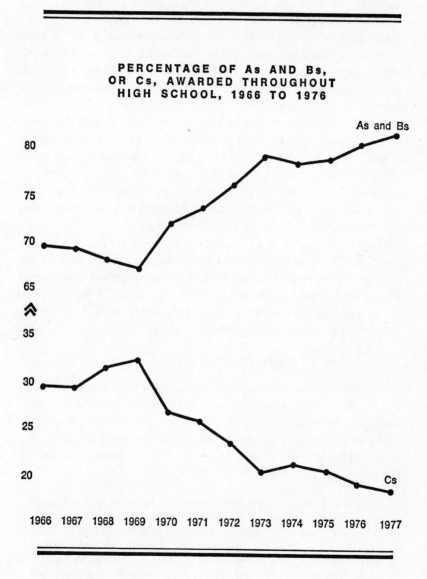

PERCENTAGE OF As AND Bs,
OR Cs, AWARDED THROUGHOUT
HIGH SCHOOL, 1966 TO 1976

tenuous relationship between effort and reward. This is a very danger-ous lesson to teach and bodes ill for the future of our country."[17]

Recent surveys show that while grades have gone up, course re-quirements in both high school and college are going down, in some cases as much as 23 percent. Can you believe it? At tax-supported col-leges, students are getting credit for horseback riding, witchcraft, monster literature, or contemporary trends—that is, anything that the students want to study.

No wonder taxpayers and parents are becoming both disillusioned with our public schools and increasingly vocal about their discontent!

Many conscientious educators are equally concerned. A survey of college professors revealed that 94 percent of the nation's college and university professors view grade inflation as "a significant if not seri-ous problem of academic standards," and two-thirds admit to granting higher grades than student work had warranted.[18]

Diagram 2 is based on a 1975 study of grade inflation by the Univer-sity of California at Berkeley. It was confirmed later by a 1976 Carne-gie Foundation report that shows the trend has worsened. The number of As and Bs awarded students between 1969 and 1976 had increased 20 percent (from 54 percent to 74 percent). Either students are getting smarter, or grading is getting easier.

Teachers Who Can't Teach

One fundamental of teaching is central to the problem: "You cannot impart what you do not possess." A nonmusician will never teach someone to play the piano. Nor will an English teacher who does not know and use good grammar be able to produce good writers.

Unfortunately, many modern schoolteachers are unqualified for their jobs. Dr. Paul Copperman states:

How many of our public-school teachers are adequately discharging their responsibilities . . . ? My personal estimate is about half. My judgment is that from 5 to 10 percent of our public-school teachers are superb, another 15 to 20 percent are good, 25 percent are adequate but should be better, 30 to 40 percent are inadequate but trainable, and 10 to 20 percent are so bad they should not be teaching under any cir-cumstances. . . . My estimates are based on personal observation of the public schools, and conversations with numerous parents and school

Diagram 2[19]

GRADE-POINT AVERAGES UP

	2.8	2.7	2.6	2.5	2.4	2.3
1975						
1970						
1965						
1960						

officials during my eight years as the director of my private reading school in California. These estimates have been reinforced in conversations with a number of extremely competent and experienced educators, who consult widely in public schools around the country, and who are directly involved in university programs of teacher training.[20]

I have been associated closely with educators for over seventeen years and have come to the conclusion that the teaching field is like the ministry or any other profession—you can make it what you wish. An industrious worker will give it his best and become a laborer worthy of his hire. A goof-off will find public education an ideal place to loaf and get paid for it. The real losers, however, are the children, their parents, the taxpayer—and ultimately America herself.

A Gallup poll has found that teacher laziness and lack of interest are the most frequent accusations of half the nation's parents, who complain that students get "less schoolwork" now than 20 years ago. Whether the parent perceptions are fair or not, there is no doubt that circumstances have certainly changed some teacher attitudes. At a Miami senior high school this spring, one social studies teacher asked his pupils whether their homework was completed. Half the students said no. The teacher recorded their answers in his gradebook but never bothered to collect the papers. Says the teacher, who has been in the profession for 15 years and has now become dispirited: "I'm not willing any more to take home 150 notebooks and grade them. I work from 7:30 A.M. to 2 P.M., and that's what I get paid for." A longtime teacher in a large suburban school outside Boston told TIME it is common knowledge that some of her colleagues, anxious to preserve their jobs as enrollments dwindle, fail children simply to ensure hefty class size the next year.[21]

Educators are not only extremely sensitive to criticism from without, but most refuse to police their own profession. They seem to be saying, "We are experts! Just pay your taxes, send us your children, and trust us—everything will work out okay." But it *isn't* working out, and the public is getting tired of paying the salaries of educators who autocratically refuse to improve a very sick school system. In fact, many parents fear that the doctors in charge are the cause of the patient's sickness.

In the fall of 1979 it was announced in Dallas: "535 first-year teachers in the Dallas school system took a test of basic academic skills, and officials were shocked to discover that one out of three did worse than the average high school junior in both mathematics and English."[22] In Louisiana only 53 percent of those applying for teaching jobs passed competency tests in 1978, and 63 percent in 1979. When asked about teacher applicants who failed, the director of certification for the state of Louisiana, Jacqueline Lewis, replied, "Obviously they're moving out of state to teach in states where the tests are not required."[23]

The Pinellas County school board of Saint Petersburg and Clearwater, Florida, instituted a policy in 1976 that "required teacher candidates to read at an advanced tenth-grade level and solve math problems at an eighth-grade level. Though all had their B.A. in hand, about one-third of the applicants (25% of the whites, 79% of the blacks) flunked Pinellas' test the first time they took it in 1979."[24]

The "no pass, no fail" theories of our educrats, so popular a few years ago, are culminating in teachers who hold bachelor's and master's degrees, yet can't teach.

The sad part of all this is that the people who have caused the problem—the humanist educrats (the elite heads of many teachers colleges, administrators, and many superintendents and principals who are determined to jam atheistic, amoral humanism, with its socialist world view, into the minds of our nation's children and youth, kindergarten through college)—are the only ones who can change it. Unfortunately, they like the status quo and aren't about to create positive changes—unless forced to by taxpayers and parents. Only when a sufficient number of citizens decide to elect school-board members committed to traditional moral values and a high degree of literacy and learning, will the situation be modified. After all, they are the ones who hire the superintendents who, in turn, hire school principals. These high-salaried administrators could revolutionize our schools, if they wanted to and were held accountable for doing so.

Actually, public schools could be transformed in three to five years if school boards would institute standard reading and learning tests, to be administered at the end of each year. By making it clear to the superintendent of the district and each principal in the system that their employment the following year was contingent upon an improvement in SAT scores, these administrators would see to it that schools became serious about educating our nation's children. First they would have to

Who Controls Our Public Schools?

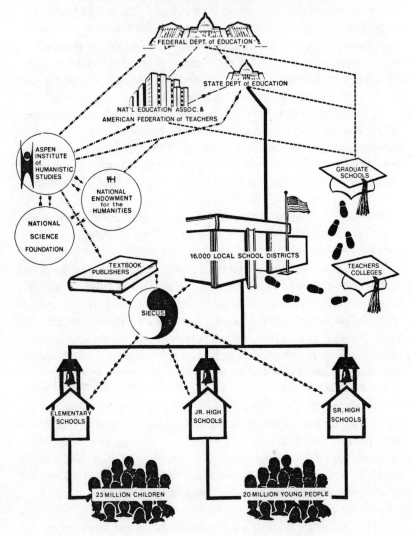

FEDERAL DEPT. of EDUCATION

STATE DEPT. of EDUCATION

NAT'L EDUCATION ASSOC. &
AMERICAN FEDERATION of TEACHERS

ASPEN
INSTITUTE
of
HUMANISTIC
STUDIES

NATIONAL
ENDOWMENT
for the
HUMANITIES

NATIONAL
SCIENCE
FOUNDATION

GRADUATE
SCHOOLS

TEXTBOOK
PUBLISHERS

16,000 LOCAL SCHOOL DISTRICTS

TEACHERS
COLLEGES

SIECUS

ELEMENTARY
SCHOOLS

JR. HIGH
SCHOOLS

SR. HIGH
SCHOOLS

23 MILLION CHILDREN

20 MILLION YOUNG PEOPLE

make it clear to all classroom teachers that their employment next year was dependent on their pupils' learning improvement at the conclusion of the current year.

And that puts the finger on the core of the problem in our public schools. They simply are not accountable to parents and taxpayers anymore. All across the land, humanistic educators and liberal politicians, using the school board for a stepping-stone to higher office, sit on school boards, letting educators set their own budgets, teaching policies, and philosophy. We need to return to a sane educational policy in this country, demanding that the public schools become a viable reflection of the community that pays their bills and supplies the children. As autocratic and bureaucratic control of our schools by atheistic humanism has increased education and learning have decreased. That is always the case with humanism! Given enough time, it destroys everything it touches. The shambles of our schools is just one example.

The Gallup Poll of 1979 indicated that 84 percent of the American people believe the Ten Commandments are still valid today, and an astounding 94 percent believe in God. Apparently a high percentage of the 6 percent who disbelieve in God are educating our children, kindergarten through college. That is the principal reason why we are losing the battle for the minds of our children.

Humanists demand freedom—freedom to do their own thing with the minds of the young. Years ago they realized that the key to humanizing America was to infiltrate the educational system, kick out Christianity and traditional moral values, and bring in humanism's amoral values. Who can deny they have succeeded? But as we have demonstrated they have done a very bad job of educating in the process.

And this is only the tip of the iceberg. If all of this makes you angry, just wait until you find out *why* Johnny still can't read.

Why Johnny *Still* Can't Read

Our schools just are not doing an effective job of teaching our children to read—and that has become a national and educational disgrace! At the urging of John Dewey and his disciples humanist educrats have adopted an ineffective theory of reading instruction that has set our educational system back twenty-five years. Not properly tested before its use, the system was nothing more than an idealistic theory, and it has retarded the educational development of millions of citizens.

Even more tragic than its propagation is the refusal of educrats to admit their failure and return to phonics, the best reading system ever designed. Eighty-five percent of our public elementary schools still use the look-and-say, or picture, method of teaching reading, which cheats millions of our children out of one of their "inalienable rights." For in this technologically advanced day, it is next to impossible to enjoy "the good life" if one is not a good reader.

Twenty-five years ago Dr. Rudolf Flesch, a reading expert, wrote a book that shocked the educational community and brought welcome relief to thousands of nonreaders. It was entitled *Why Johnny Can't Read,* subtitled *And What You Can Do About It.* With devastating clarity, Dr. Flesch proved how inferior look-and-say was to the time-honored phonics method of learning to read.

Instead of honoring him for his contribution to the education of our schoolchildren, educrats viciously attacked him. They labeled him an "ignoramus, a propagandist . . . a crank, a menace to the cause of good education." But they never answered his charges or disproved his evidence that phonics is a much superior method of teaching reading than the humanistically inspired look-and-say technique.

In May of 1981 Dr. Flesch published his second book on the subject, *Why Johnny Still Can't Read*. After a quarter of a century, the nation's educrats have guaranteed an educational tragedy. They have spent billions of dollars on a second-rate reading system, and our current literacy rate proves just how second-rate it is. Dr. Flesch reports that 85 percent of our nation's public schools "still stick to old, discredited look-and-say."[1]

In 1977 a blue ribbon twenty-one-member advisory panel, headed by former Secretary of Labor Willard Wirtz, issued a report on the decline in the SAT scores. "The panel members," it said, "share strongly the national concern about the increasing signs of functional illiteracy ... (but they could find) no *one* cause of the SAT score decline."

However, in an appendix to the report, Professor Jeanne Chall of Harvard University offered a clue to that one basic cause. The student's low SAT scores, she wrote, had a "clearcut" statistical relationship to the reading instruction program used ten years earlier in first grade. The program had been based on a series of "look-and-say" readers.[2]

For a nation that prides itself on education, it is tragic to admit that 23 million adults in our country are functionally illiterate. For this "education" we have paid over $2 trillion in the past twenty-five years. Does that make you suspicious that something is drastically wrong? It should! Particularly in view of the recent test scores indicating that Christian and other private schools are doing a better job of teaching reading with considerably less money.[3] Interestingly enough, most private schools are teaching phonics.

An incredibly interesting case history of a thirty-six-year-old woman, a typical victim of the look-and-say reading method, appears in Dr. Flesch's second book. Born into a home of college-trained parents (her father was a university dean), she was a disappointment both to herself and to her parents. Before going to kindergarten, she seemed happy and bright, and she enjoyed having her parents read to her. Soon after beginning school she became "sober and timid," and her "eyes hurt all the time." Although her mother became upset at her slow reading progress, her father counseled that they should give the school more time, because they were introducing a new reading system that he (like many unsuspecting parents) thought would be an improvement.

Finally, in third grade she did so poorly that her parents transferred her to a private school, where she was compelled to repeat third grade and begin the study of French. In the seventh grade she studied Latin. She did well in both foreign languages, though she was still a poor reader of English. Often embarrassed by her slow reading, poor spelling, and weak writing in junior high and high school, she lacked a strong self-image and almost did not attend college.

At the urging of a family friend, who just happened to have been her Latin teacher and was convinced of her superior intelligence in spite of her difficulties with English and reading, her parents sent her to college, where she majored in French but included courses in Spanish, German, and Russian. She earned a 3.5 grade average in the foreign languages (all studied by the phonics method), but her ability to read well in five foreign languages did not overcome her feelings of inadequacy at her poor showing in English.

When her second-grade son (another victim of public-school look-and-say teaching) began to have trouble with his reading, she sought out Dr. Flesch's book *Why Johnny Can't Read*. Until then, although familiar with phonics in French and other languages, she had not thought to try that approach in English. Since Dr. Flesch included phonics instruction to parents and a list of words in his first book, she began to "play with it" in her spare time. Within three weeks she had doubled her reading speed and comprehension. She testified, "I had finally learned, at the age of 36, to read my native language!" Now she claims to read "10 times as much" as she used to.

> Best of all, I no longer feel guilty and baffled by my general ignorance. Much of it has been overcome, and I know that what remains is not my fault, but the fault of those who introduced the word method, that "new reading system," into the school I attended for the first three grades.[4]

Today she runs a reading tutorial program in New York City. I cannot help wondering how many millions of bright, capable individuals across America are needlessly struggling with self-doubt and other unnecessary feelings of inferiority, functioning in careers well below their creativity level simply because they were not properly taught how to read.

Beware Educrat Propaganda!

Many readers who have heard the propaganda coming out of the public schools to the effect that look-and-say is a good method of learning to read (in spite of declining reading scores) owe it to themselves and their children to read Rudolph Flesch's *Why Johnny Still Can't Read,* for he carefully documents his findings.

> Mitford Mathews, the wise old author of *Teaching to Read, Historically Considered,* wrote . . . : "The fact is that the method, prior to its adoption, had never been scientifically tested in competition with any other. . . ."
>
> Mathews didn't mean, of course, that no such studies have been made. On the contrary, since the first was done in 1911 there have been 124 such studies, carefully comparing the results of phonics-first and look-and-say. How many of them proved the superiority of look-and-say? Not one—not a single, blessed one.
>
> This sounds unbelievable, I know. In fact, it is unbelievable, considering the near-monopolistic rule of look-and-say for the past fifty or sixty years of American education. Nevertheless it's true. I can prove it by citing chapter and verse. If any educator wants to cite a single contrary research finding, he or she is welcome to do so.[5]

He then carefully introduces the groups of tests made, comparing the two methods, starting with the eleven tests made prior to his first book, which he had already cited. Of those he says:

> When I wrote my book *Why Johnny Can't Read* in 1955, I listed eleven studies that had been done up to that time. All of them gave results in favor of phonics-first; not a single one favored look-and-say. The scientific proof was complete and overwhelming.[6]

He then lists three other groups of studies that encompassed all the other 113 tests. "This brings the total count to 124. As I said, *not one* of those 124 studies showed results favoring look-and-say."[7]

A study of the 124 tests, comparing the look-and-say technique with the time-honored phonics method, proves that race, IQ, background, and socioeconomic level cannot account for the startling diversity of success rates. In every case the phonics-trained children were the better readers.

My enthusiasm for phonics is not based on my educational qualifications, for I have never taught reading. I am, however, vitally interested in education and have been heavily involved in it for over seventeen years as founder of a Christian high school and school system. All our elementary schools teach phonics, and we produce good readers.

Teachers in Christian and private schools stress phonics, and gradually many in public education are beginning to recognize its superiority to the method that, for decades, has retarded our educational process.

According to Dr. Barbara Bateman of the University of Oregon, "Near failproof methods for teaching all children to read are already available. Continued failure of schools to employ these [phonics-first] programs is at best negligent and at worst malicious."[8]

As one remedial-reading teacher observed, "If we use phonics to improve poor readers and it works, why don't we just start children on phonics in the first place?"

The Humanistic Origin of Look-and-Say

Since the look-and-say method of reading is so harmful to the education of our children, has never compared favorably in competent tests with phonics, and has consistently deteriorated our students' learning levels, we are forced to inquire, "Why is it still used in 85 percent of our public schools?" Before answering that question, we must first examine the origin and development of look-and-say. Keep in mind, phonics had already proved its value by producing the best foundation for reading for the largest number of children in history and had permeated the greatest educational system in the world with a higher literacy rate than we possess today.

Professor Fredrich Gedike, of Germany, wrote the first look-and-say primer entitled *Children's Book for the First Practice in Reading Without the ABC's and Spelling.* Gedike was an ardent believer in the educational theories of the atheistic humanist philosopher Jean Jacques Rousseau. He advocated that teaching should follow nature: it was natural for children to learn, and thus they should be free to pursue their curiosity. They should perceive nature as a whole—for example, viewing a tree as a whole. Therefore, instead of learning to read *t-r-e-e*, they would learn faster if they saw the whole word at once: *tree*. Interestingly enough, recent tests prove that children *don't* look at words the way they look at nature. Instead, most children (and adults) read by looking at the initial letter first.

Gedike's book caught on quickly because it seemed to make the learning of words easier and faster. But one problem surfaced immediately: how could children sound out letters in order to read unfamiliar words? After three editions, Gedike's book dropped out of sight.

It was not until 1836 that the first look-and-say primer was published in America. Thomas H. Gallaudet had successfully taught deaf mutes to recognize fifty key words, so he applied that method to normal children in *A Mother's Primer*. Josiah Bumstead, John R. Webb, and Samuel Worcester also produced look-and-say primers.

The look-and-say book which received the strongest promotion was written by Mary Peabody Mann, wife of the Unitarian-humanist Horace Mann, who became the first commissioner of the Department of Public Education for the state of Massachusetts and later for the United States government. Horace Mann was to education in the nineteenth century what John Dewey was to the twentieth century. Both exercised a harmful influence upon education, and both were humanists. Mann lead the campaign that made public education compulsory so that future humanist educators could fill the minds of their charges with humanist philosophy. He injected humanist teachings and values alongside religious concepts. Dewey made the teaching of humanism exclusive by getting traditional religion and its values expelled from the public schools.

The unproved theories of humanism, like the untested look-and-say method of learning to read, have proved disastrous to our nation's schools. As we shall see, humanism is the origin of rampant drugs, sex, violence, and self-indulgence in our schools, which are not conducive to the learning process. I find it supremely ironic that our public schools are supported largely by the 84 percent of our taxpayers who believe in God and religious values. Yet in order to give their children an education without humanistic fallacies and anti-Christian attacks, many must pay a second time in order to enroll them in private schools.

Like most humanists, Horace Mann did not hesitate to promote the work of fellow humanists, even his wife's book. While secretary of the Board of Education for the state of Massachusetts, he penned a supportive review:

> "It is a beautiful book," he wrote. "It is prepared on the same general principles with those of Worcester, Gallaudet, and Bumstead; and it contains two or three reading lessons and a few cuts for drawing, in addition to a most attractive selection of words."
>
> In 1843 Mann went with his wife to Europe and spent an hour in a Prussian classroom during a reading lesson. Although he didn't know a word of German, his wife interpreted for him what was happening. Nevertheless, he misunderstood completely what the teacher was doing—he was using the by then standard "normal word method"— and thought this was a demonstration of look-and-say.
>
> When he came back to the United States, Mann wrote his famous Seventh Annual Report to the Massachusetts Board of Education and recommended passionately the use of look-and-say. He wrote about the methods used by Gallaudet, Bumstead, Worcester, his wife, and the Prussian schoolteacher, mixing it all together in a frontal attack on the prevailing method of teaching children with the alphabet and *ba, be, bi, bo, bu.*[9]

Other Boston educators were not willing to roll over and play dead for what they considered a harmful method of teaching reading, so they organized a committee of thirty-one grammar-school masters to study the situation. Eventually they issued a lengthy attack on the new method, charging that it didn't work when the student approached unfamiliar words and, in addition, it produced poor spellers. That was 137 years ago. Look-and-say still manufactures poor spellers and hesitant or slow readers with poor comprehension.

After the "great debate" in Boston, look-and-say became unfashionable, and phonics continued to dominate the American educational system for many years. Then in 1883 the city of Chicago hired Francis Wayland Parker, a humanist thinker from Massachusetts, as the principal of the Cook County Normal (or teachers) School. For sixteen years that ardent advocate of look-and-say taught this method to the prospective young teachers of Illinois. The results were so disastrous that he was fired. Unfortunately for American education, one of Parker's admirers was Mrs. Anita McCormick Blaine, the daughter of inventor Cyrus McCormick. Interested in educational reforms, she donated a million dollars to the University of Chicago to establish a modern school in which Parker could influence future education.

In 1908 Edmund Burke Huey wrote *The Psychology and Pedagogy of Reading,* which Flesch labels as "the Bible of the movement." Psychology as a "science" was coming into prominence at that period of time (invented and promoted largely by humanists, which ultimately led to it being called humanistic psychology). Consequently as psychologists recommended look-and-say because of Huey's endorsement, it was granted a respectability beyond what its results merited. Gradually publishers began to introduce texts based on the look-and-say method.

Originally the American school system gained its teachers from Harvard, Princeton, and Yale, all founded to advance the Christian faith. Harvard, the oldest college in America (founded 1636), was almost totally commandeered by the Unitarians in 1805 and became a hotbed of Unitarianism, German rationalism, skepticism, biblical criticism and humanism. Even so, it was not totally atheistic. That was not the case of Columbia University, in New York City, which by the turn of this century was probably the most atheistic humanist citadel in America. Columbia served as the headwaters of modern education after humanist John Dewey accepted the head post of Columbia Teachers College. No other college in America (of which there are 3,000) has exercised more influence on modern education than Columbia University. It "embraced look-and-say together with progressive education, and the University of Chicago and other institutions followed suit."[10]

The two foremost leaders were Professor Arthur I. Gates of Columbia and Professor William S. Gray at Chicago. In 1929 the Scott, Foresman Company invited Professor Gray to revamp their Elson Readers, and this marked the birth of Dick and Jane. A year later, Professor Gates joined up with Macmillan and produced a look-and-say series for them. Gradually most major textbook houses fell in line and the "Dismal Dozen" of basal readers came into being.

By the middle thirties look-and-say had completely swept the field. Virtually all leading academics in the primary reading field were now authors of basal reader series and collected fat royalties. They had inherited the kingdom of American education. Inevitably that huge bonanza created problems. Look-and-say, after all, was still essentially a gimmick with no scientific foundations whatever. As it had for 150 years, it produced children who couldn't accurately read unfamiliar words. From the fourth grade up, textbooks in all subjects had to be "dumbed down" to accommodate them. Grade promotions had to be based on age rather than achievement. High school diplomas were given to functional illiterates. Colleges had to adjust to an influx of students who couldn't read. The national illiteracy rate climbed year after year after year.[11]

Publishing Is Big Business

There are publishers, and then there are publishers. The production of textbooks is an enormously profitable business, if it is done on a large scale. Just 5 percent of the textbook market for 43 million school children K through 12 boggles the mind. Before his book came out, Dr. Flesch had studied the field carefully and listed the following seventeen major publishers of school texts in two categories, according to reading technique.

THE PHONIC FIVE

1. Addison-Wesley Publishing Co., 2725 Sand Hill Road, Menlo Park, Calif. 94825
2. Distar, Science Research Associates, 259 East Erie Street, Chicago, Ill. 60611
3. Economy Company, 1901 North Walnut Street, Oklahoma City, Okla. 73125
4. J. B. Lippincott Company, East Washington Square, Philadelphia, Pa. 19105

THE DISMAL DOZEN

1. Allyn & Bacon, Inc.
2. American Book Company
3. Ginn & Company
4. Harcourt Brace Jovanovich
5. Harper & Row
6. Holt, Rinehart & Winston
7. Houghton Mifflin Company
8. Laidlaw Brothers
9. Macmillan, Inc. (regular series)
10. Macmillan, Inc. (Bank Street Readers)

THE PHONIC FIVE	THE DISMAL DOZEN
5. Open Court Publishing Co., P.O. Box 599, La Salle, Ill. 61301	11. Rand McNally & Company 12. Scott, Foresman & Company[12]

Until recently the Phonic Five publishers listed above supplied texts for 15 percent of American schools. The Dismal Dozen publishers sold textbooks to the other 85 percent. (Now perhaps you can understand why the Dismal Dozen provide seminars, "experts," and other inducements to keep the schools using their products.) Because of an increased interest in phonics, some of the Dismal Dozen have announced their intention to produce phonics texts. However, some have just added a small amount of phonics to the look-and-say method.

When Dr. Flesch or other courageous authorities speak against the incompetence of look-and-say as a reading technique, publishers are quick to rush "reading experts" (in their employ) into the fray—people who are quick to reassure teachers and educators that critics of look-and-say are just distorting the facts.

But what are the real facts? Too many Johnnys and Janes are weak readers, and 21 percent of the others are functional illiterates. The problem is getting worse, not better.

Many perceptive educators feel that reading ability will continue to decline until we determine to make a massive return to phonics.

Why Do They Use Look-and-Say?

In the face of the alarming decline in reading ability, the increasing concern and outspoken condemnation by qualified reading experts, the drastic decline in SAT scores during the past decade, and the growing disenchantment of parents with the public schools, it is legitimate to ask, "Why do 85 percent of our tax-supported schools persist in using an inadequate method of teaching reading?"

Actually, a number of reasons come to mind. As the American school system totals over 2 million classroom teachers and probably an equal number of administrators, it is safe to say that close to a million educators are involved, one way or another, in the teaching of reading at the elementary-school level. But only a small number of these set policy! Most of them follow the orders of those who do. Among that million people, we will encounter a variety of reasons why some favor look-and-say over phonics. Consider the following possibilities:

1. Human Greed   We have already established that textbook publishing is a multimillion-dollar-a-year business. Over a decade it is worth billions. Eighty-five percent of the nation's textbook business, divided among twelve major publishers, offers staggering possibilities. In the book industry there is probably no more lucrative business than the production of textbooks.

Look-and-say requires more and bigger textbooks than phonics. The fact that it costs the taxpayers more is lost to the publishers in the light of the enormous profits that are generated. Look-and-say involves learning to read by pictures, which take up more room. Pictures can be made with color, and students will need several picture-book readers, not just one. The program also requires workbooks, flash cards, and other gimmicks—all for a high price.

Not only the publishers profit, for as Dr. Flesch indicates, "Virtually all leading academics in the primary reading field were authors of basal reader series—and collected fat royalties."[1] Not many people, even educators, could be objective about the merits of phonics when making an evaluation, if switching from look-and-say would cost them thousands of dollars a year in potential royalties.

The publishers are clever. They don't ask some gifted first-grade teacher with a unique ability to produce superb readers to write their texts. (To their credit, many such caliber teachers still work in the public schools.) No, teachers don't have enough influence. Publishers would rather have the department heads of teachers colleges author their texts. That insures that such schools will continue to brainwash another decade of prospective teachers with the look-and-say technique.

2. *Progressive Education = Progressive Brainwashing*   The difference between educating a child and brainwashing is indoctrination. Education trains a child in the basic skills necessary for learning and objectively exposes him to the facts of history, geography, science, government, and so on. Brainwashing indoctrinates the child with a biased world view.

Progressive education, in essence, is socialism. John Dewey and his disciples were all socialists, and Dewey didn't even try to hide his political views. That is why our children know more about the "merits" of socialism than the facts of history will substantiate. But we are getting ahead of our story.

"Progressive" (socialist) educators favored look-and-say teaching techniques. In the twenties they looked upon phonics as an enemy that must be replaced. To them, look-and-say was a theory based on their atheistic, humanistic beliefs and a potent vehicle for indoctrinating (brainwashing) a whole generation of children's thinking. First they made teachers of phonics seem archaic so they could be replaced with the new look-and-say teachers, who with their modern reading techniques, had also been heavily indoctrinated at Columbia University and other such schools with a socialist world view. In addition, they wanted to get rid of those phonics textbooks because they were pro-family, promorality, pro-America, and pro-work ethic and free enterprise.

If you doubt that, try to find some of those "pros" in the look-and-say textbooks used by 85 percent of our schools.

3. Naiveté   Many sincere and dedicated teachers actually believe that look-and-say is the best method of teaching reading. Some Christian teachers interviewed for our Christian school system's elementary schools have to be rejected because they do not perceive phonics as a better method of teaching reading than look-and-say. Why? Because that is what they were taught!

Educators tend to respect educators. It is natural for an education major to accept as "gospel" what the head of his state college's Department of Education says about reading. After all, "He has a PhD and serves as a consultant with a nationally known textbook company!" That young teacher simply doesn't realize that Dr. Brainwasher earned his doctorate sitting at the feet of John Dewey or Robert Gates (or their disciples) at Columbia University, where he learned about the merits of look-and-say, progressive education, and world socialism. He may also make extra money from that textbook company as an apologist for and a promoter of the look-and-say method.

To the conscientious look-and-say teacher, I would like to extend a challenge. Instead of getting angry at me for castigating the approach, study the problem. Here is a list of relevant books:

Chall, Jeanne S.; Conrad, S. S.; and Harris, S. H. *An Analysis of Textbooks in Relation to Declining SAT Scores.* New York: College Entrance Examination Board, 1977.

Chall, Jeanne S. *Learning to Read: The Great Debate.* New York: McGraw-Hill, 1967.

Copperman, Paul. *The Literacy Hoax.* New York: William Morrow, 1978.

Flesch, Rudolf. *Why Johnny Can't Read and What You Can Do About It.* New York: Harper & Row, 1966.

Flesch, Rudolf. *Why Johnny Still Can't Read: A New Look at the Scandal of Our Schools*. New York: Harper & Row, 1981.

Mathews, Mitford M. *Teaching to Read: Historically Considered*. Chicago: University of Chicago Press, 1976.

When you have finished that list of books, visit phonics reading schools and compare their students with yours. Then make up your mind.

This may seem like extensive research—and it is—but if you plan to spend a major part of your life teaching children to read, you might as well utilize the best method possible.

4. The Conspiracy Theory   Most educators scorn the conspiracy theory, not because they have researched it, but because they were taught to reject it. Many people, however, maintain that a conspiracy has been operating, first in Europe and presently in our country, in an attempt to destroy traditional Judeo-Christian moral values. Doubtless you have heard of such groups as the Illuminati, Bilderbergers, Council on Foreign Relations, and more recently, the Trilateral Commission. These are only some of the suggested groups. One of their avowed purposes, according to the theory, is to reduce the standard of living in our country so that someday the citizens of America will voluntarily merge with the Soviet Union and other countries in a one-world socialist state.

To do so, the theory goes, they would have to lower the literacy level in the western countries, particularly America, and raise it in the Soviet Union, until the economy of Russia equaled that of the United States. They would also use open access to drugs, pornography, free sex, and a guaranteed-income philosophy to demotivate youth in the West. As bizarre as that sounds, I read such accusations over twenty-five years ago, and the material had been in print twenty-five to fifty years before that. Fortunately, democracy as we know it and the free enterprise system of this country have proved so powerful, and Russia's socialism so retarded, that the economic levels of the two countries are still worlds apart.

Personally, I do not know if the conspiracy theory has any validity. I am aware, however, that John Dewey, the father of progressive education (which turned out to be regressive education and set the American school system back at least two decades) was a committed world socialist. He spent three years in Russia, *after* the Bolshevik Revolution. Whether he was really working for the socialists or Marxists during his years in American education would be difficult to prove, but who can deny that education in its modern form wouldn't be much different if he had?

We should also note that while our educators have used the inferior look-and-say method of teaching reading and have raised the grades of our children to cover their falling reading scores, Russia is still using phonics. As our learning requirements and standards have dropped, Russia's have risen.

I find it fascinating that the elite educational leaders of both countries are for the most part atheistic humanists or humanistic thinkers. All Communists are secular humanists, but all secular humanists are not Communists. They are, however, predominantly socialistic in their world view. Now why would the humanist educrats of America destroy a once-great educational system while their Soviet counterparts are stressing learning, hard work, and discipline? Remember, true secular humanists espouse a socialist world view. Just read the 1933 and 1973 *Humanist Manifesto* (signed mainly by educators), and you will discern it plainly. To most humanists on both sides of the ocean, a united socialist world, with a planned economy (planned by them, of course), is the only solution to war, hunger, pollution, and so on.

Now don't misunderstand, I am not saying that all educrats are part of a gigantic conspiracy. I don't even know if there is one. But if a few humanist educrats, responsible for some of the terrible trends and decisions that have been made in American education during the past fifty years, were part of a conspiracy, it would certainly explain a number of things. Just a few persuasive leaders in key positions of power could accomplish the task. And humanists are notorious for helping each other up the administrative ladder to positions of maximum influence, particularly in education. That would explain why so many humanists have flooded the upper echelons of administration, from elementary-school principals to university presidents.

It has been my observation that educators, liberal politicians, equally liberal media personalities, and secular humanists usually ridicule the conspiracy theory. Yet they are the ones who benefit most by having the populace at large disbelieve it. If a majority of our nation's citizens ever get suspicious that atheistic humanists have been working for years to overthrow the traditional moral values upon which this country was founded, they would rise up at election time and elect school-board members deeply committed to preserving morality, not destroying it.

Of one thing I am certain: if a genuine conspiracy had been operating for over seventy-five years in this country and throughout the western world, moral, educational, and governmental conditions would be very similar to what they are today. The majority of our schools would be using look-and-say reading techniques and, in general, doing a poor job of educating our nation's children.

5. Change for Change's Sake Some educrats jam look-and-say into the minds of our schoolchildren because of their addiction to the unscientific theory of evolution. I hear them refer to "the evolutionary flow of history," applying this flow to marriage, family, values, and practically everything else.

Somehow humanists look suspiciously on anything traditional as if something tried and proven must be improved upon. So they give the impression that a really progressive person or educator will be subject to change and that change brings advancement. Unfortunately, some changes result in failure—like the "new math" launched with such gusto a few years ago, which turned out to be bad math when the SAT scores were made public. However, the undaunted humanist, with his philosophy heavily grounded in the theory of evolution, will rarely return to basics, but will use his failure as an excuse to initiate another change. That is why "progressive education" has shown itself to be so regressive within the learning process. Reluctant to leave success alone, humanists love to make changes: in textbooks (at least every five years), visuals, teaching styles, and learning methods. To an educational change artist, any successful program must be modified. "Success" is not measured by improvement but by the fact that significant change has been implemented.

If you find that logic a bit too difficult to comprehend, don't worry.

You're just too basic, and your mind is not sufficiently humanized—
for which you should be grateful.

6. Academic Arrogance Humility is not a humanistic aspiration; consequently, degreed humanist educators find it very difficult to admit their blunders. In fact, now they are on a campaign to do away with testing, which exposes their educational deficiencies for too many parents and taxpayers to see. Dr. Paul Copperman describes it well:

> A wide-scale campaign is currently under way to ban the use of all standardized educational tests, including IQ tests, achievement tests, and aptitude tests. If this movement is successful, American school-children will no longer be tested with such tests as the Stanford Achievement Test, the Comprehensive Tests of Basic Skills, the Iowa Tests of Educational Development, or either the SAT or ACT. The recent actions of the states of New York and California in banning all group IQ tests are indicative of the growing strength of this movement, as is the ongoing campaign by the National Education Association (NEA), the nation's largest and most powerful educational organization, for a complete moratorium on the use of standardized educational tests.
>
> The antitesting movement has also found support in a number of recent Supreme Court and lower federal court decisions, and a number of government regulations, restricting the use of educational tests in employment. One of these decisions prevented a Mississippi school district from using a minimum score on the National Teacher Examinations put out by ETS as a criterion in the employment of teachers. Another prevented a New York school district from using a procedure for selecting school principals that relied in part on tests of general intelligence and cultural breadth. A whole series of decisions and regulations prevent private industry from using IQ or educational test scores as criteria for employment.
>
> The antitesting campaign is one of the most acrimonious in the history of American education.[2]

Copperman then goes on to comment:

> In my opinion the success of this campaign would jeopardize the education of every American child, by preventing parents from monitoring the educational progress of their children, by encouraging educational experimentation on America's children without the safe-

guards of proper evaluation procedures, and by insulating the schools from the scrutiny of an informed public. I am well aware that standardized educational tests are imperfect measuring instruments, and that they can be used unwisely and their results misinterpreted. Nonetheless, they are uniquely useful educational tools that make a real contribution to the education of America's young people.[3]

It would be so much simpler if our progressive educators would admit to their multibillion-dollar blunder and return to phonics, but don't hold your breath.

7. The Secularization of Our School System   Some modern educators use look-and-say instead of phonics because the material enables them to secularize our once God-conscious school system.

A God-conscious school is much different from a religious or sectarian school. A religious school specializes in teaching religion; a God-conscious school simply acknowledges an almighty Creator. Our public schools were God-conscious before John Dewey. To rid our students of the "God intoxication"—the clearly announced intention of humanists back in 1933—our schools had to be completely secularized. The process began with textbook modification: phonics texts inculcated too many character-building principles, moral values, and acknowledgements of a Supreme Being. The best way to assure change was to replace the reading system.

These seven possible reasons for the continued use in our schools of an inferior reading system are certainly not exhaustive, and no one is exclusive. But they provide an insight into some of the reasons why Johnny still can't read after years of disastrously declining reading scores and why, in the face of the evidence, our humanist educrats show no signs of admitting their fifty-year failure and announcing a return to a proven reading technique, phonics.

I hope the groundswell of resentment from parents will yet be heard in the ivory-towered conference rooms of academia.

4

What Can Parents Do About Johnny's and Jane's Reading?

After decades of automatically sending their children to the nearest neighborhood school, parents are being forced to consider other options. Next to a child's spiritual moral life, nothing is more important than his acquisition of basic learning skills. Almost every parent knows that in order for his child to gain a piece of the great American dream, he must learn to be a good reader, writer, speller, and mathematician. Anything short of that tarnishes a parent's dream.

However, if a large percentage of our high-school young people are not qualified for college, what can parents do? For openers, don't wait until high-school graduation, when sending your son or daughter to a junior college will remain your only viable option. Exercise your initiative in the following ways:

1. Carefully (and tactfully) examine your child's school, particularly the reading program. If your child is in one of the grades from kindergarten through third grade, using the look-and-say method of teaching reading, immediately search for a school that teaches phonics. When you find one, do whatever is necessary, within the law, to transfer your child to that school. Remember, the first three years are crucial in learning to read.

If you are Christian, consider sending your child to a Christian school. Reasons for that will be given later, but even then you should be selective. I have found that some Christian schools employ Christian teachers trained in humanistically certified public schools, bringing look-and-say reading techniques and other humanistic fallacies into private education. The environment will be better for your child, but will the education? Bill Gothard has bemoaned this process on the college level: "Many Christian colleges provide little more than a humanistic education in a Christian environment." That is also true of some Christian elementary and secondary schools.

If you are not Christian, there are probably other private schools in your community to choose from. Or like many nonchristian parents deeply concerned about the education level of their children, you may opt for a Christian school because of the superior education offered.

2. Teach your child at home. If none of these other options are open to you, like thousands of other parents across the country, you may elect to teach your children in the friendly environment of home.

A *U.S. News & World Report* article entitled "When Parents Ask: Who Needs School?" reported that a burgeoning number of families have decided "they can teach better than the public schools. Estimates are that the number has doubled or tripled in the past decade."[1]

> Parental complaints are reflected by John Holt, a former educator and editor of a monthly newsletter, *Growing Without Schooling,* who says: "Schools are not only destructive of intellect but character. With very few exceptions, the social life of our schools is meanspirited, competitive, status seeking, snobbish, cruel, often violent and full of talk about who went to whose party and who did not."
>
> Many parents agree. Observes Frank Turano, 35, of Somerset, Mass., who with his wife Maureen has been hometeaching two daughters for two years: "There's something wrong with the education system—and it isn't the children." He pinpoints social and academic competition as the biggest poisoners of public education.
>
> Other parents cite problems of drugs, discipline and declining achievement for removing their offspring from classrooms. What many perceive to be a harmful moral climate and the inability of teachers to teach are two more reasons.[2]

Christian Liberty Academy of Prospect Heights, Ill., led by Reverend Paul D. Lindstrom, has produced a home-study curriculum for under $200. Sales are skyrocketing from 25 percent to 50 percent each year, and other curriculum publishers are joining in.[3]

Court battles are being waged as humanist educrats realize that they are losing their stranglehold on education. Instead of facing the fact that they have abused their hallowed privilege of being entrusted with the minds of our children, they blame everyone else—parents, society, fundamentalists, religion, and in some cases even the government. They evidently forget that educationally they *are* the government—unless parents choose to send their children to a private or Christian school or teach them at home, where kindergarten through fourth and even sixth grades are doing very well.

Dr. Raymond Moore, thirty-year public educator, is a pioneer in teaching children at home. He has written several excellent books on the subject, his best-seller being, *School Can Wait.* He has inspired thousands of parents to instruct their own children at home. In his *Hewitt Research Bulletin* he addresses the subject of learning readiness.

Despite early excitement for school, most early entrants (ages 4, 5, 6, etc.) are tired of school before they are out of the third or fourth grades—at about the ages and levels we found that they should be starting. Psychologist David Elkind calls these pressured youngsters "burned out." They would have been far better off wherever possible waiting until ages 8 to 10 to start formal studies (at home or school) in the second, third, fourth or fifth grade. They would then quickly pass early entrants in learning, behavior and sociability. Their vision, hearing and other senses are not ready for continuing formal programs of learning until at least age 8 or 9. . . .

The eyes of most children are permanently damaged before age 12. Neither the maturity of their delicate central nervous systems nor the "balancing" of the hemispheres of their brains, nor yet the insulation of their nerve pathways provide a basis for thoughtful learning before 8 or 9. The integration of these maturity levels (IML) comes for most between 8 and 10.

This coincided with the well-established findings of Jean Piaget and others that children cannot handle cause-and-effect reasoning in any consistent way before late 7's to middle 11's. And the bright child is no exception. So the 5's and 6's are subjected to dull Dick and Jane rote learning which tires, frustrates and ruins motivation, requires little thought, stimulates few "hows" and "whys." Net results: frequent learning failure, delinquency. For example, little boys trail little girls about a year in maturity, yet are under the same school entrance laws. HEW figures show that boys are 3 to 1 more often learning disabled, 3 to 1 delinquent and 4 to 1 acutely hyperactive. So unknowing teachers far more often tag little boys as "naughty" or "dumb." And the labels frequently follow them through school.

Socialization. We later became convinced that little children are not only better taught at home than at school, but also better socialized by parental example and sharing than by other little children. This idea was fed by many researchers. . . . Home schools are usually a highly desirable alternative. Some 34 states permit them by law under various conditions. Other states permit them through court decisions. Home schools nearly always excel regular schools in achievement. Although most of them don't know it, parents are the best teachers for most children at least through ages 10 or 12. For further information write us at 553 Tudor Road, Berrier Springs, Michigan, 49103.[4]

From Raymond and Dorothy Moore, *Home Grown Kids,* copyright © 1981 by the Hewitt Research Foundation and *Home-Spun Schools,* copyright © 1983; used by permission of Word Books, Publisher, Waco, Texas 76796.

Your first reaction to parents teaching their children at home may be negative. So was mine. That reflects the power of the educational propaganda machine. They have conditioned us to believe that only they are "qualified" to teach our children, and the earlier we entrust innocent and impressionable minds to them, the better—at least, the better to make little humanists out of them. When are we going to wake up to the fact they are doing a relatively inept job of educating our children because they are more interested in making one-world humanist robots out of them than in producing skilled workmen for the future good of America?

Frankly, many parents are doing a better teaching job at home. "But what about a child's social adjustment?" interested parents quickly ask. It may surprise you to learn that children kept at home and educated by their parents until age eight or ten have demonstrated better social adjustment when they started school in the third or fifth grade than those who enrolled as kindergarteners. This is particularly true for shy children, who gain security from their parents and are better able to cope with peer pressures at eight or ten than at five or six.

Teaching children at home is not new. Thousands of our missionaries have been doing it for years—and missionary kids are usually superior students when they reach junior and senior high school. Ironically, most missionary families felt guilty about teaching their children at home, as though they were "cheating them educationally." Now it turns out that the educational product of a dedicated parent is usually superior to that of the public school, and the child is better off socially.

Additional books on this subject can be obtained through writing and sending a self-addressed stamped envelope to Family Life Seminars, P.O. Box 1299, El Cajon, California, 92022.

Teaching children at home will entail personal sacrifice, but that is nothing new to devoted parents. It can, however, be a very unifying factor for a family in which children are still regarded as "a heritage of the Lord" and a source of blessing. God has placed in a child's heart a giant shrine for his parents, particularly during the early years of life. Because of our national romance with education, we have gradually remanded that place to the public school. That was not fatal in the days when the public-school teacher shared the same basic values as the parents, but today, except in isolated instances, it is disastrous.

Just recently I talked to a kindergarten teacher on a plane as she returned from a teacher's convention. In a small seminar of thirty-one teachers the subject concerning the use of Christmas carols in the classroom arose. A heated discussion ensued, and it was overwhelmingly decided thirty to one that Christmas carols were not appropriate in the classroom. Parents and taxpayers would have reversed the vote on this subject and many others, particularly in the field of moral values. Unfortunately, parents and taxpayers are no longer running the public school. We just pay the bills.

3. Supplement your child's education. Many parents reading this book will have children who have passed the third grade and who read poorly. Take it upon yourself to supplement their reading skills. Dr. Rudolf Flesch's first book, *Why Johnny Can't Read,* offers some excellent suggestions for parents to use in training their own children in phonics. You will find that book a very handy tool.

A wise parent understands that he, not the public schools, is responsible for the education of his child. For that reason, he must take whatever steps are necessary to determine his child's progress in his grade level and supplement his formal education, where it is deficient.

We are responsible for our children's spiritual, physical, and mental preparation for life. It is not enough to feed and clothe their bodies and take them to a good church, which provides the spiritual advantages that only the church can give. We are also responsible to God and the child to inculcate the skills needed for success in this technologically advanced age.

After more than a century of assigning the education of our children to the public schools, we can no longer do so. In many school districts that has been inadvisable for twenty years. Now parents must forcefully take charge of their children's education: at home, in a good Christian school, or with supplementary instruction.

4. Elect profamily school-board candidates. A parent is now obligated to exercise his freedom as an American citizen in order to help profamily candidates, committed to promoral values, get elected to the local school board. I say *promoral* because such candidates are never humanists. They believe in moral absolutes, which are anathema to a secular humanist.

In almost every school district across the land, humanists will actively endeavor to get atheists, freethinkers, and other humanists elected to the local school board, enabling them to determine the policies and philosophies of the district. Why? Because they realize what we are just learning—that the public school is the greatest pipeline to the minds of 43 million of our nation's 50 million children (the other 7 million attend private schools)—and they want to use it to infuse the religion of humanism.

It will happen only if we sit back and let them.

sponsored educational system. He and Luther realized that the way to inculcate religious learning in the citizenry was to educate them and provide them with the right kind of literature.

The printing press had been invented less than a century earlier, and it was expected that material with moral values or religious precepts would be printed. Therefore anything people read would have a wholesome effect on them. Our forefathers who came to America with this heritage immediately established schools, and later colleges, for every child in the New World.

These early schools unashamedly taught the religious doctrines of the Puritans or those of the community they represented. For the most part, this lasted for the first sixty or seventy years, until liberalism entered the scene; gradually the Puritan charter was replaced, and public schools, called common schools, were no longer reliable in the eyes of the Christian community.

> This did not mean a loss of interest in education. It meant a shift in emphasis and a change in organization in keeping with the other changes taking place in colonial society. Private academies run by educator proprietors sprang up to teach the more practical commercial subjects. By 1720 Boston had far more private schools than public ones, and by the close of the American Revolution many towns had no common schools . . . at all.[2]

Samuel L. Blumenfeld is a distinguished educator who has carefully researched both public and private education in America. His book *Is Public Education Necessary* makes this statement:

> Apart from New England, where tax-supported schools existed under state law, the United States, from 1789 to 1835, had a completely laissez-faire system of education. Although the idea of the town-supported common school had spread westward with the migration of New Englanders and was encouraged by the federal land grants, there were no compulsory attendance laws anywhere. Parents educated their children as they wished: at home with tutors, at private academies, or church schools. This did not mean that poor children were neglected. Some states paid the tuition of poor children, enabling them to attend the private school of their choice. Virtually every large city in the country had its "free-school" societies that built and

America's Educational Roots

Americans have always been interested in education. The humanist textbook writers cannot alter the fact that the New England colonists who founded America came here in quest of religious freedom. When the King James translation of the Scripture was completed in 1611, the common man had in his own language a copy of the Word of God that he could understand for himself—if he could read.

When we realize that the Massachusetts Bay Colony was founded by the Puritans in 1630 and the first college, Harvard, was established just six years later, we recognize that the early settlers were serious about education. This quest for learning, particularly as it reflected itself in making education available to the common child, was relatively unique to Christian communities. Prior to the sixteenth century, only the elite ruling class and otherwise gifted individuals could ever expect their children to become literate, much less broadly educated. Martin Luther changed that as early as 1524, when he wrote his letter to the German princes, urging them to establish schools for every man's child, paid for by the government.

> The first compulsory attendance system was established in Württemberg in 1559 by the duke of Württemberg. Detailed attendance records were kept, and fines were levied on the parents of truants. The Saxon and Württemberg systems became models for compulsory public schools in most of the Protestant German states and later in Prussia.[1]

A decade later, when John Calvin became the head of the government in Geneva, Switzerland, he immediately established a state-operated schools for the poor and were supported by the community's leading benefactors and philanthropists. Such schools were considered extremely worthwhile causes for philanthropy. Often these schools also received small grants from local governments in recognition of their public service. Thus, there was no need for any child to go without an education. The rate of literacy in the United States then was probably higher than it is today.[3]

From the earliest days in American history, parents seriously heeded the rights and responsibilities of educating their children as they pleased. Christians in this country assumed that the education of their children's minds was as much their responsibility as the preparation of their spirits. That is why, in many cities and villages throughout the country, ministers were the first teachers. They were usually among the few educated individuals in a community, and since they had to supplement their income anyway, it often fell their lot to become the teachers of the children Monday through Friday and the preachers at the church on Sunday. Naturally a man of God would not keep character-building values or his religious doctrines out of the one-room schoolhouse—a single dwelling that served as the schoolhouse during the week and the church on Sunday.

In the bigger cities and towns, the private school enjoyed a higher academic reputation than the common school.

> Freemarket forces were slowly shifting public favor from the poorly managed public school to the more efficiently managed private school. Only in Boston did the public schools receive unflagging public support despite the competition from private academies, mainly because of a special situation in that city: the growth of the Unitarian movement which strongly favored public education.[4]

Why would the Unitarians in Boston favor public education? For the same reason that Luther and Calvin approved government-controlled and sponsored education: so that classrooms could become conduits to the minds of their children, inculcating religious principles. The Unitarians were just copying a page from Calvin and Luther.

What makes that frightening for today's education is the fact that Unitarianism in America was the mother of secular humanism, which stalks the public-school corridors today with absolute control. Unitarianism was headquartered in Boston. Isn't it interesting that Boston was the center from which compulsory education sprang—a system that ultimately excluded traditional Judeo-Christian moral values and replaced them with Unitarian–secular-humanist amorality? They have replaced one religious system with another. As further evidence of the close kinship between Unitarianism and humanism, notice that 25 percent of the original signers of the *Humanist Manifesto* in 1933 were either Unitarian ministers or Unitarians. Additional evidence appears in the Federation of Religious Humanists, made up largely of Unitarians.

> The takeover of Harvard in 1805 by the Unitarians is probably the most important intellectual event in American history—at least from the standpoint of education. The circumstances that signaled the takeover were the election of liberal theologian Henry Ware as Hollis Professor of Divinity and the subsequent retreat of the Calvinists to a new seminary of their own in Andover. From then on Harvard became the Unitarian Vatican, so to speak, dispensing a religious and secular liberalism that was to have profound and enduring effects on the evolution of American cultural, moral, and social values. It was, in effect, the beginning of the long journey to the secular humanist world view that now dominates American culture.[5]

The first giant step toward the corruption of modern education, then, occurred at Harvard University in 1805. I say "giant step" because there were many smaller steps long before that. Within eighty years of the founding of Harvard University, liberal theologians (whose thinking process originated in the humanistic minds of Europe) tried to gain control of this citadel of Christian teaching. For almost one hundred years the controversy raged between fundamentalists and liberals. As Unitarianism grew stronger in Boston, with the influx of immigrants from Europe, many of the ministers of the larger churches traveled to Europe and were further liberalized. Upon their return, they exercised an increasing influence upon Harvard, ultimately moving it permanently into the liberal Unitarian (or, eventually, humanist) camp.

At that time in history, Germany was a hotbed of rationalism and higher criticism. In the name of academic intellectualism, Unitarianism brought this so-called scholarship from Germany to Harvard, from which it was disseminated to other schools, colleges, and seminaries, ultimately effecting the liberal movement in theology and the secular movement in public education.

Blumenfeld documents the incredible story of Robert Owen, an Englishman often labeled "the father of modern socialism," who established a socialist community in Scotland. Central to this atheist's purpose was the establishment of an educational system to condition the minds of future generations for socialism. Believe it or not, all of this transpired *before* Karl Marx wrote *Das Kapital.* In 1825 Owen transferred his efforts to New Harmony, Indiana, a communal experiment that failed within a couple of years. Owen explained that one ingredient for success was lacking: education as the prerequisite to the success of socialism. Thus the Owenites, joined by transcendentalists, Unitarians, Universalists, and other humanist forerunners, began to work insidiously for the takeover of public education.

Orestes A. Brownson (1803–1876), a Universalist minister (but later a Catholic convert) who joined the Owenites in the 1820s, revealed in his autobiography:

> that the Owenites went underground in 1829 and organized their activities nationwide in the form of a secret society in order to attain their goal of universal public education. Brownson wrote:

> The great object was to get rid of Christianity, and to convert our churches into halls of science. The plan was not to make open attacks on religion, although we might belabor the clergy and bring them into contempt where we could: but to establish a system of state,—we said *national*—schools, from which all religion was to be excluded, in which nothing was to be taught but such knowlege as is verifiable by the senses, and to which all parents were to be compelled by law to send their children. . . . The first thing to be done was to get this system of schools established. For this purpose, a secret society was formed, and the whole country was to be organized somewhat on the plan of the carbonari of Italy, or as were the revolutionists throughout Europe by Bazard preparatory to the revolutions of 1820 and 1830. This organization was commenced in 1829, in the city of New York, and to my own knowledge was effected throughout a considerable part of New York State. How far it was extended in other states, or whether it is still kept up I know not, for I abandoned it in the latter part of the

year 1830, and have since had no confidential relations with any engaged in it: but this much I can say, the plan has been successfully pursued, the views we put forth have gained great popularity, and the whole action of the country on the subject has taken the direction we sought to give it. I have observed too that many who were associated with us and relied upon to carry out the plan, have taken the lead in what has been done on the subject. . . . It would be worth inquiring, if there were any means of ascertaining how large a share of this secret infidel society, with its members all through the country unsuspected by the public, and unknown to each other, yet all known to a central committee, and moved by it, have had in giving the extraordinary impulse to godless education which all must have remarked since 1830, an impulse which seems too strong for any human power now to resist.[6]

This group of influential intellectuals seemed to have a strange fascination for freethinking, atheistic educators.

During the 1830s a battle royal raged between the Friends of Education (a title describing a coalition of socialists, Unitarians, atheists, educators, and others who favored tax-supported, government-controlled public schools) and those who were committed to private schools. The former believed it was the government's duty to educate our young; the latter were convinced that parental responsibility came first. Naturally, the Friends of Education did not want government to run the schools. They just wanted government to pay the bill and let them, the educational elite, exercise control. After all, they were the only ones qualified to do so. Yet theirs was an education established without God and thus without His moral values. Nonhumanists realize that a society without moral values will end up in chaos. According to Blumenfeld, "The simple truth is that by 1832 the Bible had already been excluded from the curriculum of secular public education."[7] The husband of Harriet Beecher Stowe in 1836 advised, "Without religion—and, indeed, without the religion of the Bible—there can be no efficient school discipline."[8] The anarchy in today's public schools is the national result of excluding the Bible and its morals from our tax-supported curriculum.

The nineteenth-century humanist educrats devised three basic steps to their plan of taking over the public schools.

1. Make school attendance compulsory.
2. Establish government-sponsored "free" schools. This plan was sold to the nation on the basis that "free" would insure education for all the poor. Ironically, according to an 1817 survey, 96 percent of the children of Boston, where this scheme was hatched, were in some school at the time, and the other 4 percent had access to "charity schools" if their parents so desired.[9] In other words, like everything else liberals sell to the public, they didn't need them in the first place.
3. Establish teacher-training schools—controlled by the elite, of course. At first these were called normal schools (like denominational seminaries, where ministers are indoctrinated with denominational theology and practice). In these teacher seminaries future educators were taught how to secularize education—in other words, how to teach facts without God. That is only one step away from making our schools atheistic—which is only one step away from making them amoral. First evict God from the curriculum, then expel morals. Remember, that was the goal of the Boston Friends of Education back in 1835. Now do you understand why our twentieth-century schools are so antagonistic toward God, religion, morality, and particularly Christianity? If you don't believe that, just try holding a Bible class on campus one time—even after school hours.

The Nineteenth-Century High Priest of Public Education

Horace Mann is usually considered the father of public education. Actually, the present secular humanist course of public education was already set in motion while he was still a struggling attorney. In Boston, the Friends of Education, led by atheist socialist Robert Owen (father of the Owenite movement), Josiah Holbrook (who entered Harvard in 1806, one year after the Unitarian takeover of that institution), and other atheists, Unitarians, and transcendentalists, had laid well-entrenched plans for the takeover of public education and its use as a pipeline to the impressionable minds of our children long before they created the office of secretary of the Massachusetts Board of Education in 1837.

Seven years previously, at one of Holbrook's Lyceum meetings for school teachers and educators, the delegates voted to form the American Institute of Instruction.[10] These humanist forerunners of education campaigned vigorously for a state-supported school system financed by property taxes. Their campaign slogan: Crusade against ignorance. Now, after 147 years under humanism, the same policies could be promoted under the slogan, Campaign to perpetuate ignorance.

It is significant that Horace Mann was selected as the first secretary of Public Education for any state in the United States and, because of that position, ultimately occupied a similar post in the federal government—significant because he had never been an educator, unless, of course, we include the two years he spent in a tutorship at Brown University in 1820 and 1821, where one day his students "hissed and hooted him out of class."[11] This was to be his only firsthand experience as an "educator." Horace Mann was selected for his Massachusetts post because he was a brilliant Unitarian skeptic whose many associates were board members of the Friends of Education. As a lawyer he had distinguished himself as a sterling orator; he had successfully run for public office; and he was highly respected among the Unitarian elite of Boston.

One of the little-known facts about Horace Mann's life is that he was born in 1796 of strict Calvinistic stock with strong Puritan roots. Even as a boy he had difficulty with the austere misrepresentation of God advanced by the hyper-Calvinism of New England. At twelve years of age, he was taken by his parents to revival meetings, where he fell under deep conviction, but unlike thirty of his youthful associates, he did not accept Christ. He later wrote:

> I remember the day, the hour, the place and the circumstances, as well as though the event had happened but yesterday, when in an agony of despair, I broke the spell that bound me. From that day, I began to construct the theory of Christian ethics and doctrine respecting virtue and vice, rewards and penalties, time and eternity, God and his providence which . . . I still retain.[12]

Ultimately, this "theory of Christian ethics and doctrine" was nothing more than the Unitarian denial of a personal God, a fallen nature, a divine Savior, and the need for a personal conversion experience. Like many others who have rejected the conversion experience and turned to skepticism, he seemed to retain a lifelong antagonism toward true Christianity and the reliability of Scripture.

After graduating from college and pursuing his studies in law, Mann distinguished himself as an orator and made many Unitarian friends, who had a profound influence on him. Gradually the voices of conviction within him subsided, replaced with a strident antagonism toward the Christian faith.

The great controversy at that point in history regarding the nature of man pitted the biblical view of the Calvinists that man is a sinful, fallen creature in need of a Savior against the notion of Unitarians and other freethinking atheists (basing their philosophy on the theories of humanist Jean Jacques Rousseau) that man is really very good. The assumption that man is naturally good and, if left to himself, will come to right conclusions and pursue moral ends is idealistic sophomorism at its apex. Historically, it has proved to be a disaster. That, however, does not deter humanistic or Unitarian educators from their continuing campaign toward "the perfectibility of man."

Horace Mann: The Prophet of Education

Most people do not think of Horace Mann as an educational prophet. However, his first annual report to the Massachusetts Board of Education on January 1, 1838, contained a prophecy that radiated frightening overtones.

> And what citizen of Massachusetts would not feel an ingenuous and honorable pride, if, in whatever direction he should have occasion to travel through the State, he could go upon no highway, nor towards any point of the compass, without seeing, after every interval of three or four miles, *a beautiful temple,* planned according to some tasteful model in architecture, dedicated to the noble purpose of improving the rising generation, and bearing evidence, in all its outward aspects and circumstances, of fulfilling the *sacred object of its erection?*[13]

Who has not seen these "temples of learning after every interval of three or four miles"? Mann was referring to the thousands of elementary, junior and senior high schools that occupy some of the most valuable land and possess the finest facilities and equipment in the nation—but propagate their anti-God, anti-Christian, antitraditional moral values and anti-American religious doctrine of secular humanism. Our public schools are temples of the religion of atheistic humanism. It is known by many names—liberal humanism, secular humanism, scientific humanism, atheistic humanism—but it is ever the same: a religious dogma without God, without morals, deifying human nature and possessing a socialist world view that is destructive to the long-range good of America.

No wonder public educators have expelled Bible classes, Youth for Christ clubs, release-time classes, prayer meetings, or any other religious activities from the campus. They do not want *their temples* to propagate a belief in God and basic moral values—even though we, the God-fearing taxpayers of America who make up the overwhelming majority of our population, are obligated to pay for them.

We do not object to humanists operating schools for children of humanist parents. Because America is a free country, one can teach almost anything. We do object to the way in which humanists forcibly appropriate our taxes and arrogantly expel all religious teaching but their own. As we shall see in a future chapter, not one of the basic beliefs of humanism is scientific or provable. All must be accepted by faith. Therefore their humanistic brand of secular philosophy is a religion and should have no place in our government-controlled, tax-supported "public" schools.

Originally our nation's schools were controlled by local school boards of five or more people elected by the community. If these trustees permitted educators to initiate such policies and programs that counteracted the values of the community and its homes, they could be recalled or voted out of office at the next election. We still go through the motions of such elections, but for years the educators themselves or other like-minded humanists have been seeking such positions, and thus local school boards have tended to give the educrats of their district everything their humanistic hearts desired. Gradually Christians and others committed to traditional moral values are waking up to the fact that those are *our* schools! As taxpayers, we have a right to use our influence in our community schools. But even when we do gain local representation, we make a horrifying discovery: one school-board president confided to me, "We local trustees have very little control over our districts. By the time the state board of education and the federal Department of Education get through with their state or federally funded programs, we have little choice but to go along."

Under Mann's control, the board of education pushed for compulsory school attendance and established public-school libraries, stocked with the writings of "approved" authors—that is, Unitarians, transcendentalists, and other atheists—but excluding "sectarian books." He also launched normal schools so he could be assured that future generations of teachers would know the Unitarian/humanist line. Today's schools bear tragic evidence that Mann and his followers were enormously successful.

> To Mann, who believed the Normal School to be "a new instrumentality in the advancement of the race," the linking of state power to teacher education was indeed a crowning circumstance, creating what James G. Carter had described in 1825 as a powerful "engine to sway the public sentiment, the public morals, and the public religion, more powerful than any other in the possession of government." And once a nation's teachers' colleges become the primary vehicle through which the philosophy of statism is advanced, this philosophy will very soon infect every other quarter of society, for the most potent and significant expression of statism is a state educational system. Without it, statism is impossible. With it, the state can and has become everything.[14]

Horace Mann moved from the Massachusetts Department of Education to become the first secretary of the Department of Education for the federal government. What he did for education in Massachusetts he ultimately duplicated for all of America:

1. Education was made compulsory and public, which finally drove private schools out of business. Millions of parents found out too late that a "free" public education is incredibly expensive, for it opens their children's minds to the flow of secular humanism's antimoral education.

2. State teachers colleges were established, where all teachers could be indoctrinated in the new nonsectarian (or anti-God) philoso-

phy of education. These American teachers sat at the feet of Unitarian educators who had traveled to Europe, the home of French skepticism and German rationalism, Hegelian statism, and other forms of secular humanism. Gradually our schools and libraries reflected the atheism of Europe, not the God-consciousness of our founding fathers.

3. Control of our schools was taken from parents and local communities and given to the "state," which meant humanist educrats were hired by the state to train our youth. But typical of religious zealots, the humanists in control of state schools are more interested in the indoctrination of our youth with the theories of humanism than in academic-achievement scores.

Horace Mann was followed by other humanists like John Dewey, who promoted his devastatingly harmful progressive education. To further the destruction of our government schools, he introduced look-and-say reading, child-centered teaching techniques, and challenged moral absolutes. After him came the new math, open classrooms, sex education, values clarification, and a plethora of programs that have bilked the taxpayer, undereducated the child, and defrauded the parents.

State-Controlled Education Is a Failure

Samuel L. Blumenfeld has described it well:

> After more than a hundred years of universal public education, we can say that it nowhere resembles the utopian vision that drove its proponents to create it. It has not produced the morally improved human being the Unitarians insisted it would, nor has it changed human nature in the way the Owenites predicted. (Ironically, one of the public school's biggest problems today is the physical safety of its teachers!) It has turned education into a quagmire of conflicting interests, ideologies, and purposes, and created a bureaucracy that permits virtually no real learning to take place. Nonsectarian education has become secular humanist indoctrination, as biased in its worldview against religion as Calvinism was in its favor. The Catholics were aware enough to see what it would all lead to and bolted the public school rather than accept the destruction of their faith. As for the Normal Schools,

they have blossomed into state teachers' colleges that cannot produce competent instructors in basic academic skills. The whole experiment has been a colossal failure. . . .

Is public education necessary? The answer is obvious: it was not needed then, and it is certainly not needed today. Schools are necessary, but they can be created by free enterprise today as they were before the public school movement achieved its fraudulent state monopoly in education. Subject education to the same competitive market forces that other goods and services are subjected to, and we shall see far better education at much lower overall cost. Instead of a "crusade against ignorance" to reform the world, we shall have schools capable of performing the limited and practical functions that schools were originally created to perform.

The failure of public education is the failure of statism as a political philosophy. It has been tried. It has been found sorely wanting. Having learned from our mistakes, would it not be better to return to the basic principles upon which this nation was founded? Education was not seen then as the cure-all for mankind's moral diseases. But it was on that premise that the reformers built the present system. They were wrong. The system cannot work because in a free society government has no more place in education that it has in religion. Once Americans grasp the full significance of this idea, they will understand why the return of educational freedom is essential to the preservation and expansion of American freedom in general.[15]

The best thing that could happen to public education in America is the establishment of competition in education, permitting parents to educate their children where they please without having to pay twice, once through taxes to subsidize the religion of humanism and once through tuition to private schools. This could easily be done by giving parents (or grandparents) tuition tax credits, allowing them to deduct from their income taxes the amount of their child's private-school tuition (which usually is one-half the cost of educating the same child in public school).

Within ten years 51 percent of our nation's children would be attending private (largely Christian) schools, and the public schools would be forced to improve their product to remain competitive. The humanists wouldn't like it, however, for they would have to make training our children in basic skills their number-one priority instead of what it is today: indoctrination in the religion of secular humanism.

Religion Takes Over the Schoolhouse

Secular humanism, the official doctrine of public education, has all the markings of a religion. Consider the following:

1. A well-defined Bible or "Scriptures"
2. A stated doctrine or dogma
3. An object of worship
4. A priesthood
5. Missionaries
6. Seminaries
7. Temples
8. An established life-style
9. A support base
10. Its roots are grounded in ancient religions
11. Recognition by the Supreme Court as a religion
12. Vigorous opposition to theistic religion
13. A world view
14. A view of death
15. Open acknowledgement of its position

This religion monopolizes the minds of our nation's 43 million public-school children and 13 million college and university students. If you don't believe that these characteristics of religion are currently operating in our nation's controlled (or "public") schools, I suggest that you read on.

What Is Religion?

According to a typical dictionary definition, a religion involves "any system of beliefs, practices, ethical values, etc. resembling, suggestive of, or likened to such a system (humanism as a *religion*)."[1] Note that even a dictionary published in the mid-seventies equated *humanism* and *religion*.

Does the term *religion* imply a belief in God? Only in the narrow sense of the word. For instance, in a court case involving the Washington Ethical Society and the District of Columbia, the former wanted its building to qualify for tax exemption as a religious society, insisting that belief in a Supreme Being is not necessary for religious tax-exempt status. The court ruled that the Ethical Society did indeed qualify as a religious corporation.

Contemporary courts and academicians, then, have repeatedly defined *religion* in the broadest sense of the word, and as we shall see, humanists look upon their system of thought as "true religion."

Does the preponderance of atheism in education indicate that a belief in God, the Bible, and moral values is based on superstition rather than fact? No, but it is one confirmation of the power of brainwashing in the name of education. In actuality, very few educators have ever examined the evidence for biblical authority or Christianity. If one investigates only one side of the evidence, that is the side he will most likely accept—whether or not it is true.

Educators are not unbelievers because of lack of evidence but because of inadequate exposure to it. I have personally led several educators to Christ, and in each case they were willing to consider the vast evidence for Christian truth objectively and then make a decision. After their conversion, they acknowledged that they were unaware that any apologetics for Christianity existed. The Institute for Creation Research has led scores of educators and university-trained people to a saving faith in Christ by confronting them with the evidence *for* biblical truth.

Faith in Christ is not based on the whims of feeling or superstition, as the humanists would have us believe. It is founded upon the testimony of the Scriptures, which is available to anyone who will examine it. True faith is based on reason, which in turn rests firmly upon the

Word of God. That is what God meant when He said, "Come now, and let us *reason* together, saith the Lord: though your sins be as scarlet, they shall be as white as snow; though they be red like crimson, they shall be as wool" (Isaiah 1:18, *italics added*).

Why Atheists in Education?

Why is the field of education so attractive to atheistic humanists? Primarily because it is the most effective arena in which to make converts to their religion—and get paid for it. Humanists do not give tithes and offerings to support their religion. (Some rich humanists will do so if they receive tax deductions.) The rank and file will not support humanist churches or humanist Sunday schools; that is not their style. Secular humanists have gravitated to four major fields for three centuries—and in this order.

1. Education—from day-care centers to graduate schools.
2. Government—the promotion of antimoral legislation.
3. Law—the best professional springboard to politics, but also a controlling influence over the judicial system.
4. Media—the most effective way to communicate their ideology to the masses as:
   a. Journalists
   b. Writers
   c. Publishers
   d. TV and radio owners, producers, script and screen writers, directors, actors, newscasters and talk-show hosts

An Object Lesson From History

By the seventeenth century, most colleges and universities of Europe had been founded by religious orders: Catholics, Lutherans, Calvinists, and the Church of England. Even Voltaire and Rousseau attended Jesuit colleges. But the French skeptics, German rationalists, and other atheistic forerunners began to infiltrate the professorships of these universities and colleges for the purpose of reaching the minds of the bright youth of the next generation.

The plan worked so well that these professors gradually found their students becoming the teachers of Europe's children on both the elementary and secondary levels. And because European churches did not inaugurate Bible institutes, schools, and colleges, their young people became followers of religious humanism (in the name of *enlightenment* or *free thought* or *secularism*), instead of followers of the faith of their parents or church.

Dr. Francis Schaeffer notes that Europe crossed "the Existentialist line of despair around 1880," while America, because of its more substantial base of biblical knowledge, did not pass that point until the 1930s. Since then the Western world, including America and Canada, has become increasingly secular—that is, a-God. Western civilization for hundreds of years was the result of Reformation thinking, based on biblical truth. Gradually, however, we have been secularized. And don't think for a moment it was an accident! It was all planned by the humanists. Their strategy:

First: Take over the colleges and universities, turning them into religious citadels for the teaching of the religion of humanism while excluding or ridiculing the teachings of the traditional religions based on the Bible.

Second: Train the next generation of journalists, lawyers, politicians, educators and other molders of "public opinion."

Third: Get former students now in government to pass laws and regulations favorable to humanist causes and vote them large amounts of money collected from taxes to support their work.

If you assert, "That couldn't happen in America," I would respond, "Have you visited a college or high school lately where only humanistic teaching is tolerated? Have you found public libraries where humanist books are welcome and promoral books are *persona non grata?*"

Even a cursory study of federal government grants reveals that the U.S. Office of Education, the National Institute of Education, the National Science Foundation, and projects financed through the Elementary and Secondary Education Act (ESEA) have had a profound influence on the development and selection of materials placed in our local schools. People who speak of local control over such matters are naive indeed. Many local school boards have merely rubber-stamped Federally-funded curricula.[2]

The only remedy to all of the above is to send legislators to Washington and your state capital who (1) understand that secular humanism is the enemy of everything that is good and wholesome and (2) will subsequently cut all future government spending for humanist causes. After all, our Constitution forbids that the government do anything to establish or advance religion. And secular humanism *is* a religion!

The Religious Characteristics of Secular Education

Don't be deceived into thinking that humanism is merely a philosophy. That is a masquerade humanists have utilized for over three centuries to deceive millions in the Western world. And don't be duped into thinking that because religious people believe in God, those who do not believe in God are not religious. That is another mass deception the humanists have used to good advantage for years.

Belief and disbelief are both matters of faith, for neither can be proved empirically. In fact, it takes more faith to believe that the universe, the earth, man, and animals all came into being without a Creator than it does to conclude that order and design demand some super-being who oversees the entire process. Consequently, both belief in God and disbelief are evidences of religious conviction or faith. Labeling them secular or rational or educational changes nothing, though it may fool the naive.

A very revealing article in the *Journal of Humanistic Education* (a journal for teachers, which usually contains articles by such educators as Simon and Combs), written in the spring of 1981, is entitled "Eastern Sources of Power and Joy," by Dr. David Ryback. After making it clear that he does not approve the Puritan ethic and that it should be replaced with "the philosophies of the East, particularly Buddhism, Taoism and Confucianism," he suggests they "may have something to offer as we extend outward to more sources of power and joy." He then exults, "Buddha began to teach his doctrine of humanistic personal growth through one's own effort . . . Buddha taught that man is master of his own fate, or can be if he so chooses . . ." (which, of course, is consistent humanist doctrine). Regarding Confucianism, he says, "We in the West struggle for individual freedom and expression with the inevitable result of competition and feelings of alienation. In the East the struggle is for selfless consideration of others . . . and collective achievement." (Evidently he has forgotten the Red Brigade of China, which massacred millions of their own countrymen. Confucianism has produced a very low view of human life that allows abortion, euthanasia, the right to suicide, and even infanticide.) He also lauds the Confucian philosophy: "as it applies to the classroom, it can be characterized by the following statement: Life should be so ordered in the classroom and in each student and teacher, as to allow the fullest development of what makes us truly human. . . ." In other words, we *become* "truly human"—we are not born that way.

Ryback then goes on to state that "open classrooms" originated in Confucianism. "Laotzu may have been the first exponent of the open classroom. In a classroom setting, Laotzu would focus on the space within rather than on the walls. As a Taoist, he was much more process oriented than goal oriented. Mystical awe of the universe is more important in Taoism than trying to change our environment."[3] (Quoted from newsletter published by the Barbara M. Morris Report, P.O. Box 756, Upland, CA 91786 $20/10 issues.)

In case you have wondered about the derivation of the open-classroom teaching technique that has proved to be so aggravating to parents and so unsuccessful as a teaching style to children that it is being abandoned by many quality educators, Dr. Ryback identifies it. His humanist friends in the religion of Taoism established it.

This article to educators not only confirms the religious nature of the theories of humanism but also explains why in the past few years a new interest in courses entitled "The History of Religion" or "Comparative Religion" have invaded the public school. If these follow the usual humanist education program, they will be nothing more than thinly disguised opportunities to teach the mystical religions of the East to our Western children at taxpayers' expense—unless those taxpayers rise up and protest, "We have had enough of these false religions in our public schools."

Comparative Religions

"Comparative Religion," a relatively new course infiltrating high schools nationwide, should raise all our eyebrows. In the first place, it is inserted at the expense of time spent on more basic learning areas. Second, in most cases the course is a humanistic affront to Christianity. The teaching technique is really very simple. Representatives of the local religions in a community come in and lecture to the class. What could be fairer? Protestant and Catholic children are exposed to the beliefs of Unity, Unitarianism, Buddhism, Taoism, Mohammedanism, Hare Krishna, and other Eastern religions. Although Eastern faiths may represent only 1 or 2 percent of the population, 90 percent or more of classroom time is spent on them.

As a sop to the traditional religions of the community, a liberal rabbi, liberal Catholic priest, or liberal Protestant minister, all of whom tend to agree philosophically more with the Eastern religions and humanism than the fundamentalists of the same religious persuasion, may be asked to address the class. Only rarely will a school invite a representative of the fundamental churches of the nation, even though they represent the majority view held in this country. Why? Because humanists know what few conservatives realize: humanism is the outgrowth of the Eastern religions, a perversion of Christian thought with what we call liberalism. Actually, there isn't a nickle's worth of difference between the philosophy of an Eastern religionist, a liberal theologian (whether Protestant or Catholic), and a secular humanist.

Does that shock you? It should—because that will be the religion of the Antichrist during the tribulation period—liberalism, humanism, and Eastern religion.

The Ecumenical Church of Revelation 13 and 17, we must repeat, will be an amalgamation of theological liberalism, humanism, and Eastern religion. You will be able to investigate the details in another book of this series, yet to be written, on this subject.

The Fifteen Identification Marks of
Secular Humanism

1. Secular Humanism Has a Well-Defined Bible or "Scriptures"   In my first volume on humanism, I spent an entire chapter on the humanist Bible, the codified position of humanism, contained in two volumes: *Humanist Manifesto I,* written by John Dewey in 1933; and *Humanist Manifesto II,* updated and expanded in 1973 by Paul Kurtz. In all probability the humanists in education wish these sacred writings had never been distributed—not because they do not contain their basic ideology, but because they have been so widely disseminated by Christians and other citizens committed to moral values and have thus become the Achilles heel of the humanist movement.

Humanist Manifesto I & II are so shocking to any believer in God that his first reaction is one of disbelief. When he discovers that it was signed by some of the most influential people in education today, Mr. Taxpayer is invariably appalled. The only individuals I know who do not perceive the dangers within these documents have not read them, are humanists themselves, or do not understand that they form the basis for the principles being taught regularly in many of our nation's public schools.

2. Secular Humanists Have a Stated Doctrine or Dogma   All religions hold to a doctrinal statement of faith. That is certainly true of Baptists, Catholics, and Jews, whose religious doctrines are well-known, even by those outside of their religion. Like other religions, humanism can be identified with a body of beliefs.

In *The Battle For the Mind* I went to great lengths to document the existence of the five basic doctrinal tenets of secular humanism in their own writings: (1) atheism, (2) evolution, (3) amorality, (4) autonomous, self-centered man, and (5) a socialistic one-world view. Sometime later, in a national magazine, Corliss Lamont, the leading spokesman for the humanist movement during the past forty years, acknowledged that I had quoted him profusely in my book. He did not, however, deny that I had accurately interpreted his doctrinal position and that of the humanist movement he represents. The following diagram, taken from my first book, should be read from the bottom up.

Summary of
Humanist Manifesto I & II

(read from bottom up)

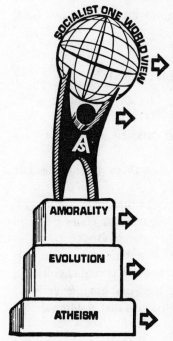

"We have reached a turning point in human history where the best often is to transcend the limits of national sovereignty and move toward the building of a world community . . . the peaceful adjudication of differences by international courts."

"We believe in maximum individual autonomy—reject all religious, moral codes that supress freedom, . . . demand civil liberties, including right to oppose governmental policies—right to die with dignity, euthanasia and suicide."

"Ethics is autonomous and situational . . . and stem from self interest—favor right to birth control, abortion, divorce and choice of sex direction."

"Religious Humanists regard the universe as self-existing and not created. . . . the human species is an emergence from natural evolutionary forces."

"We find insufficient evidence for belief in the existence of the supernatural . . . as nontheists we begin with man not God . . . no deity will save us; we must save ourselves."

The Gablers on the Teachings of Humanism

Mel and Norma Gabler of Garland, Texas, are acknowledged by secular humanists, Christians, textbook publishers, and even the press of the United States to be the most informed individuals in the country on the content of public-school textbooks. They are so influential in the state of Texas that some publishers, desirous of gaining their approval, check with the Gablers before they go to press with their texts. After years of research, the Gablers have listed the following nine basic tenets of humanism found in our children's textbooks. You will note that each one fits neatly under one or more of the five basic dogmas listed above.

THE TEACHINGS OF HUMANISM

- EVOLUTIONARY DOGMA   the idea that evolution is unquestioned scientific fact
- SELF-AUTONOMY   the idea that children are their own authorities
- SITUATION ETHICS   the idea that there are no absolute rights or wrongs
- CHRISTIANITY NEGATED   the idea that there is no supernatural (salvation, heaven/hell; many humanists claim belief in deity, but place their faith in man rather than in God)
- SEXUAL FREEDOM   the idea that public sex education is necessary, but without morals; belittles modesty, purity, chastity and abstinence/accepts abortion, premarital sex, and homosexuality
- TOTAL READING FREEDOM   the idea that children should have the right to read anything
- DEATH EDUCATION   the idea that there is no hope beyond the grave
- INTERNATIONALISM   the idea that world citizenship is preferable to national patriotism
- SOCIALISM   the idea that socialism is superior to private ownership[4]

© 1981 The Mel Gablers

The Gablers, after reading hundreds of school textbooks, state: "Humanism is a no-God religion and as much a religion as Christianity. This no-God religion is being passed on to our children through public education, in a subtle but effective manner."

3. Secular Humanists Have an Object of Worship   Mankind cannot tolerate a vacuum regarding God. Humanists do not understand that many yearnings of mankind are intuitive or inborn. One of these is his instinctive hunger for God. This can be verified by any observer of ancient cultures. I have traveled in forty-four countries and do not know of a single one in which there are not some ancient religious edifices rising out of primitive stone. The people who worked for the erection of these monumental structures were extremely poor, and their giving came at great sacrifice. They did so, however, to satisfy their urge for worship. Even Lenin showed he was aware of this craving by man, when he said, "Man is incurably religious."

When the Communists took over Russia, they tried to eliminate God from the entire culture, but failed utterly. They turned cathedrals and churches into museums; they disbanded most of the clergy; and they educated people with a total void toward God. In 1977, when my wife and I spent five days in Moscow, we were impressed (as we had been after nine days in Poland) that Lenin has become the god of Communism. Not only is his body encased in a tomb, to be viewed by the masses, but his emblems and statues are everywhere. The Russians and Poles and people of all nations need someone to worship. If they do not worship God or man, they will give obeisance to animals, as they do in India and other countries of the world.

Thus it is with secular humanists: they must have a God to worship. The humanist god is man himself. In fact, humanism is pure "manism." Pythagorus, one of the earliest humanists, said, "Man is the measure of all things." The basic humanistic misconception about man concerns his nature. Humanists view man as good, as potentially perfectible. In fact, humanists in education look upon education as the key to that perfectibility. From this view has sprung the idea that man by nature will do the right thing, if unfettered by the laws of religion, culture, or authority. Therefore, the humanist cries, "Liberty, freedom, equality," as if this will automatically guarantee man's total freedom and happiness. What they have produced is little more than a self-indulgent, pampered generation that thinks the world owes it a living.

The word *humanism* is very appropriate for this new (about one-hundred-year old) secular religion. It is made up of two parts: *human,* meaning "man," and *ism,* meaning "religion" (like Protestant*ism,* Catholic*ism,* or Confucian*ism*). *Humanism,* then, means, "the religion of man." This "manism" religion finds its embodiment in the prophetic number 666 of Revelation and will occupy much of my attention in a future volume in this series.

4. Humanism Has a Priesthood   All religions have a priesthood, no matter what it is officially called. From the Levites of Judaism to the Buddhist monks, there must be an elite leadership that propagates the "gospel" and formulates the religious plans that influence the next generation.

Since the religion of humanism chose public education as its vehicle to control the thinking of future generations, we should expect their priesthood to be the *Who's Who* in education. An examination of the history of public education will not disappoint us: the personnel abound with humanists. Horace Mann was the nineteenth-century high priest of education. He associated with his socialist, atheist, and Unitarian Friends of Education like Holbrook, Channing, and Owens. Included in this priesthood would be William Barton Rogers (an atheist married to a Unitarian activist), who founded the Massachusetts Institute of Technology in 1861.

John Dewey, the father of progressive education (otherwise known as regressive education) was the high priest of twentieth-century humanism. He stamped his version of atheism, evolution, antimorality, and socialism on this century's schoolchildren. It is important not to underestimate how harmful this man's ministry of promoting the religion of humanism has been to America's children. Every high priest has his lesser priests—in this case such disciples as George Counts, Robert Gates, and others who went out to instruct the teachers of our current public schools. It would be safe to assume that almost every head of a major teachers college is a secular humanist.

Additional luminaries in the priesthood of humanism would be Albert Ellis and Joseph Fletcher, who contributed greatly to the situation-ethics mentality so rampant today. We must also add B. F. Skinner and Carl Rogers of behavioristic and humanistic psychology fame and all of the SIECUS board members, such as Lester A. Kirkendall (known as the father of the sex-education movement) and Mary Calderone, the evangelist of sex education, formerly president of SIECUS (now replaced by Sol Gordon). This religious hierarchy has helped produce the national wave of sex activity rampant in our country. Additional high priests include Sidney Simon and Lawrence Kolberg, of values clarification, the teaching technique that more than any other, confuses this generation's children about morality. And the list goes on and on—a priesthood and high priesthood that earns its living communicating the religion of humanism in our public schools.

5. Secular Humanists Have Missionaries Every religion must have its missionaries who actively move out into the hinterland and provide the grass-roots work of recruitment.

Before the religion of humanism became the official dogma of our public schools, teachers were trusted educators of our young, who took seriously their responsibility for teaching reading, writing, arithmetic, and the other necessary skills of life. That is no longer the case. Today's teachers, according to some educators, are "change agents"— that is, agents of social change. As incredible as it may seem to you, their objective is to change our nation's generation of children from their commitment to traditional moral values and the values of their parents to the new humanist values (which in my studied opinion are no values at all).

As of 1981, we have a president who campaigned on a platform of traditional moral values; he was elected by individuals who clearly wanted a national leader committed to such traditional values. The high priests and missionaries of education represent opposing values. One educator, for instance, declares:

> We need to de-emphasize tradition and the past.... Educators can no longer afford to deplore and resist change. Too many teachers are still insisting that things must be done the "right way.".... [5]

All teachers, of course, have not been given advanced training as change agents, and many would resist it if they were. However, it is very difficult for parents and, in some cases, even concerned administrators in public education to identify these radical missionaries of humanism, for academic freedom guarantees them the privacy to teach anything they wish behind the closed door of the classroom. This was acknowledged by one educator in a warning to teachers that they eventually may have to face the results:

> When a teacher closes the classroom door in the morning and is alone with the students, the real curriculum begins . . . eventually the time of reckoning may come with cries and community furor.[6]

6. Humanism Has Its Seminaries   Like other religious denominations and groups, humanism has its seminaries, although they have been disguised under other names. Most graduate schools in the United States have been completely taken over by secular humanist thought, particularly in the field of education. It is almost impossible to get a PhD degree from an accredited college or university that is not overwhelmingly humanistic in its philosophy and teaching. This was one of the original targets of the humanists for implementing their control of the educational system, for they knew that in order to indoctrinate an entire generation of students, they first had to train the teachers. Virtually every teachers college in America is manned by PhDs who have had their minds immersed in the religion of secular humanism, which explains why all teachers colleges approach teacher preparation from a humanist perspective.

Present-day teachers seminaries are called teachers colleges. Some are state schools; others are divisions within universities, such as the Teachers College of Columbia University. Before that these teachers schools were called normal schools; in fact, even today some of the older colleges still have, engraved over the doorpost, the name Normal College.

Most people have no idea how easily a small number of influential humanist educators in key positions in the teacher-preparation field can have an impact on the morals, values, and objectives of millions of children. Church history, however, shows that entire denominations have in time been changed from conservative to liberal because liberal theological professors were granted key seats in theology and Christian ethics in the denomination's schools. It takes less than fifty years to change the entire direction of a denomination. Horace Mann and his friends established these teachers seminaries over a hundred and thirty years ago.

7. Secular Humanists Have Their Own Temples Many public schools are the citadels for the propagation of the religion of secular humanism. We have already seen that the humanists have temples, as Horace Mann referred to them in his previously quoted first annual report to the Massachusetts Board of Education.

Naturally, most educators do not use the term *temple,* not because it is inaccurate, but because use of it would inflame the many God-conscious taxpayers who would realize that they had been subsidizing humanism's religious buildings in the form of universities, colleges, high schools, junior high schools, and elementary schools by the thousands.

It takes no stretch of the imagination to conclude that believers in God have spent several trillions of dollars subsidizing the temples of the humanists, in the name of public education. These humanistic temples are the most elaborately equipped educational facilities in the world. I have visited multimillion-dollar multimedia centers that are absolutely incredible—if utilized. One media center specialist in charge griped, "The professors just won't take the time to use the equipment adequately." That observation is equally relevant to elementary and secondary schools. Paul Copperman observes, "Many inner-city schools are virtual technological laboratories of sophisticated electronic gadgetry that nobody uses. These funded schools are saturated with nonteaching adults. Investment in these secondary services has little relevance to educational process, and practically no impact on educational outputs.[7]

An indication of the religious bigotry of secular humanists appears in the way they dispose of unnecessary public-school properties. Due to the population decline and the flight to private education during the past decade, many public schools are standing idle and must eventually be sold. A pastor of a booming church in northern California shared with me that one of the local public schools was put up for sale, but when it was turned over to a realtor, a proviso forbade him to sell it to a church or Christian school. Since all the church people in that area had contributed to the original purchase of that school through their property taxes, such an action only confirms what most of us in Christian school leadership have already discovered: to the religious humanists, we are the enemy. And that enmity exists in a country that boasts of its religious freedom, tolerance, and equality.

8. Secular Humanists Create a Life-style   Almost every Christian is aware that Christianity produces a change in life-style. In fact, if a sinner does not change his ways after his conversion, we have serious doubts that he has really been born again. In the early days of Christianity, the followers of Jesus were called "followers of the way" because of the different way of life Christianity introduced.

We have already observed that many change agents masquerading as school teachers use every opportunity they can for social engineering. Some educators even admit it. Kenneth S. Kenworthy has said, "The basic personality patterns may have been formed before children ever enter school. They can be changed but the later that is postponed, the more difficult is the process."[8] Barbara Morris quotes Sidney Simon, one of the principal advocates of values clarification, which has swept like wildfire through many of our nation's schools during the past decade. Referring to his teaching at Temple University, he stated:

> I always bootlegged the values stuff under other titles. I was assigned to teach Social Studies in the Elementary School and I taught values clarification. I was assigned Current Trends in American Education and I taught *my* trend.[9]

Heed the testimony of a man who teaches the teachers of our nation's children!

The effects of humanistic thought on a person's life-style become startlingly evident in the personal testimony of educator Dr. Bill Freeman as published in *Christianity Today:*

> For 25 years, including my first two years of college and three years in the navy during World War II, I was associated with a rather conservative environment. I was reared in a small farming community in central Texas by parents devoted to their Christian faith and who brought up their four children to abide by biblical standards.

The first crack in this relatively solid foundation occurred during my latter undergraduate college years at Southern Methodist University, where I encountered many liberal professors. The crack almost became a break in the early 1950s, and I completed a master's degree in the domain of John Dewey at Teachers College, Columbia University. It was there that I was fully indoctrinated into the permissive philosophy of education and life.

I was introduced to the idea that there are no absolute standards: judgments depend only on circumstances. At the time, I was fascinated by situation ethics. Academically, that meant the teacher emphasized social development as much as intellectual progress, and that he expected less from students than formerly. Also, I began to believe that the group was more important than the individual. Many of my grades were determined by such nebulous criteria as group progress, social interaction, and future potentialities. I found myself enjoying the ease of achieving high marks (what we know today as grade inflation was just beginning).

Soon after receiving the M.A. degree, I put many of these permissive ideas into practice as a classroom teacher and principal in one of the state's better school systems, in Austin, Texas. I led in shaking up the basic curriculum. For example, I advocated the "progressive" idea that writing, reading, and arithmetic should all be integrated into the social studies program, letting these basic skills more or less "emerge."

... Relativism also influenced my moral philosophy, because I had accepted the idea that, regardless of my personal beliefs, what other people did was all right. I could keep my own position, if I desired, but I should not hinder "progress" for others. So I kept silent as society became more and more permissive while it abandoned traditional moral values.

However, I began to wake up as my two older children, then a high school junior and a college freshman, alerted me to the world of evangelicalism. As they became involved in evangelical campus groups, I realized they had a commitment and personal faith that I lacked.

Dr. Freeman began a thorough research of the writings of Dr. Francis Schaeffer and even visited L'Abri, Switzerland.

I could see that I had been submitting to the kind of humanistic forces that give man credit for the creation of the universe. I had seen the degeneration that occurs when humanists take God's truth out of human life. ...

After L'Abri, I tried to look at our culture more realistically. As I read newspaper and magazine reports, I saw that once highly regarded positions of leadership in our society were being eroded by immoral and illegal practices. Judges, ministers, police officers, mail carriers, bankers, senators, representatives, and even presidents were all found guilty. Yet, more and more the public was accepting these practices as permissible.

To be specific, I came to see seven deadly perils in permissiveness: *Self-centeredness.* We are becoming dedicated to self. The feeling of "damn the other person" is rampant. Because of this egocentricity, we are often able to justify any "self-fulfilling" act.

Laxity. We are coming to reject standards, authority, and adherence to laws, commandments, beliefs.

Dishonesty. We are becoming oblivious to lying, deceit, and shady deals. We are approaching a day when we no longer trust anyone.

Greed. We are becoming dedicated to self-gratification, dissatisfied regardless of our affluence.

Apathy. We are becoming indifferent to the needs of others, believing that it is best not to get involved—what is going on is none of our business.

Hatred. We strive for acceptance, care, friendship, love; yet we often demonstrate hatred by failure to build up people through praise. It is peculiarly difficult for us to say, "I love you."

Irresponsibility. We are losing our self-discipline. If things get tough, we move on because we live in a disposable society. If our work gets too hard, we quit; if our marriage gets difficult, we divorce; if our parents are "no good," we run away; if our schools are dull, we drop out.

As an educator he:

became specially aware of the results of permissiveness in the public schools. I came to see such problems as grade inflation, promotion for merely social reasons, laxity in discipline, lower academic standards, and general disrespect for people and property as reflections of our culture and its system of education. . . .

Young people today need specific, concrete answers—not endless talk about relativism and freedom of choice. The only freedom comes within a structure of absolutes, and if our teachers deny that structure, then they are really locking their students in bondage—the bondage of meaninglessness.[10]

I have quoted this excellent testimony at length because the author has traveled the superhighways of academia—the university, the teachers college, the classroom—and is reflecting the very issues that concern me. Secular humanism is creating a dangerous life-style.

9. Secular Humanists Have a Support Base   In spite of the crocodile tears shed by educators over the need for more funds to finance their lavish buildings and pay for their theoretical stratagems, they are rapidly spending our country into financial bankruptcy. All churches and religious orders have a support base. The one with which I am most familiar, as taught from both the Old and New Testament, involves tithes and offerings voluntarily given by believers. Secular humanists loudly bemoan the fact that churches and religious orders are granted tax exemptions as if this represented an abuse of the separation of church and state. They fail to concede that their temples never pay taxes; in fact, the high priests live off the forcible collection of taxes and probably have twenty times the funds at their disposal that all the religious groups in the country have, put together.

The supreme irony, of course, is that the bulk of this money comes from those who do not share the humanist value system. America's schoolchildren will be infinitely benefited when a sufficient number of taxpayers rise up and require that legislators cease and desist any further funding for the religious ideology of secular humanism. This would force our educators to get back to the serious business of teaching Johnny and Jane the basic skills so essential to their future.

10. Humanism Is Rooted in Eastern Religions   The concepts of modern humanism are not new, but can be traced back to Aristotle, Socrates, and Pythagoras. In their *Humanist Manifesto* they announce:

> Humanism is a philosophical, religious, and moral point of view as old as human civilization itself. It has its roots in classical China, Greece, and Rome; it is expressed in the Renaissance and the Enlightenment, in the scientific revolution, and in the twentieth century.[11]

If the truth were known, humanism, or the worship of man, goes back to Babylon, the source of all religion in which man substitutes worship of the creation for worship of the Creator. I am confident that if Nimrod were living today, he would be a humanist.

11. Humanism Is Officially Identified by the Supreme Court as a Religion Rather, than repeat the details listed on pages 128, 129 of *The Battle for the Mind,* where I give the historical and legal precedents in which the Supreme Court officially accepts humanism as a religion, I will only list them here:

1. *Torcaso* v. *Watkins,* 367 U.S. 488, 495 (1961)—The Supreme Court included secular humanism with the other religions of the world.
2. *United States* v. *Seeger,* 380 U.S. 163 (1965)—Decreed that religion included "atheists, agnostics, as well as adherents to traditional theism."
3. *Reed* v. *Van Hoven,* 237 F. Supp. 48 (W.D. Mich. 1965)—stated "as between theistic and humanistic religions. . . ."

Additional information can be found in the *Texas Tech Law Review* (Winter 1978) by attorneys John Whitehead and John Conlan.

12. Humanists Vigorously Oppose Theistic Religion The humanists' much ballyhooed quest for "human rights," "the brotherhood of man," "peace among mankind," and "pluralism" stops short of religious tolerance. "Academic freedom" is an educational charade! It means freedom for homosexuals, lesbians, feminists, abortionists, Marxists, and almost every other conceivable antimoral, anti-American teaching, except the recognition of God the Creator or the traditional moral values that Jews, Christians, and others share.

In essence, "academic freedom" is religious intolerance. Several times the church I formerly pastored for twenty-five years in San Diego had rented the 3,300-seat community auditorium in downtown San Diego for large church meetings. Consequently, you can imagine my surprise when, in 1971, our church in El Cajon, a city ten miles west of San Diego, tried to rent the community auditorium in that city but was denied permission. I verified that the building was indeed available that night, but it seems that a special proviso was included in the agreement when that auditorium was constructed. It was a joint venture between Grossmont Junior College and the city of El Cajon, on a 50-50 basis. The college had insisted that the contract contain an exclusion clause wherein the facility was never to be rented to

The Religion of Secular Humanism

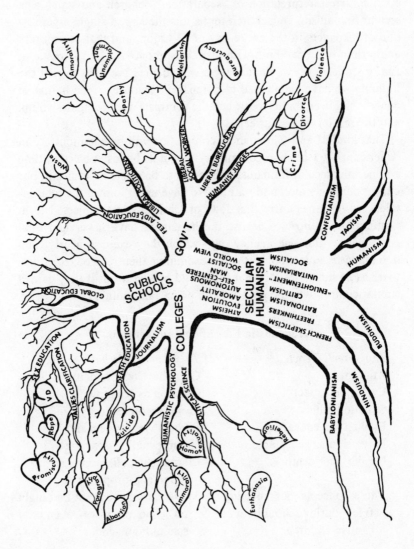

churches. It has been the scene of rock concerts, symphony concerts, and other kinds of activity, but *churches are forbidden!* This is just another bizarre interpretation of "separation of church and state" a la secular humanism. Our church represents the largest single organization of taxpayers in the entire city of El Cajon, and that community auditorium had been built with taxpayers' money, as had Grossmont Junior College, yet we as taxpayers were denied the right to rent the building we have been taxed to purchase. Obviously, some humanist educrat had been on his toes when the contracts were being drawn up, and the rest of us were asleep.

That kind of anti-Christian discrimination will be common fare in America if the Christian community sits on its hands at election time and permits secular humanist politicians to be elected to office in our cities, counties, states, and nation. We have never known the total intolerance in our country that Jews or Christians are subjected to in Communist countries, because the humanists have never had total control here. But one agency over which they exercise nearly total dominance is education. It is worth examining their religious tolerance there as an indication of what life would be like for us if they gained similar control over the government, police, and military.

Humanistic Educational Intolerance

They Freely Teach	They Totally Forbid Teaching
Atheism	God the Creator, deity of Jesus
Evolution as fact	Creation as scientific
Situation ethics	Moral absolutes
Explicit sex education	Biblical view of sexuality
Perversion as acceptable	Homosexuality as wrong
No life after death	Eternal life, heaven and hell, judgment, prophecy
These concepts can be taught freely during school hours to captive children.	These concepts cannot be taught on school premises—even after school hours end.

Whatever happened to religious tolerance in this country? Whatever happened to pluralism? They are both *dead* in public education and on public-school campuses, because humanists exercise virtual control there. If the day ever comes when they regulate the FCC, we will lose our rights to broadcast and televise—just as humanists have censored Christians out of those areas in Europe.

If humanists ever achieve the same oppressive authority over the IRS that they have in education, churches will lose their tax exemptions, as will Christian schools. This same intolerance has already been experienced by some churches in cities where humanists control the city council or the county board of supervisors. When a church needs a building permit or a conditional-use permit, the humanists vote as a block against the church, whereas the conservatives or the traditional moralists vote for them. Humanist legislators just do not see any value in churches.

This is not to say that all humanists are intolerant or immoral. It is accurate, however, to label them amoral—that is, neutral on morality. Christians are committed to the absolutes of morality. Humanists demand that society take a neutral position, which often leads to or condones gross immorality. Humanist control will result in humanist totalitarianism, no matter how neutral or "fair" some humanists may be, because history shows that the ruthless Joseph Stalin, Mao Tsetung, or John Dewey types will arise to discriminate against their victims.

If enough Christians awaken to the ever-increasing danger of humanism in our country, we will not be as controlled in the rest of society as we currently are in education. I hope their intolerance in this field will warn Americans that they are not to be trusted with control in other areas of influence. In fact, education would improve measurably if that control were removed.

Americans must awaken to what *religious freedom* or even *separation of church and state* really means to the religious humanist elite who control our schools, media, courts, and government bureaucracy. They mean by those terms that humanists must have the freedom to teach their religion of secular humanism—in the schools, government-controlled TV or wherever they please—*at taxpayers' expense!*

13. *Humanists Have a World View*   A person's world view affects every decision of his life. Like rose-colored glasses, it changes everything he sees; consequently it affects his thinking process.

Like a Christian, the humanist has two major time stages in his world view: immediate and eternal. For a Christian the immediate stage of his world view causes him to look on the world compassionately as a "white harvest field" of needy souls. That is why Christians have been the world's great humanitarians. Our people have built the orphanages, hospitals, schools, and other humanitarian agencies—not the humanists. Our people have voluntarily given billions to feed the hungry and supply the needs of suffering souls. Admittedly, we could and should do more in obedience to our Lord's command to help the poor, but Christians do not need to be ashamed of their past record when confronted by liberal humanists, who are not givers but takers. Their method: "take [forcibly, through taxes] from the rich and give to the poor"—create jobs for more liberals and humanists. Like welfare, which, I am told, takes thirty-two dollars in taxes to give nine dollars to the poor, the humanist cause benefits the humanist far more than the needy. The humanist gains votes from the poor to keep in office liberal politicians who vote more taxes from the working people—and the humanists call that humanitarianism.

The eternal stage of the humanist world view is ineffably dangerous. They believe, "When you're dead, you're dead"; there is no life after death. This causes some to foster a libertine philosophy: "Eat, drink and be merry, for tomorrow you die." Unlike the Christians, who believe that God controls the future, humanists are out to control it. Instead of being content to let the world exist as independent countries, they are eager to bring the nations into a one-world government based on socialism. They blame the capitalist countries for the poverty of the third-world countries and insist that only elite humanists are qualified to plan a world economy that will bring peace and equality to this planet. Because they do not believe in life after death, they are more actively driven to create a socialist heaven on earth. The master humanist planners of UNESCO, UNICEF, WHO, and other United Nations agencies are working feverishly to bring about what they call "the new world order." Their primary vehicles for causing American policy to share in this view and become its principal source of leadership and provision are (1) our public schools, kindergarten through university, (2) the media, both TV and press, and (3) government bureaucracy, the millions of humanists who have infiltrated every conceivable department of the federal and state government. The 14 million bureaucrats in government represent the highest concentration of humanists of any agency except education and media.

Be sure of this: during the next generation, we will hear and see increasing amounts of propaganda from education, media, and government bureaucrats about the new world order. It is a segment of their religious quest—a very dangerous element for those who love liberty and morality. Socialism, whether national or international, always advances on the wheels of oppression.

14. Humanists Have a View of Death   Humanists have developed a view of death. Of course, everyone holds some view of death, for that is part of living. But your view forms a special component of your religion. Even if you reject the concept of life after death, that is a religious view. It has always been so. Whether it's the Indian's view of the Happy Hunting Ground or the Hindu view of a better life the next time around, both are part of a religion. In atheism, a cornerstone of the humanist belief system proclaims stringently, "There is no life after death."

Science cannot prove or disprove life after death, but humanists teach as fact that it does not exist. How can they be so dogmatic on the subject? By faith, of course. Consequently their view of death and eternity is part of their religious perspective.

If the Christian premise concerning death is unwelcome in the public school, why is the humanist view so freely taught? Because ours is wrong and theirs is right? Or because theirs is legal? Certainly not! Humanists *control* the public schools, and their fellow humanists in the ACLU stand as voluntary watchdogs to see that only humanistic views are taught.

15. Humanists Admit That Humanism Is a Religion   The reluctance of some Christian educators and ministers to recognize that humanism is a religion has amazed me. They must be passivists at heart, who by nature would rather switch than fight. For once a Christian faces the fact that humanism is indeed a religion, he is compelled to oppose it with all his influence. Otherwise he is willingly supporting—with his taxes—the most dangerous religion in the world.

Humanists themselves are neither confused about their philosophy nor reluctant to proclaim its tenets. Paul Kurtz, a leading spokesman for humanism, states in *Humanist Manifesto II:*

> Humanists still believe that traditional theism, especially faith in the prayer-hearing God, assumed to love and care for persons, to hear and understand their prayers, and to be able to do something about them, is an unproved and outmoded faith. Salvationism, based on mere affirmation, still appears as harmful, diverting people with false hopes of heaven hereafter. Reasonable minds look to other means of survival.[12]

In all, *Humanist Manifesto I* calls the humanistic belief system a religion *nine times.* Consider the following examples:

1. In order that religious humanism may be better understood we, the undersigned, desire to make certain affirmation which we believe the facts of our contemporary life demonstrate.
2. Today man's larger understanding of the universe, his scientific achievements, and his deeper appreciation of brotherhood, have created a situation which requires a new statement of the means and purposes of religion.
3. To establish such a religion is a major necessity of the present.
4. First: Religious humanists regard the universe as self-existing and not created.
5. Eighth: Religious humanism considers the complete realization of human personality to be the end of man's life and seeks its development and fulfillment in the here and now.
6. Ninth: In place of the old attitudes involved in worship and prayer the humanist find his religious emotions expressed in a heightened sense of personal life and in a cooperative effort to promote social well-being.
7. Twelfth: Believing that religion must work increasingly for joy in living, religious humanists aim to foster the creative in man and to encourage achievements that add to the satisfactions of life.

8. Thirteenth: Religious humanism maintains that all associations
   and institutions exist for the fulfillment of human life.
9. So stand the theses of religious humanism.[13]

Until a sufficient number of citizens recognize that the trouble with
our public schools is not a lack of money, facilities, or time in
school—it is the use of the public school for the teaching of the most
harmful religion in the world, secular humanism—the best thing we
can do for modern education and our 43 million public-school children is to expel secular humanism and get back to teaching basics
resting on the traditional moral values upon which our nation was
founded.

How to Make Sexual Animals Out of a Generation of Children

In 1969, as a concerned parent and local pastor, I appeared before our school board in opposition to the new brand of sex education that was sweeping the country. The next year, as a fledgling author, I penned a well-documented booklet entitled *A Christian View of Radical Sex Education.* In 1972 I was invited to address a summer-session sex-education class at San Diego State University, all of the students serving as sex educators in local schools. Needless to say, I was extended reservedly polite, but hostile, treatment.

In each of these experiences I predicted that this new, explicit brand of sex education, taught to mixed classes, kindergarten through twelfth grade (though, at the time, the primary focus was on junior high and high school), would result in a massive wave of youthful promiscuity, teenage pregnancy, and an unprecedented epidemic of venereal disease. (Since I did not anticipate the 1973 Supreme Court decision to make abortion legal, I omitted the mass murder of the unborn, which has now resulted in over 10 million deaths.) Teaching explicit sex education to unmarried teenagers, I advised, was tantamount to pouring gasoline on emotional fires.

Today I am sorry to report that promiscuity among teenagers has reached incredible levels. According to the 1981 Guttmacher report on teenage pregnancy, "It is the exceptional young person who has not had sexual intercourse while still a teenager. Eight in 10 males and seven in 10 females report having intercourse in their teens. . . . About *85 percent* had intercourse before marriage."[1] Teenage pregnancy was recently reported as the number-one problem in the Washington, D.C., school system, and that can be repeated throughout the country. Teenage abortion seems to be a major contributor to the increase in teenage suicide among girls. And for the past five years, the United States Health Department has indicated that the number-one health hazard in the United States for young people under twenty-four years of age is venereal disease. But that does not tell the full story. The rest of it is that a new strain has arrived on the scene called herpes simplex II—and, as of this writing, it is incurable!

Now the secular humanists in our public schools have the audacity to inform parents that the only way to solve the teenage pregnancy and venereal-disease problem is to supply our young people with *more* sex education in the public schools. That is like asking Jesse James to solve the problem of bank robbery! If our humanist educrats were as interested in teaching Johnny and Jane to read, write, and do math as they are in making them sexually active before marriage, we would have a nation of teenagers with academic skills, instead of a country of youthful fornicators.

There Is a Place for Sex Education

I am not opposed to sex education per se. As a matter of fact, I have written a book entitled *The Act of Marriage,* which has become the leading manual on sexual adjustment for married couples within the Christian community.

No, I do not oppose sexuality or sex education as long as it is confined to the one expression laid down in the Word of God: marriage. All sexual expression outside of marriage is clearly condemned in the Bible. However, the Scriptures teach that sexual freedom and an undefiled relationship as they exist between a man and wife are pleasing to God (Hebrews 13:4). Unfortunately, the value-free teachings of secular humanism make no allowance for moral absolutes. Consequently, explicit sex education has made sexual animals out of a generation of young people.

Secular Humanism and Sex Education

For years I have closely monitored the sex-education movement and have noticed that with few exceptions the leading exponents of today's brand of radical, explicit sex education have been atheistic humanists.

Since secular humanists do not believe in God, they tend to adopt the theory of evolution as their favorite explanation of man's origin. Consequently they do not perceive a need for morality. According to their theory, animals are amoral, and since man is an animal; he should be free to act in an amoral manner. This is the primary cause for the sharp clash between humanists and traditional moralists raging in our country today. We believe that moral absolutes exist; they do not. Thus we disagree on almost every moral issue.

Unless your school district is blessed with a superintendent who has courageously resisted the state or federal educrats, with their perverted compulsion to make sexual animals of our youth, you would be shocked by the explicit nature of the local high-school sex-education curriculum. In fairness to those quality educators still in the system, a number of locally produced programs are not nearly so offensive as those produced at the national level. In fact, I know one Christian who has served twelve years as sex-education curriculum director for a large school system in order to keep it from falling into the hands of an amoral humanist, who would adopt a SIECUS-approved or government-funded program designed to destroy the morals of our youth. The spontaneous outcries of parents and others, from Miami to Seattle, and from New Jersey to California, suggest that such courage is now universal. At present we are experiencing a new attempt to make the radical sex-education materials of the late sixties and seventies look like Sunday-school literature by comparison to that of the eighties.

Jacqueline Kasun Blows the Whistle

Jacqueline Kasun, professor of economics at Humboldt State University, Arcata, California, is the concerned woman who blew the whistle on the human-sexuality course that the federal and state educrats almost imposed on California's schoolchildren in 1979. As an educator herself, she is appalled that so few of the "sexologists" who would inflict their values on children, whether parents like it or not, are really qualified for the roles they have assumed. According to Dr. Kasun:

> The movement's leaders and disciples are not biologists but mainly psychologists, sociologists, and "health educators." Their principal concerns are less with the physiology of procreation and inheritance than with "sexuality," a very broad field of interest running the gamut from personal hygiene to the population question, but largely concerned with attitudes and "values clarification" rather than with biological facts.
>
> Thus, though the new sex programs are rather thin on biological facts, they do not skimp on information about the various types of sexual activity. From instruction in "French" kissing to the details of female masturbation, the information is explicit and complete. The curriculum guide for the seventh and eighth grades in my city of Arcata, in Humboldt County California, specifies that "the student will develop an understanding of masturbation," will view films on masturbation, will "learn the four philosophies of masturbation—traditional, religious, neutral, radical—by participating in a class debate," and will demonstrate his understanding by a "pre-test" and a "post-test" on the subject. A Planned Parenthood pamphlet, *The Perils of Puberty*, recommended by my county health department for local high school use, says: "Sex is too important to glop up with sentiment. If you feel sexy, for heaven's sake admit it to yourself. If the feeling and the tension bother you, you can masturbate. Masturbation cannot hurt you and it will make you feel more relaxed."[2]

Who's Responsible?

One school superintendent protested, "I can't be held responsible for everything that is taught in all the classrooms of my district." My answer to him was very simple: "Why not?" That is one of the problems with public education today: accountability. Educators demand the right to "experiment" with the most precious possession a parent can share with them—the mind of his child—without being held accountable for the results. They "innovate," "change," and "upgrade" at will—without parental consent—and then pass the buck whenever anything goes wrong. Why shouldn't the superintendent be accountable? We pay him $50,000 and provide him with deputy superintendents, assistants to the superintendent, executive secretaries—at times an excessive support, it would seem—to administrate his system. Then why shouldn't he be held responsible? To be honest, he does not want the responsibility, but he cherishes the authority.

In San Diego County I couldn't even get the superintendent to discuss with me the 1979 controversial course, *Education for Human Sexuality,* which was eventually rejected by the state Superintendent of Education (in time for him to run for reelection). There is no excuse for any superintendent not to know what is taught in his district's sex-education classes. He is responsible for hiring the sex-education-curriculum director, and he oversees the program—or should.

Parents and taxpayers must hold superintendents and school-board members fully responsible for the condition of their schools. If they permit humanistic antimoralists to pervert the morals of our young by teaching sex courses that would make a stevedore blush, they should be replaced, by whatever legal means are available, with those who are committed to what President Reagan calls traditional moral values.

Responsible educators should be honored. That is, those who make academic achievement their number-one priority—with a vital emphasis on hard work, discipline, respect for authority, and vocational preparation—should be applauded when they do not endeavor to undermine the moral values of parents by using the classroom to advocate "alternate life-styles." But aggressive humanists, whose obsession with social and moral engineering is creating the present disenchantment with our public schools, should be expelled. If they want to perpetuate their religious doctrine of humanism (which is little more than antitheistic Unitarianism in academic regalia), they ought to be honorable enough to do it at the expense of the 15 million or so humanist taxpayers in America, not at the expense of the 160 or more million who desire their children to be taught moral absolutes. However, don't expect them to do so willingly.

In spite of parental outcries over the explicit nature of sex education, it has been jammed down the throats of our children. One of the biggest lies told by our educrats is, "Parents demand it." The truth is, parents resent it, finding it excessively detailed and inflammatory. It should never be taught without a balanced view of virtue, self-control, and marital commitment.

Sex Education Was Not "Spontaneous"

Of one thing you can be certain: the national teaching of radical sex education has not been spontaneous or "community developed." In fact, it is largely the work of fewer than 300 atheistic humanists whose access to the minds of our nation's 43 million public-school children has done more to corrupt the morals of America during the past two decades than any other influence, except for the widespread dissemination of pornography. A handful of leaders created the entire debased program: Aldous and Julian Huxley, F. Brock Chisholm, Margaret Sanger, and others. They were joined by sexologists, educrats, and humanists, all of whom have in common a strong antagonism toward religion in general and Christianity in particular. In addition, they are adamantly opposed to any kind of moral absolutes.

Prior to 1960 little or no uproar was heard concerning sex education in the public school, because it was almost nonexistent. Some physical-education teachers supplied the basics, and in many schools human sexuality was introduced in biology classes. Rarely was it explicit or presented in mixed classes in such a way as to have a humiliating effect on impressionable and sexually excitable youth. Almost never was it presented as an open attack on parental and traditional moral values.

The massive sex education movement generated in the early sixties—which is big business today—was not spontaneous or accidental, but carefully planned. To understand its origin, one must know who started it and why. And the best place to start is with the most powerful single force behind the entire movement: SIECUS. The Sex Information and Educational Council of the United States was founded in 1964.

Claire Chambers has written the most carefully documented work I have read on the subject, which is *Siecus Circle of Humanist Revolution.* In it she details the history, background, and personalities of the founders and prime movers of the sex-education movement. Serious students of sex education should read her 550-page book, for in it she documents how the United Nations sponsored organizations United Nations Educational, Scientific and Cultural Organization (UNESCO) and World Health Organization (WHO) have worked with

Planned Parenthood to establish sex education in our public schools in the name of "population control." Instead of controlling unwed pregnancies, sex education has measurably increased them by creating a teenage wave of sexual activity unmatched by any generation in the history of the world. What do these organizations have in common? They were all headed by secular humanists whose moral values conflict with those upon which this country was founded, which, by the way, are still held by the majority of the American people.

Chambers also points out that many of the same people were the originators of SIECUS, have served as board members or have contributed materials or have lectured for it. This connection is important because it explains part of the reason for the drastic change, since the mid-sixties, in the moral tone of sex-education teaching, from traditional moral values to the United Nations humanistic, antimoral values.

First I find it interesting that the past president of SIECUS, who served as its chief spokesman for many years, was married to the number-two man in the World Health Organization. That could be coincidence and so could the fact that the sex-education curriculum of SIECUS is more in line with WHO's permissive values than it is with America's traditional moral values. But it also could be by design.

The public school has served as an excellent conduit to the minds of our youth, for getting the international New World Orders of humanism to replace the values of their parents. Read Chambers' book and see if you agree that today's explicit sex-ed policies that have caused incalculable suffering and heartache in parents and teenagers have strong international humanist connections. You will find her evidence quite convincing.

Why Are They So Successful?

The success achieved by SIECUS, AASECT (its front organization that is made up of sex therapists and representatives of the public schools who are responsible for sex-education programs), and Planned Parenthood in overthrowing traditional moral values in the minds of our youth is really quite simple. They just arrange seminars, conferences, or institutes for sex educators, obtain foundation grants or federal or state funding for tuition, and then invite sex-education teachers or prospective teachers to attend by offering free tuition, board, and room, and academic credit. Those who are turned off by the crass crudities that emanate from the antimoral humanist lecturers selected by SIECUS or AASECT drop out of the program in disgust. Those who share their humanistic values and those educators too naive to understand what is going on absorb what they learn and take it back to their local school district. By this means a handful of humanists have succeeded in corrupting the morals of an enormous pecentage of our nation's youth (aided, of course, by pornographic literature, X-rated movies, and antimoral TV programming).

Not all teachers who attend such conferences are humanists or naive educators. Some are committed to traditional moral values but elect to wade through the filth in order to expose these people as intellectual charlatans. Consider the testimony of Barbara Morris, a nationally recognized authority on the philosophy of contemporary education:

> Up until 1970 when I attended a conference sponsored by SIECUS (Sex Information and Education Council of the U.S.) I could not believe sex education in the schools could be a problem. I would not believe the schools would dare to intrude in this very private area of children's lives. But I learned differently, very quickly. Unfortunately, many parents still believe sex education is nothing more than providing just "the facts of life". They would know differently if they could attend the meetings sex educators attend.
>
> At that SIECUS meeting in New York, I learned that homosexuality would be promoted in sex education as a legitimate alternative lifestyle. Under the guise of exploring the definition of "intimacy", the attendees were exposed to the opinions of a panel of "experts", group discussions and a desensitizing film that promoted homosexuality. There was also the appearance of newspaper columnist "Dear Abby" who gave her approval and congratulations to the panel of experts, saying she liked their candor and their willingness to confess to others. Her praise for the meeting was emphatic and lavish.
>
> At the same meeting, Dr. Harold Leif, M.D., a past president of SIECUS, told the group that sex education in the past dealt with the "plumbing aspects" of human sexuality but in the future, the shift would be to a greater concern for values. In sex education, students would be taught to search for intimacy, autonomy and independence in diverse life styles. He said that by 1980, sex education would be

taken for granted. Only the goals would be hotly debated. How right he was!

Dr. Mary Calderone was also on hand, pleading for an end to the use of the word "deviant" in describing homosexuality. She insisted it was a value term and that henceforth, homosexuality should be considered an alternate lifestyle.

All of this, remember, took place in 1970. Where are we today? Are we still going to believe that sex education in government schools provides just the facts of normal sex?

In 1972, the American Association of Sex Educators and Counselors (AASEC, which was later to become AASECT, adding "Therapists" to the name), had a meeting in Washington, D.C. Dr. Patricia Schiller, executive director, opened the meeting, assuring the sex educators that "you are the cream of the country."

Dr. David R. Mace, the sex educators' symbol of respectability, delivered a devastating repudiation of religion in general and railed against Christianity in particular. Also at the same meeting was the darling of the more liberated sex educators. Dr. Albert Ellis, who was given enthusiastic applause for mockery of God and four-letter obscenities.

At the same meeting, prior to showing explicit sex films intended to desensitize the viewers, the press was asked to leave because it was a closed meeting and legal counsel had warned of possible arrest for showing such films in an open meeting.

The following year, AASEC had another meeting which was bolder than the previous meeting, even though an effort was made to give the event an aura of respectability. But just as little can be done to cover the stench of decaying garbage, little could be done to add respectability to the meeting. But try they did. Dr. David Mace was back again, but this year he did an about face. In his cultured British voice, ringing with the expertise of an accomplished preacher, he spoke highly of those religious figures in history who put humanness ahead of their religion, such as St. Francis of Assisi and "Pope Paul the twenty-third". To St. Francis and the mis-named Pope, he added Rev. William Genne, coordinator of Family Ministries of the National Council of Churches of Christ. Rev. Genne spoke approvingly of lesbian and homosexual "marriages" and "various types of communal experiences".

To keep in touch with the reality of who and what they are, Dr. Albert Ellis, who makes no pretense of being intellectual about sex, again delighted the sex educators with obscene language, a lambasting of parents and the "goddam" Catholic church.[3]

On 6 November 1981, the Sex Education Coalition of Metropolitan Washington held a sex-education-teaching-methods conference in the nation's capital. Participants included "teachers, sex educators, Planned Parenthood representatives, and others." Two of the others who had slipped in were my personal friends—Sandy McKasson, active opponent of explicit sex education in Dallas, and Karen Davis, president of Christian Women's National Concerns of Fort Worth, Texas.

The woman lecturer and leader for the day was billed as an "AASECT Certified Sex Educator" and "Family Life/ Sex Education Teacher" with seven years of experience in the Falls Church, Virginia, junior- and senior-high-school system. "Her classes have been used as model classrooms for the development of many public and private school programs," the officially distributed notes read. My friends brought a tape recorder to the sessions and have subsequently printed a verbatim report. At the outset the lecturer explained that one way to make youngsters comfortable in sex education classes is to "make them feel special"—by declaring that they would be trained as sex educators to their peers. "She said she gave the book, *Our Bodies Ourselves,* to her students and suggested that they pass this information along to their peers when they have a friend that needs information."[4] That book, incidentally, is probably the most objectionable sex education book in public-school libraries today.

The teacher of sex-education instructors bemoaned the fact that "adequate" teaching materials were not available because the field has only been opening up since the late 1960s. Of sex education in general she noted, "It is absolutely on the cutting edge. It is in the pioneering stage at the moment." She added, "There isn't a textbook for high school that I find adequate. There is a book that Sol Gordon wrote called *Parenting.* The first chapter is very short and dynamite."[5] (Moralists would tend to label it *pornography,* not *dynamite.*)

Speaking of anatomy and physiology, she observed, "You can do with that what you want to. I think that I will have difficulty with my administrators convincing them that in the eighth grade I am going to want to talk about sexual arousal to orgasm. I think I will be able to do it. Those are just such catch words to people." Explaining that her use of language seldom matches that used by traditional biology teachers, she stated, "But I fool them. When I say 'anatomy and physiology,' I mean sexual response, erections, orgasms, all those good things. That's not what they mean at all."[6]

In discussing the overall content of a sex-education course, she listed the following as being of prime importance:

Non-marital sex
Homosexuality
Masturbation
Abortion
Contraception
Rape
Incest[7]

The "professional" sex educator spoke at some length about the new sex-education fad labeled "guided fantasy." This methodology asks the teacher to suggest a setting between two or more people and encourage the young people to fantasize about it—with no limitation.

> Remember, I've been teaching this course for 10 years and have a lot of trust and parent education.
> Now, I take them on a guided fantasy, and I have them walking down the beach, and I have them see this special person, and that person walks slowly to them. I tell them to "experience" what turns on their feelings in their bodies, in the upper part of their chest [to the workshop participants she said, "You have to go through this yourself in order to tell them what to look for"], on to their shoulder muscles, arms, what are their feelings in their body. What do they feel tingling? It's so special. Then, have them parting.
> They [the kids] always say, "Why did you bring us back?" They don't want to come back. It is a wonderful experience. I say to the parents that the reason I do that is to get them in touch with the facts—to get them in touch with legitimate physical responses.[8]

"Legitimate responses"? Sexually aroused teenagers at a time of high libido and low moral commitment, stimulated by a "professional" sex educator in their own tax-supported schools, are hardly in a position to know the difference between "legitimate" and "illegitimate" responses. What *should* teenagers do with their passions, drives, and urges? Why aren't they encouraged to ask their parents? After all, parents pay the bill for this "education," and they have to bear the responsibility when their teens get pregnant or contract VD. This kind of irresponsible teaching is criminal. It causes untold emotional and physical suffering never experienced as a result of the teaching of chastity, morality, and responsibility.

SIECUS: The Sin-Sick Sex Council of the United States of America

What seemed to many like spontaneous sex education springing up across the United States was not spontaneous at all. It was the result of a plan carefully laid by people whose objectives can scarcely be limited to education. This cleverly structured organization was labeled by *McCall's* magazine as "A high voltage, non-profit organization . . . which is without doubt the most important single force in sparking sex education in our schools. . . ." The National Education Association (NEA), which has worked closely with SIECUS from the beginning, had this to say about them in the early days:

> A new, voluntary health agency, SIECUS (Sex Information and Education Council of the United States) has just been established in New York City. One of its many purposes will be to provide assistance to communities and schools wishing to embark on sex education programs. SIECUS will act as a clearinghouse for research and education in sex, as a source of information about sex education in the schools, and as a public forum where consideration of various aspects of man's sexuality can be carried out in dignified and objective fashion.[1]

In 1970 the NEA was obviously no protector of America's schoolchildren, for they did not bother to warn or even mention to their teachers that SIECUS was the illegitimate offspring of UNESCO and the World Health Organization, themselves the outgrowth of the

United Nations. What do these elite leaders of the UN, UNESCO, WHO, SIECUS, and the NEA have in common? It isn't nationality, profession, or hobbies, but their religious belief in secular humanism. Dan Smoot, a careful researcher, reported in 1969:

> SIECUS . . . was organized in May, 1964; began active operations in July, 1964; and formally announced its existence in January, 1965. It has federal tax exemption as a "non-profit, voluntary health organization." Its principal sources of income are gifts from tax-exempt foundations—Commonwealth Fund, Ford, and others.
>
> Dr. Mary Calderone, organizer and founder of SIECUS, runs the organization as executive director, with a small staff. She has a 51-member board of directors composed of 26 persons from the academic field; 5 from business; 4 from the federal government; 4 from the social services field; 3 from the publishing field; 2 from Catholic organizations; 1 from the National Council of Churches; 1 Rabbi; 1 county judge; 1 from a state government; 1 from a TV station; 1 from a research foundation; 1 from the National Education Association. SIECUS is not a membership organization. The only people officially affiliated with it are its staff and board members.
>
> The SIECUS role is primarily that of persuader and consultant. Dr. Calderone and various members of her board are perpetually crisscrossing the country, participating in sex-education conferences, speaking to PTA groups, school boards, community organizations, selling the idea of establishing sex-education programs, with the SIECUS slant, in all grades of all schools.
>
> SIECUS itself produces little material for direct classroom use. It has published eight SIECUS Study Guides, intended to disseminate SIECUS ideas about sex education, rather than to serve as classroom aids. It publishes a quarterly newsletter . . . which is largely devoted to reviews of sex-education materials approved by SIECUS. SIECUS also sells "SIECUS Reprints"—reproductions of magazine articles, speeches, and lectures, most of which were prepared by Dr. Calderone and various members of her board.[2]

The purpose of SIECUS was spelled out very carefully in its own newsletter of October 1968, by Dr. Calderone:

> The purpose of sex education is . . . engagement of the individual, whatever his age, in a process by which, while acquiring a fund of basic knowledge, he may also be helped to develop at least the beginnings of insights and attitude changes that might enable him to make

sound, rational decisions regarding the use that he will make of that knowledge, whether professionally or in his personal life.[3]

The official stationery of SIECUS notes that its aim is: "To establish for all responsible elements in our society an understanding of the basic role of sex in interpersonal relationships, that is, the personal and social significance of human sexuality."[4]

In her speech to the Texas PTA State Convention on 21 November 1968, Dr. Calderone stated, " 'The concept of sexuality as the totality of expression of the individual's entire self as male or female is, I believe, the essence of the purpose for which SIECUS was established . . . As a 10th grade boy put it, "There's more to sex than just doing it." ' "[5]

The Radical Sexologists of SIECUS

Since it is their admitted purpose to foster attitudes about sex, we had better take a close look at the attitudes or principles of those who make up the SIECUS organization. It is impossible to separate the subject of sex from that of moral values and principles; therefore it is worth the time and space to examine carefully just who makes up this powerful, morally subversive organization. Fortunately, their publications clearly introduce their originators and directors. Be sure of this: the moral values and principles regarding one of the most delicate and significant subjects in the world will be no higher than the moral values of those who direct it. As an old saying counsels, "A stream never rises above its source."

Dr. Mary Calderone: Founder and Former Executive Director

Dr. Calderone, a grandmother in her late seventies, is a niece of Carl Sandburg; a daughter of Edward Steichen, a well-known photographer; a graduate of Vassar; a Quaker; and a member of the Family Life Committee of the National Council of Churches. She previously served as medical director of the Planned Parenthood Association. Dr. Calderone is evidently a dynamic and forceful personality, for early in the history of SIECUS, she was referred to by *McCall's* magazine as the "Commander-in-Chief of 'sex education' forces."

Though described by the *Saturday Evening Post* as a Joan of Arc for sex education, Dr. Calderone is more often referred to as "a sweet-faced, silvery-haired grandmother" who shocks audiences by using four-letter words to make her point, excusing herself by insisting that euphemisms in sex discussions are dishonest. Her motto is "tell them everything and tell them early." According to the *Post:*

> Contrary to the views of most child psychoanalysts, Dr. Calderone holds that sex education should start in the nursery. Around the age of three the child should assimilate such knowledge, along with the correct terminology, such as "The penis of the father is made to carry the sperm into the mother through the vagina." Kindergarten teachers should then impart additional clinical details.[6]

She insists that it is improper to tell a five-year-old child that the father "places" the seed of a baby in the mother, so she will describe the sex act in detail, using explicit terms and naming the sexual organs involved during coitus.

Dr. Lester Kirkendall: Cofounder and SIECUS Board-of-Directors Member

For many years a professor of family life at Oregon State University and apparently the second most influential figure in the advancement of the SIECUS cause, Dr. Kirkendall is:

> ... A prolific author of sex books and magazine articles about every conceivable sexual foible, [he] will never be accused of being an old fuddy-duddy by even the hippiest of the pornopoliticians. Still, Kirkendall is referred to by *Reader's Digest* as "without question, one of the most respected authorities in the whole field of sex education and family life." He has, according to the *Digest,* "helped to create today's new generation of sex educators."
>
> Lester Kirkendall says he believes that, "if present trends continue, premarital intercourse will almost certainly increase." But, the Professor adds, he doesn't feel this is necessarily bad. He writes in *Sex and Our Society* that if couples "do experiment with sex only to have their relationship flounder, their honest efforts to understand and be responsible to one another may well have been more gain than loss."[7]

Lester Doniger: Former President of SIECUS

Lester Doniger is "said to be the former Publisher of *Pulpit Digest,* Director of Pulpit Book Club, and President of the Pulpit Press [ultraliberal Protestant organizations that have tried to influence ministers to the left for many years]. Curiously, Doniger's autobiographical note in *Who's Who in World Jewry* does not mention his Protestant publishing business, and he has variously listed his birthplace as Raczki, Poland, and Vienna, Austria."[8]

Mrs. Elizabeth Koontz: SIECUS Board Member

Mrs. Koontz was president of "the million-member National Education Association. . . . It is thus not surprising that N.E.A. has been in the forefront of promoting S.I.E.C.U.S. throughout the nation, and that Mary Calderone has been a contributor to the *NEA Journal.*"[9] Mrs. Koontz was named by President Nixon to direct the Women's Bureau of the Department of Labor.

Dr. Isadore Rubin: SIECUS Treasurer

A founding board member and treasurer from the early days of 1964 until his death, Dr. Rubin was one of the most influential men on the board.

> . . . Rubin was on May 3, 1955 identified in sworn testimony before the House Committee on Un-American Activities as a member of the Communist Party by Mrs. Mildred Blauvelt, an undercover operative within the Communist Party for the New York City Police Department. Rubin was subsequently Editor of the *New York Teacher News,* published by the New York Teachers Union—which was expelled from the A.F.L.-C.I.O. when it was found to be controlled by the Communists. So total was his commitment to the Reds that he even had to be dismissed from his job as a teacher in New York City because of his refusal to deny his membership in the Communist Party.[10]

Reverend William H. Genné:
SIECUS Board Member

Reverend Genné, another cofounder of SIECUS, was at one time secretary of the organization. He also served as coordinator for the National Council of Churches Commission on Marriage and Family Life.

These are only a few of the members of the board of directors, but they are certainly the most well-known and seem to be the most influential in forming the organization's ideology. Although they are few in number, do not be deceived; this is a determined, hard-core group whose teachings will, in my opinion, succeed in destroying the moral values of America's 43 million public-school children.

Parents who rebel at having the public school lead their children into the pit which proved so disastrous for the Scandinavians are astonished to find that they have run into a veritable Leftist buzz-saw. The S.I.E.C.U.S. proponents even hold seminars [for teachers and educators] on how to deal with their conservative opponents. At one of these seminars, Dr. Lester Kirkendall characterized all such opponents as "a fringe group of dissidents who don't think rationally." He maintains that those who oppose the program to "change America's sexual attitudes have hangups about sex." To skirt these "sick" people, Kirkendall recommends: "Just sneak it [the sex program] in as an experimental course. ... Go to your P.T.A. and get support. That's where the power lies. ... Don't say that you are going to start a sex education course. Always move forward. Say that you are going to enrich, expand, and make it better. The opposition can't stop something that you have already started."

This strategy puts the opponents in a position of being "aginners" who are "out to destroy our modern, progressive Family Life course."

Another strategy used by the ... sex educationists is to form a committee of civic leaders including doctors, clergymen, and businessmen to endorse the introduction of the program into the local school. Many, if not most, of these men are not aware of just what they are endorsing, but feel that sex education is generally a good idea. Once having committed themselves, pride and ego require them to defend their stand even as the educationists turn a presumed course in physiology into out-and-out indoctrination for premarital sex and amorality.[11]

Dr. Kirkendall alleges, "Parents become traumatic about their youngsters engaging in sexual activity, because they do not realize that premarital sexual intercourse, even for children, is all right, provided 'consideration is given for the partner.' "

He notes that sexologists are able to:

> Slip sex education into school curricula without unduly alarming parents, if they will start with the premise that all children receive some sex training by simply living. "Any school," he claims, "is fully warranted in saying that it is 'expanding and improving' rather than 'starting' a sex-education program. The public is less afraid of expanding than of innovating. . . ." He suggests weaving sex education into regular school courses, in preference to establishing it as a separate course, because, he says, "the more sex education can be set within the normal program the less it will be singled out as unusual and threatening."[12]

If this expression by Dr. Kirkendall is a true reflection of the determination of SIECUS board members, then it should prove worthwhile to examine some of the other activities of these people.

The Radical Background of SIECUS Board Members

Dr. Isadore Rubin, SIECUS treasurer, not only was "one of the most influential board members" but probably had the worst public record. In addition to his morally subversive work for SIECUS, Dr. Rubin was at the same time an editor of the notorious *Sexology* magazine. One reporter suggested that:

> Although S.I.E.C.U.S. proclaims that one of its purposes is to counter exploitation of sex, its own officers are involved in the wildest sort of sex exploitation. Rubin's pulpy *Sexology* magazine dwells on sex sensationalism, with lurid pictures of men and women in the most intimate positions, presenting crass articles dealing with the worst sort of perversion. Examples of features in recent issues include: "Can Humans Breed with Animals?," and "Witchcraft and Sex—1968," and "The First Sadists," and "Wife Swapping in Naples," and "My Double Sex Life (the story of a bisexual)," and "Gangs that Hunt Down Queers," and "Why I Like Homosexual Men," and "Unusual Sex De-

mands," *ad nauseam.* In addition, *Sexology* also features film reviews
of the latest "adult movies," carries advertisements for rank sex books,
and has published its own titillating work on *Tranvestism.*
Mr. Rubin's *Sexology* periodical has for years been available at certain seedy stores around the country (often from behind the counter,
with the pages stapled together), but bigger and better things are in
store for the magazine. Speaking in December of 1968 to a group of
educators at an institute on "sex education" sponsored by the International Business Machines Corporation, S.I.E.C.U.S.'s Lester Kirkendall revealed that *Sexology* is currently being revised with a different
cover and titles so it can be used in the schools.[13]

Several years ago, during a TV program, a national celebrity was
asked if there was any truth about the allegation that SIECUS treasurer Rubin was a Communist. "Absolutely not!" he replied. "No
proof has ever been given to show that he was convicted of being a
Communist." This is a typical left-wing maneuver: ignore the real accusations and answer what has not been asked. No one had claimed
that Rubin was convicted of being a Communist. But it is a fact that he
invoked the Fifth Amendment rather than tell whether or not he was a
Communist, after being identified as one in sworn testimony. His defenders are reluctant to admit the reason why he was dismissed by the
New York School Board in 1951.

Dr. Lester Kirkendall served for some time with Dr. Rubin as an
editor of *Sexology* and was a director of the anti-Christian American
Humanist Association. He ". . . defines his religion as a 'respect for and
a belief in people, and a concern for true brotherhood among men.' "

> Just as Kirkendall rejects God for "people," he also rejects patri-
> otism, actually going so far as to brand defense of one's country as im-
> moral. In "Searching for the Roots of Moral Decisions," he writes: "A
> tremendous feeling of national unity, a sense of closeness, good will,
> and harmony may result from fearing another nation or from the ef-
> fort of trying to destroy another nation. Such unity . . . is immoral."[14]

It is interesting that a man who does not consider adultery, premarital sex, homosexuality, abortion, or incest immoral does think that pa-

triotism and a genuine concern for Communist Russia's worldwide aggression is immoral.

Dr. Lester Doniger reflects a liberal theological background. In addition:

> ... The *Great Neck* [New York] *News* of February 14, 1947, carried an article entitled "US-USSR Committee Announces Meeting," which reported that a forum would be held under the auspices of the Great Neck Committee of the ... National Council of American-Soviet Friendship, Inc. Among those scheduled to appear was Jessica Smith, wife of Communist Party attorney John Abt and widow of Communist Hal Ware of the notorious Soviet spy ring called the Ware Cell. Mrs. Abt was editor of *Russia Today*. The article stated that tickets for the Council affair were obtainable from Mrs. Rita Doniger, wife of SIECUS President Lester Doniger. [This organization is described by the federal government's *Guide To Subversive Organizations* as being "created by the Communist Party in 1943." It was also cited on the United States Attorney General's list of subversive organizations as "subversive and Communist."][15]

Dr. Mary Calderone has been associated with liberal causes for years. She formerly served as medical director of the Planned Parenthood Association. Her husband, Frank Calderone, was chief administrator of the World Health Organization when it was directed by:

> ... Canadian Brock Chisholm, who spelled out the foundations for the "New Morality" when he wrote in the February, 1946 issue of *Psychiatry* ... "The re-interpretation and eventual eradication of the concept of right and wrong which has been the basis of child training, the substitution of intelligent and rational thinking for faith in the certainties of the old people, these are the belated objectives of practically all effective psychotherapy. Would they not be legitimate objectives of original education.... Freedom from morality means freedom to observe, to think and behave sensibly ... free from outmoded types of loyalties.... This is a new kind of world and there is no ethical or moral system that is intended for anyone in this world."[16]

During the years she was the director of SIECUS, Mary Calderone did all she could to bring in the "new kind of world" without the hindrances of "right and wrong."

Rev. William Genné was the representative of the National Council of Churches. It would not take much imagination to realize that he could be the transmission belt from the left-wing radical sex-education board to the left-wing radical NCCCA. Could he be the reason that the same sex-education materials that were pushed by SIECUS were available to the churches through the NCCCA? The "Reverend" Genné, . . . offers the view that . . . "Wherever healing takes place, Christ is present, no matter what the Church says about fornication. . . ."[17]

These five top leaders of SIECUS, though academically qualified, have skeletons in their closets that would appear to disqualify them from being entrusted with the responsibility of producing a national sex-education course for children ages five through eighteen. Somehow I get the feeling that they are interested in far more than sex education.

The Radical Moral Values of the SIECUS Sexologists

It is almost impossible to be totally objective. Everything that a writer writes or a teacher teaches will inevitably reflect his own attitudes. This is particularly true of sex education. Sex is such a universally significant subject that it will definitely be influenced by the teacher's or writer's moral perceptions. The printed or public statements of SIECUS evangelists are so filled with "new morality" (amorality) that had they made them thirty years ago, those individuals would have been locked up as public menaces. The Bible says of their kind, ". . . Having their conscience seared with a hot iron . . ." (1 Timothy 4:2).

Dr. Mary Calderone may look like "a sweet-faced, silvery-haired grandmother," but when she gets on her sex-education soapbox, she has been known to turn it into an academic platform that does not include traditional Judeo-Christian moral values. Her attitude is succinctly revealed in a ninety-minute lecture given to 320 adolescent boys at Blair Academy, a prep school in New Jersey, back in the mid-sixties. According to the 8 March 1966 issue of *Look,* Dr. Calderone queried:

What is sex for? It's for fun, that I know, for wonderful sensations. ... Sex is not something to be feared or degraded or kicked around or used. Sex is not something you turn off like a faucet. If you do, it's unhealthy. We are sexual beings, legitimately so, at every age. Don't think that sex stops at the age of 50. It doesn't.

We need new values to establish when and how we should have sexual experiences. Nobody's standing on a platform, giving answers. You are moving beyond your parents. But you can't just move economically or educationally. You must move sexually, as well. You must learn how to use sex. This is it: first, to separate yourselves from your parents; second, to establish a male or female role; third, to determine value systems; fourth, to establish your vocational role. Our sex expresses itself in everything we do. Sex ... is not just something you do in marriage, in bed, in the dark, in one position.[18]

According to a *Look* magazine article, Dr. Lester Kirkendall, the number-two evangelist for SIECUS, believes:

Any absolute moral standard is utterly unthinkable—aside from the absolutism of non-restraint. As a past director of the American Humanist Association and writer for *The Humanist* magazine, we can expect Kirkendall to elevate man and declare God expendable. Morality, he writes, cannot be found in context of "supernaturalism or a supernatural deity."

". . . Forty or 50 years ago," Kirkendall reminisced, "sex education scarcely recognized the possibility of choosing among alternative patterns of sexual behavior. There was only one 'right' way. Only one course of action was considered acceptable: renunciation of all sexual expression in nonmarital situations. . . . Quite a different situation now exists. There is now a very real freedom for adolescent couples." The humanistic orientation of Dr. Kirkendall is clearly expressed by this final statement: The sexually adjusted person ". . . will not be driven by guilt, anxiety, or compulsion to engage in sex with little regard for what this means to other persons or to his total situation. . . . He is in a position to direct and manage his sexuality."[19]

With attitudes like this, it is little wonder that SIECUS's materials, when served on the academic platter of "education," make the schoolchildren morally ill. It is no accident that where these concepts have been taught, there has been a marked increase in teenage pregnancy, illegitimacy, and venereal disease, not to mention psychological disturbance and old-fashioned heartache.

Dr. Albert Ellis, called by Rubin of *Sexology,* "One of America's leading sexologists," has authored such books as *If This Be Sexual Heresy, Sex Without Guilt,* and a vitriolic pamphlet entitled *The Case Against Religion.* "In his SIECUS recommended book, *The American Sexual Tragedy,* Ellis with warped logic denounces 'men who cannot be sexually satisfied with any form of sex activity but coitus' as 'probably fetishistically attached to this idea.' He recommends psychotherapy to alleviate the problem."[20]

On 3 March 1969, Dr. Ellis' activities were reported in the *Anaheim Bulletin.*

> Albert Ellis, Los Angeles psychologist, has told 1,000 Oklahoma State University students that "sex activity before marriage usually is not harmful or immoral." He said that as long as sex acts do not go against the "self-interest" of the persons, "anything is all right." Ellis also told the students he was "in favor of abortions freely administered with no legal restrictions." Ellis is a regular contributor to *Sexology* magazine. Dr. Lester Kirkendall appeared with Ellis in a three-day symposium paid for by the student government. The symposium was entitled "Sexpo-68."[21]

Dr. Sol Gordon, presently SIECUS executive director, looks at sex from the typical humanist viewpoint. A professor of child and family studies at Syracuse University, Dr. Gordon may eventually serve to scuttle the SIECUS ship. He is so outspoken that he is helping to cause a groundswell of opposition to the current explicit brand of sex education. Spontaneous groups of parents are organizing in antagonism to his leadership; in some places his appearances have been publicly opposed. In 1981 he was billed this way at a National Family Sex Education Week Event, at which he addressed "students, teachers and parents at Lincoln High School, Wisconsin Rapids and at Berg Gym, University Wisconsin—Stevens Point":

> Many parents protested Dr. Gordon coming to speak to the students. They called themselves CITIZENS CONCERNED FOR OUR YOUTH and objected to books authored by Sol Gordon that are used in many sex education courses and available in the Public library, such as: "YOU," "THE TEENAGE SURVIVAL BOOK", and other

written works such as "LET'S MAKE SEX A HOUSEHOLD WORD", "FACTS ABOUT SEX FOR TODAY'S YOUTH", "YOU WOULD IF YOU LOVED ME" and "ZING COMIX".

An advance Seminar on Sol Gordon's writings, films and educational materials was held at Assumption High School in Wisconsin Rapids to introduce parents, some teens and clergy to the materials. The programs were scheduled for three nights and for some of the materials teenagers were excluded because the materials were so repulsive and disturbing even for the adults.[22]

A major parental concern is that the values and beliefs of the SIECUS officials listed above have sifted into the curricula recommended for many public schools.

Dan Smoot observes:

> Actually, the SIECUS sexologists . . . do infinitely more harm to children than is done by sleazy characters who hang out on the fringes of school yards to sell filthy pictures to kids.
>
> Some parents approve, or accept, the teaching of obscenity in classrooms because "if the children don't learn it there, they will learn it in the gutter." Very well, let them learn it in the gutter. They will then know it is gutter talk, not fit to be used around respectable people; and most of them will develop a properly contemptuous attitude toward it—as young people have always been doing.
>
> Graphic aids now being used in many schools include life-size models, or close-up pictures, of human sexual organs—often depicted in their condition and position during coition. Showing such material to mixed classes of small boys and girls must create in most or all of them powerful emotions—of excitement, embarrassment, disgust, or fear.
>
> Details about copulation, conception, and birth are not facts of life to small children, but information about adult behavior which they cannot comprehend or consider unemotionally. Most child psychoanalysts advise against such treatment of small children.
>
> Giving sex education to mixed classes of adolescent boys and girls, on the assumption that they will react matter-of-factly and unemotionally, is tantamount to expecting in youngsters a detached, professional attitude about sexual parts of the body—an attitude that doctors and nurses acquire only through years of living, education, training, and experience. This is not a normal or healthy attitude for children to have, even if it could be inculcated into them as it cannot be.

Why try to *push* adolescents into adult behavior before they can possibly be ready for it? It is profoundly important to let children be children, until they *grow* into adulthood.[23]

Sex is the most beautiful thing in the world when experienced properly. It should never be taught without moral values. SIECUS, because of its basic commitment to humanistic beliefs, has rendered itself incompetent to produce the curriculum on such a delicate subject for an entire generation of young people.

Sex was intended for marriage. The sex education course that does not aggressively teach its confinement to that relationship does the nation, its families, and our children a great disservice.

What Every Parent Should Know About Planned Parenthood

"The most merciful thing that the large family does to one of its infant members is to kill it," said Margaret Sanger, the founder of Planned Parenthood.

Next to SIECUS and our public schools, the Planned Parenthood Federation of America is doing more to make sexual animals out of our nation's children than any other organization in the country. The humanists who shape the course of all three organizations share the same beliefs (or lack of beliefs) about moral absolutes and pursue the same objectives.

1. They want children of all ages to be familiar with every explicit detail about sex education.
2. In the name of population control and unwanted pregnancy, they are anxious to give minors access to contraceptives "regardless of age or parental consent."[24]

It is a strange day indeed when a child must gain her parent's consent to have her ears pierced but can murder her unborn child, through abortion, without it. Planned Parenthood bears no small degree of responsibility for this ironic moral dilemma.

One sex-education opponent, a minister, Reverend Paul Marx, has described Planned Parenthood as "surely one of the most wicked forces in the world, an anti-love, anti-life, anti-family juggernaut that deserves total opposition."

Why do I call special attention to the work of Planned Parenthood Federation of America? Because it is given so much undeserved community prestige and public-school access and because it is the recipient of millions of our tax dollars to finance their abortion clinics and publications throughout the country. Many of the letters I receive come from frustrated parents, because Planned Parenthood representatives continually appear in our students' classrooms, where the alternative viewpoint is forbidden.

For example one concerned parent wrote to tell me of the experience he had with his son's school. His son's class heard a Planned Parenthood representative propounding the theory that most "responsible people" believed that masturbation was a harmless way of relieving sexual tension. The decision for "responsible sex," according to this advisor, was a personal one.

The parent visited the school's principal and was told that Planned Parenthood was approved of by the government, and schools were not responsible for what they taught. The parent was refused permission to have a medical doctor present the opposing side of the issue.

Gradually parents are waking up to the fact that "academic freedom," so glowingly heralded by humanists, is neither academic nor free. It really means that humanists have the freedom to promulgate their religious theories exclusively, and we have the freedom to keep our mouths shut—except on April fifteenth, when we are forced to pay the taxes that support their programs and materials, designed to destroy the morals of our children.

Why don't SIECUS, Planned Parenthood, AASECT, and other national organizations advocate morality, virtue, and matrimonial commitments as options for our young people? Could it be they have rejected moral absolutes? Most humanists have.

Whenever I have found morality taught in sex-education classes, it is as a result of a courageous local teacher or principal who injects traditional moral values as a legitimate option.

Recently I had a high-school teacher identify himself as a sex-education instructor "for the past fifteen years." He was selected by his principal because of his deep-rooted commitment to moral values. In commissioning him, the principal said, "I don't care what you teach, but if we have any complaints from parents, we will cancel the program altogether. We are not going to have a big controversy on this subject in our school!"

That is responsible public-school administration! That principal respected the rights and values of the parents, so he selected a sex-ed teacher with the same values.

Unfortunately, the secular-humanist principals and district superintendents have the same privilege in their selection of sex-ed teachers. How can you tell which kind your school has? It's very simple. Just check to see if SIECUS-developed materials are used, if Planned Parenthood is welcomed into the classroom, offering abortion, contraception, or pregnancy counseling *without* parental consent. Are parents welcome to visit the sex-ed classes? Usually if sex educrats act as if they have something to hide from parents, it is because they do.

Sex-Education Materials

You don't have to be a moral pervert to write sex-education curricula, but after reading hundreds of pages of the modern variety, I have come to the conclusion that it surely must help. At least that is the opinion of many traditional moralists who read the magazines, view the resource materials, and examine the movies and recommended reading material provided by some sexologists.

The most difficult task in this whole business of trying to awaken parents and taxpayers in general to the gross sex-education material is to get normal, family-oriented people to believe that it is really as bad as it is. On the one hand, I cannot bring myself to reprint the filthy pictures contained in some of the recommended materials or to quote some of the obscene language, because I would be accused of distributing pornographic literature. But be sure of this: it is there, and in far too many schools it is being used with regularity.

At this point I should warn you that reading this chapter may be hazardous to the sanctification of your pure mind. For that reason you may wish to skip this section and just take my word that some sex-education curriculum material is too advanced, too explicit, and too sexually stimulating for adults or young people. But remember, if married adults find that to be so, what must teenagers on that first wave of libido feel?

A Parent Speaks Out

A parent from Illinois sent me a mimeographed copy of a report he made of his eleventh-grade son's experience. In it, he explained that he had become concerned when he saw parents from another local school protesting the sex-education materials their school system had been using.

When he examined the textbooks used by his son's school, this parent discovered nothing objectionable. It was only later, when his son brought home mimeographed material and printed brochures, that he became seriously alarmed.

The material, provided for a class containing both sexes, was to be read without class discussion. Imagine the parent's shock to discover that the glossary of sexual terms included in this material defined *chastity* as an old-fashioned word meaning to abstain from sex. Other definitions glorified terms described by one medical dictionary as perversions. Homosexuality and sodomy were treated as acceptable lifestyles.

Another brochure described the sex act explicitly, and a third encouraged masturbation and premarital sex. A final brochure on sex and aging was described by this parent as an insult to senior citizens.

The East Coast has not been overlooked by the educrats of sexology. In April of 1980 (about the same time as the California struggle over *Human Sexuality*) a press-service reported the protest reaction of angry parents in New Jersey to a new sixth- and seventh-grade sex-education program. It reportedly included material on masturbation, nocturnal emissions, intercourse, and homosexuality. One group of irate parents protested that the "intimacy tests" being given to teenagers encouraged "favorable attitudes" toward promiscuity, homosexuality, and prostitution. They also took exception to the Zing comic books, which will be discussed later.

The parental protest culminated with eighty parents picketing outside an auditorium in the state capital where these materials were being discussed. One angry parent was quoted as saying, "the choice isn't my ten-year-old child's. It's mine and my husband's." Another mother carried a poster: BACK TO THE 3 R'S, LEAVE SEX EDUCATION IN THE FAMILY.[1]

In fairness to some of the quality educators in the state, it should be pointed out that several school boards took exception to the explicit nature of the material; they went on record as opposing it and forbid its use in their system.

It seems ironic that in America parents feel compelled to form protest rallies in order to motivate politicians to introduce legislation that forbids the schools from teaching this kind of trash. Educrats, particularly sex educrats, have betrayed the trust of America's parents and deserve all the censure they receive from outraged citizens groups that are springing up throughout the country, attempting to rescue our children from their educators. We would expect that from parents in Hitler's Germany, but in America—who would have thought that possible?

An attorney friend of mine filed a lawsuit against a state library in an attempt to determine which schools had checked out a film entitled *Achieving Sexual Maturity* for showing to teenagers *without parental consent.* He found the film "morally offensive, a how-to manual and advertisement for intercourse and masturbation." He claimed, "Its nudity and explicit treatment of sexuality makes it improper for public school use."

A group of parents invited me to speak to a parental protest meeting where 700 people gathered. Just before I was introduced, a tall, twenty-three-year-old teacher was presented for the showing of a "typical" sex-education film sample of the kind available in their local high school. The young man very naively stated, "I spent all day reviewing films so that I could present the one least likely to irritate you parents." Twenty-five minutes later the parents had to be calmed down because they were so irate at the explicit instruction and heavy ridicule of virtue, self-restraint, and traditional moral values. They hardly needed my message!

Sex Education Films Get Worse

It is very difficult to keep sex-education films from becoming pornographic and erotic, particularly if they are produced by people who see nothing wrong with pornography. Consequently, like pornography itself, each film gets more offensive, making them increasingly unfit to be seen by young people. But when these films are sanctioned by our trusted school authorities, together with receiving the official seal of approval of SIECUS and Planned Parenthood, it is difficult for young people or their parents to establish the real danger of such films. However, anyone with traditional moral values who views them will testify that they are inappropriate for our nation's children.

Any sex-education film that repulses two United States Senators should not be paid for by taxpayers, and it certainly should not clutter up the minds of teenagers during school hours. A 1 April 1981 Associated Press story by Margaret Scherf tells how shocking *About Sex* was to the senators who viewed it. Senator Orrin Hatch, (R Utah) said, "That's about as disgusting a film as I've ever seen." He called the film "Pornographic, tasteless and offensive" and apologized "to those in the hearing room who had to sit through it." The article claimed the movie had already been shown by some affiliates of the Planned Parenthood Federation of America. The film showed "scenes of a nude man and woman making love, a lesbian couple holding hands and a teenage girl describing her abortion."

With sex-education teaching aids like this, funded with almost limitless dollars from the federal government, it is no wonder that many youngsters act more like animals than responsible human beings.

A month later a report from Davenport, Iowa, reviewed an all-day seminar for school personnel on human sexuality. According to reporter Kitty Schmidt:

> In attendance were health teachers, school nurses, home economics staff, and one Catholic religious [sic]. This in-service was given by two female professors from Iowa State University, funded by the Iowa Dept. of Public Instruction, and hosted by the Mississippi Bend Area Education Agency No. 9. It was my introduction into the world of pornography. . . .
>
> One of our morning activities was the viewing of a film, "A Quickie." There is absolutely not any way that I can describe this film; you would have to see it for yourself. We watched a man and woman engage in sexual intercourse and, in my opinion, degrade the most personal and intimate relationship two people can have as though they were animals copulating in the backyard. Tied into this segment of our day was the assignment to write a simile, comparing what we saw to some other activity. "Sex In This Film Is Like . . ." One imaginative soul wrote, "Like driving through a car wash. It only takes a minute, and it's over."[2]

What kind of people would plan such lurid scenes for showing to our children? The same kind of individuals who produce pornographic literature and X-rated flicks; however, these "educators" earn their living out of the taxpayers' pocket. All funds for such programs should be cut off immediately.

Human Sexuality

The $175,000 curriculum that Health and Human Services contributed to sex education in 1979 clearly reveals the moral position and judgment of humanist sexologists. We were alerted to it in California by Jacqueline Kasun, professor of economics at Humboldt State University. Due to the uproar she inaugurated, aided by many other concerned citizens' groups in our state, we had its teaching to our sex educators halted, and the state superintendent of education fired the woman in charge. Unfortunately, this material was introduced to many other states at the same time, indicating the true nature of the federally approved curriculum. We need to know what kind of material is sanctioned, because some states have implemented all or part of this program. In addition, the people who produced it are still in charge of our national sex-education materials.

I have in my file a copy of the 164-page draft called *Education for Human Sexuality*. The following overview of material a citizens committee found objectionable, including page numbers of references in the draft, clarifies what some humanists want our innocents to learn.

AD HOC CITIZENS ADVISORY COMMITTEE ON
FAMILY LIFE/SEX EDUCATION IN SAN DIEGO

These are samples of objectional teachings in the new *Education for Human Sexuality* draft curriculum that has not been approved by any reputable board in the State—yet is being taught to sex education instructors—kindergarten through 12th grade.

This program provides explicit instruction not only in human sexual intercourse but in alternative sexual "life styles," abortion, masturbation, and other disputed topics.

Beginning in pre-school or kindergarten with a mixed group restroom visit, followed by a description of the male and female genital organs (pp. 93–94), the program calls for children of ages 3 to 5 years to study human sexual intercourse (p. 99). At age six, children begin their study of the male and female reproductive systems, learning the "similarities and differences . . . between a vagina and a penis" (p. 96).

From the age of nine on, the new curriculum assumes that a majority of children are, or soon will be, sexually active (p. 121) although available surveys indicate that a majority of students graduating from high school are *not* sexually active. At age nine children study conception, ejaculation, nocturnal emissions (pp. 97, 102) and "all the contraceptive methods, services, and products available" (p. 121). At age twelve, children "visit a local drug store to check the availability of contraceptive products" (p. 123), and they learn that "pregnancy prevention services are available to young people . . . *without parental consent"* (p. 125). They "role play" the part of a boy or girl asking a doctor for birth control information (p. 134). They take a "field trip" to a "family planning clinic," and they go through it "from beginning to end," discussing pelvic examinations and other procedures. They fill out a patient's form for such a clinic (p. 135).

At age twelve they study "unplanned pregnancy" and they learn that the decision for an abortion is theirs alone to make, *requiring no consultation with their parents* (pp. 125, 135). They learn the addresses and phone numbers of all family planning clinics in their community and the bus routes to them (pp. 125, 135). They listen to speakers from Planned Parenthood (p. 150).

At age nine children read books and pamphlets regarding masturbation. Two recommended Planned Parenthood pamphlets tell them "masturbation is a perfectly acceptable, useful, comforting thing to do with sexual feelings" and "will make you feel more relaxed" (p. 97).

The program calls for children of ages 6 to 9 to be led in class discussions of their family problems, including problems of "sexual molestation." A suggested reference work for this unit is *Frances Ann Speaks Out: My Father Raped Me*, by Helen Chetin (Stanford, Calif.: New Seed Press, 1977) (pp. 138–139).

High school students study the "aging process" by discussing, "Sometimes Grandfather is fine; at other times he takes off his clothes, defecates on the floor . . . What are you going to do with Grandfather . . . ?" (p. 115)

After careful review of this proposed curriculum, the AD HOC Committee considers it unsuitable for California school children and suggests that educators, parents and interested groups of responsible citizens urge authorities to discontinue its use.

Not only is this curriculum suspect, but who knows what visual materials the teacher will elect to bring into the classroom? In addition to the radical sex-education manual, educators have access to some of the pornography prepared by Planned Parenthood or SIECUS, such as the one in my files that depicts mature, nude teenagers, boy and girl, with genitals fully exposed. Under the guise of teaching all about the reproductive organs, some "educators" are using pornographic pictures—and in mixed classes.

In the midst of our attack on explicit sex education, one nagging question arises: why do we have to stop it from outside the school? Why is there no outcry from within the system, censuring this kind of moral perversion being foisted off on our children? Is it because no teachers or administrators share the moral values of the nation's parents? I cannot accept that. I suspect it is because many quality educators with moral values are intimidated by the sexologists and other humanist educrats.

One dedicated teacher admitted to me, "I just can't buck the system. I've done all I can to get the schools to clean up their act. After twenty-three years I have come to the conclusion that the administrators know where I stand; I know that I'll never advance. The only thing left for me is to finish my time until retirement." Quite possibly the threat of such treatment has silenced many good teachers in recent years.

We should certainly become suspicious of the seriousness of the problem when we learn that, according to every survey taken of the professions of those parents who send their children to private or Christian schools, public-school educators represent the greatest number. Why? They recognize more than anyone else that the public school is usually unfit for our nation's children—unless, of course, parents want their children to become sexual animals, to subject themselves to an inferior education, or to develop a socialistic outlook on life. But who wants that? Only humanists, of course, and for the most part they control the country's schools and educational agencies.

Values Clarification and Sex Education

One parent sent me a copy of a story that was passed out in the "literature" course of his grandson. Under the guise of values clarification, this kind of sex education was bootlegged into an English class. Incidentally, this story, reproduced by a New York City reporter, caused no small stir among the parents living there. Designed for discussion on the eleventh- and twelfth-grade level, in mixed classes, these sheets were passed out in class, then collected for scoring (a method that insured that parents would not learn about the material). How would you like to have your son or daughter discuss this material with his or her peers, led by a humanistic sexologist who is addicted to the notion that "there are no rights or wrongs"?

THE ALLIGATOR RIVER STORY

Once upon a time, there was a river that was practically overflowing with alligators. As you may have guessed, it was called Alligator River. A girl named Abigail lived on the west bank of the river. Her boyfriend, Greg, lived on the opposite bank. Abigail and Greg were very much in love with each other and wanted very much to see each other. But there was one slight complication: no boat, and an alligator-filled river stood between them. Abigail decided to seek help so that she could see her boyfriend, Greg. She approached Sinbad the Sailor, who, as his name might indicate, owned a boat. Now this was very fortunate for Abigail, because Sinbad's boat was exactly what she needed to get across the river. She explained her situation to Sinbad and asked if she could borrow his boat. Sinbad thought for a moment and then replied: "Sure, you can borrow my boat, but only under one condition. The condition is that you sleep with me tonight." This startled Abigail, because she didn't want to sleep with Sinbad; she just wanted to borrow his boat so she could see Greg. So she told Sinbad to forget it and wandered off, seeking someone else who would help her.

After a great deal of time, Abigail was unable to find anyone else who could aid her. Discouraged, she returned home, where she sought out her mother. Explaining her dilemma and Sinbad's proposition, Abigail asked her mother about what she should do. Mom responded with: "Look, Abigail, you're a big girl now; it's about time you started making these kinds of decisions for yourself." With that, Mom turned and walked away.

Abigail thought and thought. Finally, she decided to take Sinbad up on his offer because she wanted to see Greg so very much. So that night Abigail and Sinbad slept with each other. The next morning, Sinbad, true to his word, lent his boat to Abigail. Abigail sailed across the river and saw her beloved. After spending a few delightful hours together, Abigail felt compelled to tell Greg what had happened. After she had related her whole story, Greg blew up completely: "You what? I can't believe you did that! I—I can't believe you slept with him! That's it. It's all over. Just forget the relationship. Get out of my life!"

Distraught, Abigail wandered off. She came upon a fellow named Slug. Borrowing his shoulder to shed her tears, Abigail related her tale to Slug. Slug then went looking for Greg (with Abigail close behind). Slug found Greg and proceeded to beat the stuffing out of him, with Abigail standing there, laughing.

In your estimation, who was the most admirable person in this story? Rank them in order.

___Abigail
___Greg
___Sinbad
___Mom
___Slug

According to a June 1981 *Columbia Magazine* article, this story appeared in the "Sex Education: Teacher's Guide & Resource Manual," produced by Planned Parenthood, Santa Cruz, California, to be used as a values-clarification technique. One can only wonder what high-school class discussion would ensue from a tale that poses an immoral premise, lacks psychological credibility, and offers a superficial view of motherhood.

With teenagers freely discussing such subjects in class, it is no wonder a 1979 survey of 2,600 young men and women in metropolitan areas across the country indicated that approximately "70 percent of unmarried young women living in metropolitan areas have had sexual intercourse by age 19—a big increase over four years ago."[3] The authors "speculated that the reason for increased teen sexual activity is 'more permissiveness' in social attitudes and the fact that young people now are left 'more to their own devices.' "[4]

If you think I am censuring educators unfairly, you should read my mail, some of it from teachers who are ridiculed by peers and administrators for wanting chastity, morality, and marriage taught as an optimal alternative to sexual activity and permissiveness. In 1980 an article by Dr. Max Rafferty, former superintendent of public instruction in California, excoriated the state's educators much more thoroughly than I have. He reviewed the case of a homosexual teacher who had committed sodomy with his seventeen-year-old student. When the mother found a collection of love letters addressed by the teacher to his pupil, she turned the vile material over to the school superintendent, who suspended the teacher. Subsequently a three-man panel reviewed the evidence and recommended dismissal, which was promptly instituted. But that did not end the case. The California Commission on Teacher Preparation and Licensing surveyed the evidence and decided *not* to cancel his credential. Merely chiding him for "extremely poor judgment in using inappropriate words and terms," they overlooked his actions and gently slapped his wrists for composing those "inappropriate" letters. Dr. Rafferty, himself a noted educator, makes a point of reminding us that such an incredible decision can only be understood in one context. "It's easy, once you understand the makeup of the licensing commission: all educators." They are "brainwashed," he explains, into rejecting absolutes; thus perverted action is no longer deemed "right" or "wrong," but "immature" or "inappropriate."[5] Is it any wonder that millions of parents have lost confidence in an organization that refuses to police itself, even at the expense of our children's innocence?

Explicit Beyond Belief!

If you think that the material we have covered so far is bad, I have news for you: the worst is yet to come. As I poured over my files of sex-education curricula designed for public schools, I separated them into two categories: (1) typical sex-education filth of which 90 percent or more of American parents would disapprove, samples of which you have already read; and (2) those I consider explicit beyond belief. Most of these are nothing more than pornography masquerading as sex-education literature. In my opinion, a person must be morally perverted to write, produce, sell, or teach them. Fortunately, not very many people in our country are that morally bankrupt. However, some have worked their way into extremely influential positions in the field of sex education. Frankly, I do not understand why responsible heads of education do not expose these people for the menace they are to our children.

Though many samples of sleazy sex-education materials could be used, I shall cite only three of the major offenders. The first, exposed by the Christian Defense League, is so explicit that I cannot include more than its description. Taken from Knudsen's *The True Story of How Babies Are Made,* a book designed for young children, the scene of intercourse portrays a naked father astride his equally naked wife, intent on three areas of contact: lips, breasts/chest, penis/vagina. The genital area offers an "inner" diagram, so that the child can perceive the mother's vagina and uterus; the father has inserted his penis into the vagina and is emitting sperm cells. The educational caption reads, "The father's testicles are filled with *sperm cells.* When he makes love, these come out of the tip of his penis. They move through the mother's vagina into a hollow space in the mother's abdomen called the *uterus,* or *womb.* Sometimes there is a tiny *egg* inside the mother, and a sperm cell joins it."[6]

Such graphic sexual illustrations, once rejected as pornography, are accepted by some as educational materials. Some alert principals, teachers, or administrators have refused such materials. Before you fire off a cry of protest, examine the materials in your district. You may be fortunate enough to have an administrator who is protecting your children. But you have a right to find out.

Another sample of sex-education pornography designed to give moral indigestion to our nation's teens was prepared by Dr. Sol Gordon, the new president of SIECUS. It is a series of comic books labeled Zing Comix, published by the Family Planning and Population Information Center in Syracuse, New York (near the university where Dr. Gordon is professor of family and child development). Even a casual examination will demonstrate that this humanist educator has no respect for parents who hold traditional moral values.

I cannot bring myself to reproduce this trash, but let me describe some of the sections in *Ten Heavy Facts About Sex,* designed for teenagers. Parents and doctors are derided as inadequate sex instructors. "All thoughts"—including "sexual thoughts, wishes, dreams"—"are normal—no matter how far out." That statement forms the caption for the cartoon depicting a male fantasizing about naked women. On the next page masturbation is described as "a normal expression of sex for both male and females. Enjoy it. There's no harm in masturbation no matter how often you do it." Oral sex is likewise approved as normal, along with homosexuality and lesbianism. Next to a picture of males and females reading "spiffy scenes" from a lurid magazine, the professor announces, "Pornography is harmless. After a while it gets boring. If porno is your bag, you don't have much of an imagination of your own." The comic ends with a review of birth-control devices and with sections explaining when "sex is a drag" or when "sex is cool." Remember, the author directs the activities of one of the nation's most prestigious sex-education and information councils in the United States—and he is a primary influence on some of our public schools.

Probably the rawest sexual presentation I have seen is the relatively new SIQ (Sex Imagery Quotient), designed by a former member of the New Jersey state board of education's Family Life Education Curriculum Guidelines Committee. He was "charged with writing the guidelines for the newly mandated sex education curriculum"[7] that must be initiated by 1983. His publication *For Kids Only,* an imagination and fantasy trip, is explicit beyond belief. Drawings of male and female masturbation and sexual intercourse appear in lurid detail. According to columnist Robert Braun, the publishers admitted that bookstores were unwilling to carry the book partially "because of its subject matter." No wonder parents raised such an outcry that the author was forced to resign from his influential position on the curriculum committee for the New Jersey sex-education course. But one question is still left unanswered: would the educators of our children have permitted such trash to work its way into our schools had the parents not cried out in protest?

Educators say, "Trust us; rely on our expert judgment." Yet repeatedly movies, books, and materials are purchased or rented for schools or libraries, using taxpayers' money, until they come to the parents' attention and furious objections are raised. At that point, of course, parents are labeled *censors, Nazis, bookburners,* or worse by the educators entrusted with the minds and morals of the children. Many responsible citizens believe it is time for educators to start policing their own profession.

Fortunately, all educators are not deceived by this humanistic assault on our schoolchildren's morals. Many superintendents, principals, and family-life educators refuse to incorporate such degrading materials into their programs. Unfortunately, we don't hear much about them. For instance, I noticed that in one western city where parents were up in arms about the junior-high sex-education program, I heard no outcry against the high-school courses in town. When I chanced to meet the high-school principal, he explained, "The reason is very simple. I refused to let our people bring that kind of material into my school." That is usually the key: the principal or district superintendent sets the pace.

Sex-Education Goals

The *admitted* goals of sex educators are almost as openly harmful as those ascribed to them by their opponents. In a report entitled "An Analysis of U.S. Sex Education Programs and Evaluation Methods," prepared for the United States Department of Health, Education, and Welfare by Mathtech, Inc., of Bethesda, Maryland, the following were proposed as goals in July 1979:

—to provide accurate information about sexuality
—to facilitate insights into personal sexual behavior
—to reduce fears and anxieties about personal sexual developments and feelings
—to encourage more informed, responsible, and successful decision making
—to encourage students to question, explore, and assess their sexual attitudes
—to develop more tolerant attitudes toward the sexual behavior of others
—to facilitate communication about sexuality with parents and others
—to develop skills for the management of sexual problems
—to facilitate rewarding sexual expression
—to integrate sex into a balanced and purposeful pattern of living
—to create satisfying interpersonal relationships
—to reduce sex-related problems such as venereal disease and unwanted pregnancies[8]

The last one is an utter fraud. The rest they are implementing all over the country. Today's young people know more about sex than any such group in the history of mankind—and they are more sexually active, just as the educators planned.

The report goes on to acknowledge that the "effects of school sex education programs" have included "changing students' knowledge, attitudes, self perceptions, skills, fears, and social and sexual behaviors." Because these are the established goals, sex-education programs should be evaluated according to the extent to which they meet these goals. To parents and taxpayers who represent traditional moral values, our schools have clearly succeeded in reaching their goals, which seems to be making our children's favorite indoor and outdoor sport promiscuous sexual activity—without benefit of marriage, commitment, or responsibility, just like the animals.

Sex Educators' True Goals

In September of 1979, a Columbia University report entitled "The Impact of Life Science Instruction at George Mason High School, Falls Church, Virginia," was released. Financed by a grant from the Ford-Rockefeller Program in Population Policy, it exposed the *real* goal of most humanist sex educators. Summing up their in-depth study, the report said, ". . . one goal of the sex education program is to alert students to the probabilities of pregnancy *and encourage only responsible sexual intercourse* using contraception, if such sexual activity occurs at all."

There you have it: an open admission that one of their goals is to encourage sexual intercourse—just so long as it is "responsible," that is, that contraception, is used.

Taxpayers Are Paying For It!

Who gave sex educators the right to encourage sexual intercourse among our youth? Did parents? Certainly not! Did the taxpayers? Of course not! But both groups are obliged to help these VD or pregnancy victims pick up the pieces of their lives. We taxpayers must pay for the abortions or births, supply a variety of medical services, and make endless welfare payments to a long stream of recipients. It is time for parents and taxpayers to unite against this national disgrace that parades in the name of "education."

Why Do They Force Explicit Sex Education on Our Innocent Children?

Have you ever wondered why the mature holder of a PhD degree, who has given himself to the profession of education, would be motivated to spend a major portion of his life trying to create sexual activity among our youth? Certainly there are far more noble pursuits in which a person with such a background could invest himself for the good of humanity—instead of this volatile subject. We have already observed that it is the most explosive issue in our schools across the country. Why do they persist in further alienating the parents in their district, particularly when parents are already on the verge of rebellion?

Actually, there are several reasons why the self-styled sexologists of education are so determined to make sexual animals out of our children. Consider the following, which in my judgment are arranged in the order of their priority.

1. They Are Amoral Humanists The prime movers of the sex education movement have all been secular humanists. Lester Kirkendall is a committed humanist. Dr. Mary Calderone was the recipient of the Humanist of the Year Award in 1974. She has probably done more to promote sex education in our schools than any single individual. Dr. Sol Gordon is a signer of *Humanist Manifesto II*. Scores of other humanists could also be cited.

As committed humanists, these sexologists passionately abhor absolute moral values. According to one of them, "There is no one up there telling you what is right or wrong." So they combine a child's natural curiosity with his first wave of libido, causing him to reject traditional moral values and adopt a life-style that violates those moral values. They have learned from history that a person will adjust his morals to his behavior, so they inspire our youth to sexual activity before they are mature enough to have established their own moral convictions. I cannot imagine a more effective method for changing the moral values of the next generation—and remember, humanists are committed to making America a humanist nation by the year 2000. The preface to *Humanist Manifesto II,* for instance, declares, "The next century can be and should be the humanistic century."

2. They Are Purposely Creating a Youthful Obsession With Sex
Teaching explicit sex education without benefit of moral values at a time of emerging sexual feeling is like putting gasoline on a fire. The sex educrats know that!

As Dr. James Parsons, a psychiatrist who has debated Dr. Mary Calderone, has stated, "The sex educators are trying to create such an obsession with sex in the minds of our youth that they will have no time or interest in spiritual pursuits." Who can deny that such an obsession has already been created among the youth of our public schools?

You must understand that, in the mind of a humanist, the worst catastrophe for a young girl is not that she loses her virtue in promiscuous sex or even becomes the rape victim of some sex-crazed pornography reader. To a humanist, the greatest disaster occurs when a young person grows up with religious taboos about right and wrong, or as many call them, moral absolutes. In 1970 Sidney Simon and his wife, Marianne, coauthored an article entitled "Sexuality in the School." They revealed their true attitude and purpose for teaching their brand of radical sex education:

> Some changes are desperately needed. Schools can no longer be permitted to carry out such a horrendously effective program for drying up students' sense of their own sexual identity. The schools must

not be allowed to continue fostering *the immorality of morality. An entirely different set of values must be nourished.*[1]

The *immorality of morality?* Says who? Certainly not almighty God! But so say the secular humanist educrats in our public schools, who are doing an effective job of making sexual animals out of our nation's youth. The humanist overlords of education usually hate God, Jesus Christ, and Christianity with a passion. They will not hesitate to stoop to any level to turn our young people away from Christianity. Most people make their lifetime spiritual commitments during their teens. What better way to keep such spiritual decisions from being made during those crucial years than by creating an obsession with sex?

Mixed sex-education classes not only ignite youthful passions, but overcome a time-honored hindrance to teenage promiscuity: parental and church disapproval. Between the ages of thirteen and twenty-two (generally speaking) a parent's influence on his children reaches its lowest level, but the school and peer group exercise the greatest influence. Consequently, any normal young person will be extremely vulnerable to sexual obsession during those years, resulting, the humanist believes, in rejection of the spiritual faith of his parents.

The whole plan sounds Satanic, doesn't it? Where do you think it came from? The humanists I have met aren't clever enough to have thought that up all by themselves.

Recently an unwed, five-months-pregnant eleventh grader came in for counseling with her mother. To my question, "How many girls in your class are sexually active?" she replied, "All of them that date." Even if she is only partially right, I find her answer frightening, and personally I blame our humanist sex educators, for if they teach people long enough that they are animals, eventually people will begin acting like them. That, mothers and fathers, is what our humanist educrats think of your children.

3. Sex Education Is a Profitable Business   The average citizen has no comprehension of the millions of dollars that can be made by SIECUS. By recommending the writings of their board members, they open a phenomenal source of revenue from books and materials that may not be good enough to pay for themselves if left to popular demand. SIECUS did not succeed in getting an exclusive corner on the lush audiovisual market of explicit sex education. As early as 19 September 1967 *The Wall Street Journal* gave a hint of just how much money was involved:

> Among the publishing concerns hoping to cash in on the demand for sex-education material is Harcourt, Brace & World, Inc. Through its Guidance-Associates division, the firm plans to invest several million dollars over a number of years to create a sex education curriculum for grades kindergarten through the twelfth grade.... SIECUS is providing consultation on the project. In June [1967], Holt, Rinehart & Winston, Inc. plunged into the field with a text called *Modern Sex Education*. Minnesota Mining and Manufacturing Co.'s visual products division and Science Research Associates, which is the educational arm of International Business Machines Corp., both say they are investing substantial sums in school health programs—texts, visual aids and the like—that will contain considerable sex education material.[2]

Don't feel too sad for SIECUS at having to share the profits of this pornographic tool of education (paid for out of our tax dollars for "good education"). Who do you think serves as consultants for these companies? You guessed it: SIECUS. Have you checked the fees being paid for consultants lately? I wonder if they are padded when companies are seeking the official approval of the people they hire as consultants?

4. Sex Education Is by Design   Pornography has always been profitable, but even that does not completely explain the purposes of some of the producers of current sex-ed material. There are people who believe they are bent on the degeneration of today's youth.

> Nationally syndicated columnist Henry J. Taylor, playing Devil's Advocate, delineated a sixteen-point program for the destruction of the United States. One of these points reads: "Preach 'permissiveness.' If 'anything goes' then, of course, everything goes. Every internal and external enemy knows the advantages of destroying a nation's standards. The rewards are as old as the Trojan horse."
> As far back as May of 1919, Allied forces in Dusseldorf, Germany,

first captured a Communist document entitled *Rules for Revolution.* Number One on that list of objectives was: "Corrupt the young, get them away from religion. Get them interested in sex. Make them superficial, destroy their ruggedness." Again, in the early 1950s, Florida State Attorney George A. Brautigam confirmed that "The above 'Rules for Revolution' were secured by the State Attorney's Office from a known member of the Communist Party, who acknowledged it to be still a part of the Communist program for overthrowing our Government."[3]

If you think it can't happen here, you are mistaken. History has a way of repeating itself, and unless concerned taxpayers and parents put the brakes on this explicit teaching method in our schools, we will surely be destroyed. Consider the following case in history. Every schoolchild used to learn that the plotters of the French Revolution (forerunners of the humanists) worked for years to destroy the morals of France. The country was flooded with pornographic literature; politicians were corrupted; faith in God was vigorously attacked by French skeptics; and the people were led into an abnormal obsession with sex.

If this kind of historic consideration doesn't give you insight into what is really going on in this country, I don't know what will. Doesn't it suggest something when you realize that at the same time pornography is increasing, movies and TV programs are unbelievably immoral? Could all this degeneration emanate from the same source?

5. They Are Attempting to Destroy Christianity and Religion Atheists tend to lack commitment to moral values. If a man does not believe in God, he is likely to think he is free to lie, cheat, steal, pander in pornography, or do as he pleases with impunity. (He is wrong of course, and one day he will give account to the God he denies. But in the meantime he wreaks havoc on the souls, minds and bodies of men or innocent schoolchildren.)

The left-wing atheist is not usually content to go his miserable way through life. Somehow he can't stand the sight of God-fearing, honest people who possess a peace and joy that he knows nothing about. Instead, he becomes an evangelist of atheism. Destroying another's faith is a sadistic challenge to him. Whether or not he realizes it, such humanist efforts parallel those of the Communist, socialist, and one-world plotters. They are bent on the destruction of Christianity and all forms of religion, regardless of the cost. It is no accident that some of the same people who believe the Bible has no place in our schools and prefer a secularized society are leaders in this nationwide, explicit sex-education movement.

Be sure of this: this program is an anti-God, anti-Christian and anti-Bible movement. It is time for Christians and other citizens committed to traditional moral values to stand up and lead our nation in a vigorous fight against this threat to our society. I am convinced that there are enough morally minded people in our country to marshal such a counterattack. Secular humanists and their ilk are in the minority, in this country, but if we don't stop them soon, they will turn our children into amoral images of themselves.

The Tragic Results of This Radical Sex Education

The explicit-sex-education movement has been in operation long enough to provide ample reports from parents all over the country, testifying to the tragic results of its highly volatile amoral ideas.

An irate mother in Phoenix, Arizona, said in a public letter that after a sex-education class she caught her twelve-year-old son trying to sexually molest their four-year-old daughter. His defense was that he had been taught about it in school and wanted to "try it out."

At Fort Worth, Texas, a mother told a radio announcer: "She had to comfort her depressed daughter who had been told in school there were no boys who did not have premarital relations. She also claims one male teacher spoke to these 14-year-old girls concerning venereal diseases and ended by telling them the different ways of practicing homosexuality."[4]

The SIECUS program, described by the National Press as "the model effort in community 'sex education,' " was early installed in the schools of Anaheim, California. *The Saturday Evening Post* labeled it "a SIECUS show window." In Anaheim, 32,000 students, seventh through twelfth grades, were annually provided with six weeks of co-educational sex education.

Gary Allen stated, in 1969:

Since the Anaheim program has been part of the curriculum for over three years, many residents have been trying to get the School Board to assess the results. Unfortunately, the School District absolutely refuses to release any statistics concerning the subsequent increase in venereal disease and illegitimate births. However, the Orange County Health Department says that venereal disease in the area is "out of control." And Richard Taylor, Vice President of the Orange County branch of the Florence Crittenton Society, which operates homes for unwed mothers, reports of this matter in the area: "The 'new Morality' is leaving a broad trail of heartbreak in Orange County."

There can be no doubt about it. When newspaper reporter John Steinbacher asked a young Marine why so many servicemen congregated in Anaheim every weekend, the reply was: "Man, everybody knows that the high school girls here are 'available.' " The comment, Steinbacher found, was typical.[5]

One report suggested that venereal disease had increased 123 percent in Anaheim. "In 1966, 300 Orange County girls had to drop out of high school because of pregnancy—30 of them from junior high schools. In 1967, the Orange County Public Adoption Agency was receiving three or four unwed mothers a day—the youngest unwed mother reported being age 13. At a home for unwed mothers in nearby Los Angeles, one out of every five was from Orange County."[6] Wake up, taxpayer! Is that why you are paying those high school taxes?

Jo Hindman, in a column on "School House Pornography" in the February 27, 1969 issue of the *Eagle,* sketches a picture that is beginning to emerge throughout the United States: "An increasing flood of revoltingly crude and pornographic material, mislabeled as 'educational' by some school hierarchies, continues to trigger childhood tragedies: unwed pregnancies, illegitimate births, incestuous brother-sister attacks, abortions and venereal diseases—welling from the bog created by the too young knowing too much too soon."[7]

Before his death, Dr. Rubin, treasurer of SIECUS, arrogantly rejected all responsibility for the moral havoc created by his work when he stated at a symposium on sex and the teenager: "For the community to ask the sex educator to take on the responsibility of cutting down on illegitimacy or on venereal disease is to ask him to undertake a task that is foredoomed to failure."[8]

In other words, he refused ultimate responsibility for the sex-education program, even though he demanded that we entrust him with our children's innocent minds and with access to unlimited funds so he and his SIECUS playmates could experiment with those minds. What can we expect from the experimental "failure"? That is about the only observation he ever uttered with which I can agree. But while educators and "sexperts" experiment, young people by the thousands are destroyed.

I don't believe that American parents want their children educated in the delicate area of their sexuality by editors of *Sexology* magazine. It is one thing in a free society to visit the corner store, purchase a pornographic magazine, and corrupt your mind. It is quite another to disseminate that kind of material in the academically acceptable environment of the public school, where the attendance of our young is compulsory.

Is is probably impossible to exaggerate when describing the human suffering caused young people and their parents by fifteen years of explicit-sex-education courses in our public schools. And I do not just mean the over half a million teenage girls who are expected to bear illegitimate children next year, nor the unknown number of teenage abortions, VD carriers, or broken hearts. How about the epidemic of Herpes II—the now *incurable* strain of venereal disease. It is said that one out of ten of our citizens carries Herpes II. When you deduct children, singles, and elderly citizens who are no longer sexually active, that translates to one-fifth or more of our nation's young people who are carriers of this dread disease. I have counseled four people in the last month who confessed to having Herpes II. For the first twenty-four years of my counseling experience I never encountered it.

Sex educators will win no popularity contests with the Herpes carriers—or with their parents.

6. *It Will Increase Marital and Mental Disturbance* As a marriage counselor I have great respect for the significance of guilt complexes, for I have seen too many people whose loose morals in youth came back to haunt them after marriage. Fortunately, I can show them how "... the blood of Jesus Christ his Son cleanseth us from all sin" (1 John 1:7); the ninth verse teaches us that we can be forgiven, "If we confess our sins. . . ." A guilty conscience can be cured when a patient confesses his guilt to Christ and understands the biblical teaching on the subject of forgiveness. But what about the SIECUS-oriented youth whose life will be strewn with uninhibited sex? After the doctors with pornographic minds have taught young people, "There is no supreme being telling you what is right and wrong," how will they deal with this guilt? Shock treatments? Expensive mental sanitariums? Padded cells? Will they free themselves from guilt during seventy-five-dollar-an-hour sessions on psychiatrists' couches?

> From Oklahoma City comes a letter from nurses at the Deaconess Hospital and Home of Redeeming Love, a home for unwed mothers. Some quotes follow:
> We now reveal the irrevocable damage, the agony, the guilt, the stinging truth of premarital sex and its consequences. If one plants sperm, babies are reaped. If it were possible, less than one day in a maternity home would convince them (the sex educators) of the misery of premarital sex. Now the guilt complex, the anguish, the torment, hell, inner unreconcilable holocaust. Abortion does not remove the intense mental agony of guilt. Permissiveness and preventives are not the answer. For every one case of well-adjusted, happy individuals we can give you a hundred examples of downtrodden, yearning, troubled and despondent cases.[9]

One of my most popular books, *How to Win Over Depression,* was published in 1974. For eight years I have watched the problem worsen—except for those who avail themselves of the supernatural resources of God, as taught in the Bible. I have particularly been concerned over the tragic increase in teenage suicides during the same period that explicit sex education has corrupted our children's morals at school.

The humanist "sexologists" who do not understand human nature fail to deal realistically with the problem of guilt. This is commonly the aftermath of premarital sex and particularly abortion. Planned Parenthood is strangely silent on the fact that many young people have committed suicide as a result of aborting to cover their sin. I should know—I have performed funerals for such families that had no church home.

It is time the American people demand from their school boards, principals, superintendents, and all elected officials a return to traditional moral values. The place to start is with sex education: excise it from school curricula, return that responsibility to parents (where it belongs), and start to hold educators responsible for teaching our children to read, write, spell, and do arithmetic. I would venture that a survey of parents and taxpayers would reveal that more than 90 percent believe we pay educators to teach those basics. Any educator who thinks otherwise ought to get out of public education and start whatever kind of educational system he wants, but he should leave our public-school children alone!

Explicit Sex Education Is an Invasion of Privacy

The current brand of explicit sex education being taught in our public schools is at best a misuse of valuable student time, at worst the creation of a perverted obsession with sex long before a child's body is equipped to handle this adult experience or his mind is psychologically mature enough to handle the resultant responsibility for his action. It is a flagrant invasion of the parental right to prolong the child's youthfulness until mind and body naturally mature—a period during which the parent teaches him his own set of moral values. Humanist sexologists have preempted the role of moral molders of our youth, and since they are committed to animal morality—"if it feels good, do it," or, "follow situational ethics," or, "don't subscribe to absolutes,"—our children are developing morals below those of their parents.

Conspiracy or Attack on Christianity?

Many knowledgeable parents and taxpayers view this current sex-education assault on the minds and morals of our nation's children as the result of a national conspiracy. They suggest that the entire package—SIECUS, Planned Parenthood, values clarification, and explicit curricula—originated as a means of so demoralizing our youth with a sexual obsession that they would lose interest in patriotism and defending their country. Consequently, they would be ripe for a Communist or humanist or one-world takeover. Whether such a plot was supposed to originate in the Kremlin, Stockholm, Manhattan Island, or Rockefeller Center is unclear.

As I have previously explained, I do not particularly hold to the conspiracy theory. Instead, I see the program as a frontal attack on Christianity. Historically, all humanists know that Christianity is their greatest enemy. Were it not for Christianity, they would have gained an absolute stranglehold on the entire world. In spite of their monopoly on the media, television, education, and government bureaucracy, their mortal enemy is the church of Christ.

Consequently, creating a generation of sexually active teens is the best possible way to keep these impressionable youth from being open to the truth of Scripture. For years we churchmen have advertised that approximately 75 percent of our converts', ministers', and missionaries' decisions were made before the age of eighteen. What better way to cut down that number than to create a national obsession with sex and to give them academic encouragement to get involved?

As devilishly clever as this plot is, I am confident that it is doomed to failure. Our Lord said, "... I will build my church; and the gates of hell will not prevail against it" (Matthew 16:18). My concern is that millions of our nation's young people will be destroyed or harmfully impaired by VD, abortion, teenage parenthood, perversions, or even sadomasochism, in the process.

This sex-education *sexploitation* of our youth by humanist sexologists has to be stopped!

The Case Against Sex Education

Traditional moral codes . . . fail to meet the pressing needs of today and tomorrow.

Humanist Manifesto II

The humanists who control most of our nation's public schools and media have created the notion that "everyone is in favor of sex education"—except, of course, those few fundamentalist obstructionists.

The truth is, the overwhelming number of parents and taxpayers oppose it, when they understand what humanists really mean by their favorite method of moral destruction. That is why I have been so extremely frank in this book. We need to shock more of our citizens into watchfulness in order to protect our children from those who would turn them into humanist robots. We must awaken the responsible majority in the teaching profession to stand up for decency and to oppose the further deterioration of our schools.

It is not difficult to build a case *against* sex education, because it is so devastatingly harmful. The problem is to get our case heard. I hope those who read this chapter will utilize it in building a counterattack against this program in their neighborhood schools.

Simply stated, sex education has proved to be a catastrophic failure. The very ills it promised to cure have multiplied alarmingly. Sold as a means of controlling teenage pregnancy and venereal disease, it has measurably increased them sevenfold. Parents, doctors, teachers, and taxpayers are emphatically censuring all facets of it. Now for the details.

The Great Sex-Education Hoax

If the public school's inability to teach our children to read, write, or do math acceptably has become, as Dr. Paul Copperman calls it, a literacy hoax, then promising parents and school boards that sex education from kindergarten through twelfth grade will halt teenage pregnancy and venereal disease has to be the sex-education hoax of the century. The results have been quite predictable: the more explicit the classroom sex education, the higher the incidence of VD and illegitimate pregnancies.

When I first opposed sex education in our school in 1969, because it was far too explicit, a high-school principal admitted, "One out of every five students who graduates from this school either is a carrier of venereal disease or has been." Thirteen years and hundreds of hours of sex education later, it is now one out of *four*.

Even the *Journal of School Health,* devoted entirely to sex education, acknowledged in 1981, "More than half of the estimated 20 million STD [socially transmitted disease] victims this year will be persons under age 25; almost one-fourth will be victimized before they receive their high school diploma."[1]

A report out of Atlanta gives no comfort to those humanists who advocate an amoral sex life for our young.

> Strains of so-called "super gonorrhea" that are resistant to all antibiotics threaten worldwide efforts to control the spread of venereal diseases, medical experts said yesterday. One of the strains was said to be very prevalent in the San Diego area.
>
> Penicillin-resistant gonorrhea strains already are well established in the Far East, speakers told an international symposium on pelvic inflammatory disease being held at the national Center for Disease Control.
>
> Even more ominous were reports from other medical researchers attending the meeting of gonorrhea strains resistant not only to penicillin but to all other antibiotics currently employed in the treatment of venereal diseases.
>
> Types of gonorrhea against which penicillin had little or no effect first turned up in this country in 1976. However, other strains, which developed through mutations of the gonorrhea bacteria, have been identified that do not respond to any antibiotics, the meeting was told.

Dr. Ronald K. St. John, of the CDC's venereal disease control division, said the mutated types of gonorrhea resistant to all antibiotics have been detected in the Philippines and are "rapidly galloping forward."[2]

Barbara Morris contributed an excellent report on the reluctant admission of sex educators that we do have a VD problem and the call of some to STD training (socially transmitted disease evidently sounds better than VD); "Some sex educators . . . feel that STD education may create 'negative attitudes' toward sexuality. I shall never forget Dr. Mary Calderone at a SIECUS meeting some 10 years ago declaring that 'we never teach about VD in sex education—it's a negative concept.'"[3]

The "it's my body I can do what I want" argument doesn't hold up where venereal disease is concerned. STDs are just that: socially transmitted diseases. Not only for consenting adults, but innocent babies. An Associated Press release dated 4–14–81 reported a hard to diagnose and widespread venereal disease called Chlamydia is causing eye infections and pneumonia in newborns. More prevalent than gonorrhea, which is at an epidemic stage, evidence of the disease has been found in up to 15 percent of women who are having babies at Grady Memorial Hospital in Atlanta. Not only does this STD affect babies, it is responsible for some 200,000 cases of pelvic inflammatory disease (PID)—a leading cause of sterility in women. Chlamydia has also been linked with medical conditions of previously unknown cause, including miscarriage, low birth weight and infant death. The tragedy is that only 14 laboratories have the expensive and complex test equipment to diagnose the disease, with routine testing some five years away.

OTHER NEGATIVE CONCEPTS

Also generally unknown to young people is the damage, often permanent, that can be done to the body by certain types of contraceptives. The IUD has come under heavy criticism recently for the role it plays in causing pelvic inflammatory disease (PID) and the resulting sterility. Does the sex education program at your school include the latest information about this problem? Not likely. It's a negative concept, you know.

According to a Washington Post article (4–4–81) contraceptive foams, jellies and creams used by at least 2 million women (including teenage "women") may cause birth defects. Is this information relayed to girls in sex-ed classes? Not likely. Again, it's a negative concept.

How about the well-known adverse effects of "the pill"? Anyone taking oral contraceptives who has not read all the possible and probable side effects listed in the information sheet (which by law must be dispensed with each prescription for oral contraceptives) is flirting with serious trouble, if not disaster. Not the least side effect is loss of hair. As one wig maker in a recent People article put it, "You'd be amazed how many girls have lost their hair while on the pill. I know. Half of them are my clients." Are teenagers told of this side effect? Not likely. That's definitely a negative concept.

THE RESURRECTION OF DR. CALDERONE

One of the people most responsible for the deadly sex-ed which exists in the schools is Dr. Mary Calderone, SIECUS' resident grandmotherly sexpert. In recent years Dr. Mary has kept a low profile, but she surfaced recently at age 75 to do an article for Family Circle (March 11, 1980) titled "The Right Way To Teach Children About Sex." It's typical Calderone. She has a knack for sugar-coated hypocrisy that is not to be believed and which shows up in a contrived questions and answers routine. For instance:

Q: Do you feel that kids are starting to have intercourse earlier?

A: Yes, there's no doubt about that. By age 16, half of teenagers have had intercourse ... That's a new trend in the last five years.

(What Grandma Mary neglected to add is that this "new trend" is precisely what her SIECUS outfit has been working for since its very beginning.)

Q: Is it because kids are maturing earlier? ...

A: ... Our society is obsessed by sex ...

(What she didn't add is that she has been one of the prime contributors to that obsession.)

Q: What books would you recommend?

A: SIECUS has a reading list that has been reviewed and selected by respected experts ...

(She doesn't identify those "respected experts.")

Q: What should you tell your child about homosexuality?

A: You should say that about six percent of the population gets more sexual pleasure only out of same-sex rather than other-sex relationships—and that's just the way it is.

Q: And if the child asks, "Is it good or bad"?

A: It's neither. It's a way of being that a person doesn't choose.

(Any responsible psychiatrist will tell you that homosexuality is a learned behavior. At a SIECUS conference I attended some 10 years ago—there was Dr. Calderone, pleading with the audience to henceforth no longer refer to homosexuality as a deviant behavior—that it should be considered a normal, desirable alternate lifestyle, and also, that in the future, that's the way homosexuality would be promoted in sex education.)

In response to a question about "a bad sexual experience" with an adult (as if a child could have a "good sexual experience" with an adult), Dr. Mary cautions parents not to tell a child "Don't go with people you don't know." (A negative concept, perhaps?) Instead, the child should be told, "Don't go with anyone to private places." What's a private place in a child's mind?

The final question, "Do you see a time when people will be comfortable and guilt free about sex?" she answered, "That's what we are working toward."[4]

No wonder the secretary of Health and Human Services (HHS), Richard Schweiker, stated: "he opposed using Medicaid funds to provide unmarried teenagers with contraceptives. HHS has $162 million budget this year to promote family planning. Schweiker said his department should not give sex education to children: 'I don't think it's the Fed's role to do it and I don't think it's the state's role unless the local school agency does it with the express approval of the parents.' "[5]

Congressman Eldon Rudd of Arizona read into the *Congressional Record:*

> Many people believe that sex education programs in the public schools, no matter how well organized or presented, inevitably increase student awareness and interest in sex, as well as unrestrained sexual activity that increases unwanted pregnancy and VD, since such courses are rarely taught in the context of what is morally right and wrong in the eyes of most families.
>
> In my judgment, Congress should make sure that federally funded health education programs and other established programs for use in educating our youth are never designed to teach or legitimize immorality, sexual promiscuity, or homosexuality.[6]

Time magazine, usually a defender of the humanists who control the teaching that imprints the minds of our public-school children, acknowledges the booming tragedy of unwed pregnancy.

> According to federal figures, illegitimate births increased so rapidly in the 1970s that 17% of U.S. babies—one out of every six—are now born out of wedlock. In 1979, the last year for which statistics are

available, an estimated 597,000 illegitimate babies were born, up 50% since 1970. Nationwide nearly a third of the babies born to white teen-agers and 83% born to black teens were illegitimate. Blacks account for more than half of all illegitimate births, but the overall black illegitimacy rate has, in fact, dropped fairly sharply over the decade. It was down 10.7%, from 95.5 births per thousand unmarried women in 1970 to 85.3 in 1979, while the white rate rose 8.6%, from 13.9 per thousand to 15.1 per thousand. Though the number of abortions has increased dramatically, among unmarried teens there are still three live births for every five abortions. Today about 1.3 million children live with teen-age mothers, about half of whom are unmarried.[7]

The cost of this rampant life-style, accelerated by humanist sexologists in our public schools, is enormous. The *Time* article adds:

> During the '70s, the rate of unwed births ran well ahead of the increase in the number of women of child-bearing age. The most recent statistics are among the worst: illegitimate births for 1979 were up almost 10% over 1978. Nobody knows when, or if, the number of illegitimate births will level off. However, one thing is certain. The cost to taxpayers for illegitimate child rearing will be high. This year alone, the federal program for Aid to Families with Dependent Children is expected to exceed $7 billion.[8]

But that is the least expensive part of the price we pay to provide humanist sexologists a lush living at taxpayer expense. Who can calculate the broken dreams of a VD carrier or an unwed mother alone in a house, sheltering her fatherless child? What about the rage when that child learns she is illegitimate or the lack of vocational productivity and opportunity due to premature parenting?

Authorities Oppose Sex Education

One of the tactics of Planned Parenthood, SIECUS, and other humanists with PhD degrees is to claim that "all recognized authorities agree upon the need for more sex education taught in school." In actuality *many* authorities disagree, but our humanist-controlled press, TV, and school systems rarely advertise their opinions. Therefore I will cite several of them here in the hope that their views will be given widespread distribution.

MELVIN ANCHELL, M.D. (PRACTICING PSYCHIATRIST, LOS ANGELES, CALIFORNIA)

Sex educators are concerned about teaching children the mechanics of mating. Such instruction is comparable to training geese to fly South in the winter . . . Trying to teach children about sex without arousing sensuous feelings is about as hypocritical or naive as trying to describe the nature of fire without acknowledging the heat produced.

Some adults expect children to express admiration and joy with learning about sex. These adults cannot believe that shattering the fantasies and doubts of children without proper aging can act as a premature seduction causing irreparable psychological harm including perversion.

MAX LEVIN, M.D. (PSYCHIATRIST, NEW YORK MEDICAL COLLEGE)

But, sadly, many of our sex educators, even among those who are highly respected, seem (in my opinion) to be confused, and they are leading our youngsters astray. I disagree with the SIECUS position that sex education "must not be moral indoctrination" . . . I speak not as a clergyman but as a psychiatrist. There cannot be emotional health in the absence of high moral standards and a sense of human and social responsibility. I know that today morality is a "dirty word" but we must help our youth to see that moral codes have meaning beyond theology; they have psychological and sociological meaning.

RHODA L. LORAND, PH.D. (PSYCHOLOGIST, NEW YORK CITY)

Twenty-five years ago, I and many other child analysts might have enthusiastically endorsed school sex education . . . because we believed at that time that emphasis on sexual knowledge could do no harm, only good. We have since learned that it is harmful to force sexual preoccupation on children of the elementary school grades . . . forcing of sexual preoccupation on the elementary school child is very likely to result in sexual difficulties in adulthood, and it can lead to disturbed behavior in childhood.

EMINENT DOCTORS SPEAK OUT
WILLIAM MCGRATH, M.D. (PSYCHIATRIST, PHOENIX, ARIZONA)

There is a phase of personality development called the latency period, during which the healthy child is not interested in sex. This interval from about the age of five until adolescence serves a very important biological purpose. It affords a child an opportunity to develop his own resources, his beginning physical and mental strength.

Premature interest in sex is unnatural and will arrest or distort the development of the personality. Sex education should not be foisted on children; should not begin in the grade schools. Anyone who would deliberately arouse the child's curiosity or stimulate his unready mind to troubled sexual preoccupations ought to have a millstone tied around his neck and be cast into the sea.[9]

Even Teachers Oppose Sex Education

A former sex educator wrote an official in the United States Department of Education, confessing his complete turnaround on the sex-education issue. A portion of his letter is used by permission:

After working for five years as a sex and family-life educator, a trainer of teachers and counselors in these areas, a contributor to many local sex education curricula, the developer of a statewide K-12 family life education curriculum, a Planned Parenthood consultant and a member of the national boards of such organizations as Zero Population Growth, I concluded that traditional public school sex education and family-life education programs were rather ineffective. Worse, I encountered many instances where these programs were actually harmful. I was especially distressed by the schools' often unintentional promotion of an extremely liberal sexual ethos. For example, public school "family life" [family life is usually used euphemistically for sex] education programs usually promote the use of the various contraceptive modalities but, paradoxically, ignore the most effective, safest, least expensive, and most widely used method of birth control among American adolescents—abstinence. And these programs are invariably devoted to developing and sustaining support systems for those students who are sexually active, but they do nothing to help the majority of students who are not sexually active or who are sexually active out of ignorance or in submission to extrinsic pressures. . . .

While working on my continence materials for DHHS, I've become quite distressed with not just the incomplete, inadequate and sometimes erroneous sexual information taught in public schools, but also with the nihilistic tenor of nearly all family-life education programs. As a rule, these programs do not encourage pro-social behavior by teaching the values of integrity, accountability, gratification deferment, planning for the future, obedience, service, and respect for the rights of others. Similarly, I know of no public-school family-life education program that uses the widely accepted findings of psychologists, sociologists, medical researchers, and economists to educate students about the importance of the complete nuclear family and discipline in order to inculcate youth with socially desirable norms and to combat the symptoms of antisocial behavior such as crime, sexual promiscuity, drug abuse, violence, and low educational attainment. In short, just as I have demonstrated to the students and parents with whom I have worked (and as I am now documenting for DHHS) that there is a very strong intellectual case to be made for premarital chastity, there is just as strong a case, based on recent and accepted research, in support of traditional family institutions, values, and morals. And I can assure you that this case can be made without reference to or reliance upon religious teachings or beliefs.

An article by Effie A. Quay appearing in the *National Catholic Register* quoted several educators who write even in NEA journals, acknowledging that sex education has been a gigantic failure. She states:

> All are agreed on one thing: Sex education in the schools has done nothing to curtail sexual activity among students but, rather, has stimulated promiscuity with a resultant upsurge in teenage pregnancies and venereal disease—the very problems sex education is supposed to correct.[10]

According to one article, the state of Michigan Department of Education admits the fact that sex education does not reduce teenage pregnancy, VD, or promiscuity:

> Sex education in Michigan schools is to train children to be competent sex partners, and to get them to examine their own sexual values—not to lower VD rates, cut down on illegitimate pregnancies, or even to curb promiscuity.
>
> This is the blunt statement made by the Michigan Department of Public Health in its book entitled, "Preparing Professionals for Family Life and Human Sexuality Education." This is the book that education officials are using to train sex education teachers in the State of Michigan.
>
> On page 9 of the book, under the title "Purpose of Sex Education," the book quotes directly from a 1973 book by Simon and Gagnon which says in part:
>
> "... but few people today take seriously the assumption that sex education will lower rates of illegitimacy, venereal disease or promiscuity.... The more viable assumption behind an interest in sex edu-

cation is that it should work to make sex a more rewarding part of people's lives—to make sex education impart competence and not necessarily constraint. . . ."[11]

Scott Thomson, executive director of the National Association of Secondary School Principals, has called sex-education programs "a charade." According to his editorial sent to the organization's 35,000 members in a newsletter, administrators must "find sufficient courage to call a halt to the charade we have been playing with the public on this issue. . . . To accept new monies for sex education programs under the prevailing situation borders on educational fraud."[12]

Obviously they have seen the statistics too: sexual instruction increases the problems they assured us a few years ago would be cured. Instead of scrapping the program, the way they should, now they just modify their approach, admit that it will not produce results as quickly as they had predicted—but it should be taught anyhow.

Learn a Lesson from Sweden and Denmark

Sweden and Denmark are far more "progressive" (*humanistic* would be more accurate) than the United States. They introduced sex education into their schools as early as 1956 and served as the basis for the SIECUS and Planned Parenthood brand of sex education. In the *Family Review* we find this revealing analysis:

> Sweden introduced mandatory sex ed in the public schools in 1956. Ten years later U.S. News and World Report (2/7/66) reported the " 'catastrophic' increase in venereal disease among youngsters, especially since 1959 . . . Physicians say that gonorrhea and syphilis are more widespread in Sweden today than in any other civilized country in the world." Look Magazine (11/15/66, pp. 37-41) reported: "Most high-school-aged Swedes regard premarital sexual relations as natural and acceptable . . . Figures in Sweden indicate that premarital intercourse is common and increasing . . . The rising incidence of venereal disease in Sweden over the past eight years, despite . . . the presence of sex education, and the easy availability of contraceptives . . . baffles the experts." Some "experts" those must be!
> Dr. Jacqueline Kasun describes a study titled *Illegitimacy,* authored by Shirley Hartley in 1975. In Sweden, after sex ed was introduced in 1956, "the illegitimacy rate . . . which had been declining, subse-

quently rose for every age group except the older group, which did not receive the special sex education. Swedish births out of wedlock now amount to 31 percent of all births, the highest proportion in Europe, and two-and-a-half times as high as in the United States" ("Turning Children into Sex Experts", pg. 7). Dr. Lorand added that, "By 1976, the illegitimacy rate in Sweden was 33 percent of all live births even though half of all teenage pregnancies were aborted" (*op. cit.*, p. 9). She then adds: "In 1963 there were 8,496 divorces or legal separations in Sweden. By 1974, the divorce and separation rate had more than tripled to 27,208. This 320 percent increase took place, moreover, during a period when the marriage rate was markedly decreasing: 7.8 to 4.8 per 1000 from 1966 to 1972."

What about Denmark? Denmark began compulsory sex education in 1970. Since then, according to the 1977 Statistical Yearbook of Denmark: assault rape increased 300%; V.D. in persons aged 16 to 20 increased 250%; V.D. in persons aged 15 and under increased 400%; abortions increased 500%; illegitimate pregnancies were up 200%; and the divorce rate was up 200%![13]

Sex Education Up—Academics Down

It is more than coincidental that our nation's educational level has receded consistently during the same period in which our young people have been so preoccupied with sex and sex education. In the pro-sex-education study of George Mason High School, cited earlier, the following chart, showing the academic characteristics of the students in comparison with their sex-education instruction, is revealing.

GRADES	TOOK SEX EDUCATION	NO SEX EDUCATION
As & Bs	31.2%	62.2%
Bs & Cs	48.7%	28.4%
C or below	20.1%	9.4%

If this study, made by the sexologists themselves, is a fair indication of what sex education is doing to our students academically, we obviously cannot scrap the program too quickly. Admittedly, further studies need to be made, but since the past thirteen years have witnessed a consistent academic decline, while explicit sex education has gone wild, we can assume from the above chart that sex education is creating an obsession with sex at the expense of academic pursuits.

The sex-education movement has been such a gigantic hoax that it is time for public schools to abolish it. For until they face the fact that our nation's children are not animals, but human beings with a moral consciousness, they are unfit to educate them—particularly in the morally sensitive area of sexuality.

It is time for our educators to stop this assault on our children's morals and get back to teaching them the basic education they need in order to make it in life—the kind of education for which we pay them.

12

How to Halt This Flow of Moral Poison

One principle you should have learned from reading this book: you cannot trust a humanist to preserve the traditional morals of this nation. Instead, expect him to undermine them because he considers them repressive, inhibiting, or evil. Be sure of this: humanists are out to change America through its schoolchildren. And if we adults sit back and say nothing, they will succeed.

That was the bad news. The good news is that this dangerous and high-powered explicit sex-education movement can be stopped! "To be forewarned is to be forearmed." Knowledge of the SIECUS and Planned Parenthood subtleties is coming to light, and the guns of opposition are being loaded. Traditionally, we Americans have regarded our children as our most treasured possession. If enough parents can be confronted with the facts, they can mount a program of opposition that will drive SIECUS, Planned Parenthood, and the explicit-sex educators out of business; but it will take the active participation of millions of parents, working in their own communities. Here are some suggestions for action.

1. Carefully examine the character building you are providing for your children. If they will be able to withstand the flood tide of social chaos resulting from this explicit program, they will need all the character training they can get.

Do you see to it that your children regularly attend a Bible-teaching church? Do you lead them in this practice? Have they personally received Jesus Christ as their Lord and Savior? Have you? If not, they could already be on dangerous ground. The best defense against atheistic-humanistic ideas is a vital belief in God, through faith in His Son, Jesus Christ. The best preventive against your young people falling victim to the free-love and other animallike notions of the explicit-sex educators is dedication of their lives—body, soul and spirit—to Jesus Christ, "who loved them and gave Himself for them."

You are the key! Your children will follow your example. Lead them in prayer at home and set consistent standards of Christian behavior for them to observe. When their class was informed by the schoolteacher that there was no God, one junior-age girl raised her hand and expostulated, "Oh, I know there is a God. My daddy talks to Him every night!" Childlike faith? Yes, and that's what our children need today to give them the moral stamina to offset the atheistic nonsense voiced at school. Remember, since the Supreme Court has ruled the Bible and prayer out of the school, you and your church are even more obligated to teach the Bible to your children.

In addition, watch what your children read. Don't just forbid them the material of the world. Give them some of the excellent books found in your local Christian bookstore. Once you are sure that your own house is in order, then enter the fight to oppose this reckless policy of inflaming young minds with adult information.

2. Take a careful look at the kind of sex education your young people are being taught in school. Be very thorough in your investigation, asking your children to tell you what they are learning and urging them to bring home materials used in class. Don't automatically assume that your school's sex-education program includes the explicit materials of SIECUS. Give your principal the benefit of the doubt. He may courageously be opposing the administrative forces that are trying to make him use it. One high-school principal I know, a fine Christian man, protested, "I would quit before I permitted that trash in our school!" Such men need your support. (Recently I wrote a note of congratulations to a local school principal for his fine editorial in the school paper and for his school's wholesome program. Later he told one of our church members that he received only two such notes. I am confident that my feeling represented the majority in our community, but they remained silent.) It is time for the silent majority to actively

support those fine educators who are sincerely trying to do a superior job of training our youth. Most of us have little knowledge of or appreciation for the inner pressures that humanist educrats exert upon them.

Many schools still send home a slip asking for authorization for children to attend sex-education classes. Make sure you know the scope and content of the course before signing it. Don't be afraid to ask to see the movie or filmstrip or to read the curriculum. Have a friend or neighbor in whom you have confidence review it. If sex educators are afraid to let you see it, perhaps they have something to hide. Check the list of movies or filmstrips and examine recommended reading material assigned junior- and senior-high-school students. Because of the anti-Christian and antimoral attitudes of their leaders, anything approved by SIECUS or Planned Parenthood could well be dangerous. Also, consider the age for which it is intended. You may find some material acceptable for older young people that would be harmful for children.

One Los Angeles area parent decided to examine the curriculum of her thirteen-year-old's sex-education class before signing the permission slip her daughter brought home. The mother was told parents were not permitted to examine the materials, so she asked to sit in and review the class. The principal then informed her, "Your presence would be a disruptive influence on the class and would inhibit the students' discussion." Then he informed the parent, "You have two options. Either sign the permission slip or reject it."

That is, sign it without knowledge of content or refuse your child admission to the class. I thought America was a free country and that our schools were "public." That kind of authoritarian elitism may be okay for Russia, but someone needs to teach these educrats that this is the United States of America. Over two hundred years ago our forefathers fought a revolutionary war to free our people from the king of England. It appears we are going to have to fight another to free our children from the clutches of this nation's educrats.

Phyllis Schlafly published an excellent checklist that has been given wide distribution in magazines, newsletters, and one national news service. It is a handy guide for concerned parents.

Sex education curricula, often disguised under the deceptive title "family life," are making their appearance in public schools all across the country this fall. Here is a checklist by which you can evaluate the curriculum proposed in your school system.

1. Does it omit all references to moral standards of right and wrong, thereby teaching only animal-level sex?

2. Does it urge boys and girls to seek help from or consult only or primarily agencies rather than their parents or religious advisers?

3. Does it require instruction and discussion to take place in sex-integrated (co-ed) classes rather than separate classes for boys and girls? (The answer to this question is always "yes" in public schools because federal law prohibits separating boys and girls.)

4. Does it require boys and girls to discuss private parts and sexual behavior openly in the classroom, with explicit vocabulary, thereby destroying their natural modesty, privacy, and psychological defenses (especially of the girls) against immoral sex?

5. Does it omit mentioning chastity as a method (the only absolute method) of preventing teen-age pregnancies?

6. Does it omit mentioning chastity and marital fidelity as a method (the only absolute method) of avoiding VD?

7. Does it assume that all boys and girls are engaging in immoral sex, thereby encouraging them to accept promiscuous sexual acts as normal?

8. Does it omit mention of the spiritual, psychological, emotional and physical benefits of premarital chastity, marital fidelity and traditional family life?

9. Does it omit mention of the spiritual, psychological, emotional and physical penalties and risks of fornication, adultery and promiscuity?

10. Does it require boys and girls to engage in role playing (pretending one is pregnant, pretending one has to admit having VD, pretending to use various types of contraceptives), thereby encouraging peer pressure to be exerted on the side of fornication rather than chastity?

11. Does it fail to stress marriage as the most moral, most fulfilling, and/or most socially acceptable method of enjoying sexual activity?

12. Does it encourage boys and girls *not* to tell their parents about the sex-ed curriculum, or about their sexual behavior or problems?

13. Does it present abortion as an acceptable method of birth control?

14. Does it use materials and references from the pro-abortion Planned Parenthood?

15. Does it present homosexual behavior as normal and acceptable?

16. Does it omit mention of the incurable types of VD which today

affect millions of Americans? Does it falsely imply that all VD can be cured by treatment?

17. Does it give respectability to VD by listing famous people who have had it?

18. Does it use a vocabulary which disguises immorality? For example, "sexually active" to mean fornication, "sexual partners" to mean sex in or out of marriage, "fetus" to mean baby, "termination of pregnancy" to mean killing a preborn baby.

19. Does it require boys and girls to draw or trace on paper intimate parts of the male and female bodies?

20. Does it ask unnecessary questions which cause boys and girls to doubt their parents' religious and social values? ("Is there a need for a wedding ceremony, religious or civil?")

21. Does it force advanced concepts and vocabulary upon five- and eight-year-old children too young to understand or be interested? (For example, selection of mate, Caesarian, pregnancy prevention, population control, ovulation, VD, sperm, ovum.)

22. Does it constantly propagandize for limiting the size of families by teaching that having more children means that each one receives fewer economic benefits?

23. Can the sex-ed curriculum reasonably be described as a "how to do it" course in sexual acts (instruction which obviously encourages individual experimentation)?

Find out what sex education curriculum is being taught or proposed in your school district. Read it and apply the above questions. If the answer is yes to many of these questions, don't be surprised if teen-age pregnancies and VD are epidemic.

3. Alert dedicated schoolteachers among your acquaintances of this dangerous form of education. I have found that the overwhelming majority of educators are very dedicated individuals, and many are fine Christians. In our opposition to explicit sex education, we must be very careful not to alienate this majority group. But they are often prone to be defensive the moment parents and taxpayers begin to criticize the public schools. For that reason be very understanding and factual in presenting your case to them.

Schoolteachers, together with ministers and doctors, have long enjoyed a privileged sanctuary in the minds of most Americans. We have a tendency to feel, and rightly so, that teachers could earn much more money in another profession. It is now time, however, that they police their own profession.

We have reached the place in American education where educators should begin to organize in order to bring morality, decency, and integrity back as standards in the public school. They have a vested interest in whether or not schoolteachers should be permitted to use profanity and filth in the classroom. Their reputation is at stake. Since many teachers become attached to the children with whom they have been entrusted over the years, why should they stand idly by while these young people have their minds crippled and their lives unnecessarily twisted to satisfy the objectives of the few? It is time that schoolteachers themselves lead a campaign that will stop this use of the public schools as a gigantic experimental laboratory disseminating sex information.

4. If you find that your school is using explicit SIECUS-approved materials, call for an appointment with your principal. It is possible that he does not know the dangerous effects of this material or the motives of those who have produced it. Kindly share your concern and urge him to read this book or other material at your disposal. If you can get him to quietly reject the SIECUS material, you have done your community a great service. If he knows that enough parents are concerned, he may revert to locally produced materials based upon community moral standards.

5. If you, like many parents, get nowhere with your principal, then either arouse other parents or find a group and join their vigorous campaigns. All community programs must begin with education. Whether you are starting a new group or joining one, the major task is to inform the parents in your community.

Give this book and other informative materials to the parents in your school. This explicit sex education is such an inflammatory program that it has been relatively easy to get parents motivated to action, but it will take work. Don't just leave the job to others or say, "Someone ought to do something about this." Your community needs *your* help. It will be worth it, for nothing is more important right now than America's children.

What can a group do? Formally appeal to the school board. They make the decision for the community, and they only understand pressure. Don't hesitate to pull out all stops, within the law, in pressuring them. You can be sure SIECUS will not be sitting on its hands, idly awaiting the decision of your educational administrators.

If that fails, consider a recall movement. Many school districts across the country have recalled or replaced school-board members who voted in these explicit sex-education materials. Any school-board member, administrator, or educator so naive or philosophically oriented that he favors SIECUS approved sex education has no business holding office. As long as our voting laws in this country grant us the power of recall and election, they should be used—whenever appropriate.

6. Participate more actively in the election of school-board officials. Concerned citizens can be assured that where Bible-believing Christians have comprised the majority of their boards, SIECUS has not been able to high-pressure school officials into adopting their course. Vigorously campaign for morally committed replacements for school-board members who back SIECUS materials.

Too long we Christians have avoided politics, calling it a "dirty business." This country was hammered out on the anvil of the Bible, predominantly by Christian men. The main problem with our country today is that Christians have retreated from politics. We need more Christians on every governmental level in this land! How can we be "salt" of the earth unless we get involved where the decisions are made?

Our country today desperately needs qualified Christians who will offer themselves to God for political leadership. It would be exciting if more than 50 percent of our leaders knew Jesus Christ and could pray for wisdom. If that were the case, we would see a deescalation of the amorality trends of today. A recent survey of the United States Congress indicates that 30 percent are "born again." We need just 21 percent more![1]

In Texas recently a nine-year veteran of the local school board picked me up at the airport. When I asked what kind of sex education was taught in their public school, he replied, "None." He then explained that all the members of the board were Christians. "When that material was introduced by our superintendent, we personally reviewed it and found it morally offensive, so we forbade its use. It is the

parents' and churches' responsibility to inculcate values and morals."
In that community, I noted, teenage pregnancy, abortion, drug abuse,
and crime were all considerably below the national average.

7. Write your president, congressman and senators. Because this is a
national problem, they should be encouraged to stop the spending of
federal monies for such pornographic education. Urge them to get the
Department of Education and Health and Human Services to disapprove the SIECUS explicit sex-education material and stop the funding of Planned Parenthood.

8. Pray for this country! We are in serious trouble when these people can get into such high positions of leadership that they can prepare
such morally degrading materials. If this country is ever to be saved, it
will have to be in answer to prayer—prayer that motivates Christians
and their leaders to action.

It's time for Christian leaders across the land to mount a charge
against this insidious cult of the pornographic. The Bible says, "Resist
the devil." Those who are ceaselessly working to destroy our children
are certainly not inspired by God. So, ministers and Christians, arise!
Get involved in this fight to enslave the minds and bodies of our youth.

13

Values Clarification

> The power of man to make himself what he pleases means . . . the
> power of some men to make of other men what they please.
>
> C. S. LEWIS

An attractive schoolteacher with a master's degree came to me for
counseling between sessions at a Family Life Seminar in a large city.
Her problem concerned values clarification in her very progressive
school district. She was the teacher of the district's teachers.

Five years before, with the aid of a government grant, this 4.0-aver-
age teacher of gifted children was sent, all expenses paid, to an extensive values-clarification seminar for teachers, conducted by a leader in
the values-clarification movement. This insidiously harmful teaching
technique—condemned by many responsible educators, psychiatrists,
ministers, and others committed to traditional moral values—is really
mortal man's most vicious assault on the minds of our children. It is a
subtle technique that combines group therapy, sensitivity training, and
peer-pressure brainwashing. It attacks the moral commitment of any
student, particularly the vulnerable children in our government-controlled school system.

Shortly after returning from the values-clarification seminar, the
head of the gifted-student department for her school system asked this
dedicated teacher to offer a seminar, relating what she had learned, for
other teachers of the gifted. (Author's note: this, in itself, is a technique
of humanistic educators: send one sharp teacher to learn a humanistic
teaching method, then bring it back into the system and indoctrinate
the other teachers, *starting with the gifted.* Why the gifted? Very simple.
They will most likely be the leaders of tomorrow, including schoolteachers, college professors, journalists, ACLU lawyers, TV personali-

ties, and others who influence the minds of succeeding generations.) After thoroughly indoctrinating all the gifted teachers, she was used in her district to train other teachers in the techniques of values clarification, so that instead of just one district teacher attacking the moral values of children, there would be several hundred.

Now do you understand why the fathers of values clarification, Sidney Simon and Lawrence Kolberg, have been so successful, within such a short time, in indoctrinating millions of teachers by holding values-clarification seminars for classroom teachers and teaching specialists all over the country? The subject matter of those seminars is readily available, for Sidney Simon, Leland Howe, and Howard Kirschenbaum published a book entitled *Values Clarification.*

The young teacher, who did not come from a Christian family and was married to an atheist in dental school, enjoyed a heady position of not only being a teacher of the gifted, but also a teacher of teachers in her district for a little over two years. Then, in the providence of God, she and her husband came under the sound of the gospel, and two years ago they were converted. In response to her newfound faith, the ingestion of biblical principles taught through her faithful Bible-teaching church, and the instinctual response to motherhood, she entertained very disturbing thoughts about being used by the humanistic system to communicate values-clarification techniques. In fact, she experienced so much conflict that she modified the entire program on her own and lived in dread that sooner or later it would come to the attention of the authorities.

I have no doubt that multiplied thousands of teachers of values clarification are unwittingly being used by the humanists in the system and that once they awaken to the harm they are doing our children and young people, they will throw off this deliberate attack on our nation's values and return to what they're really paid for: training our children in the basic skills necessary to sustain life. I hope the research of the Gablers, Barbara Morris, and many other dedicated traditionalists, which have sparked cries of protest from parents and others throughout the country, will alert these educators to the harmful effects of values clarification on their charges. I am convinced that many people who use values clarification are themselves unaware of its devastating impact on the moral values of our young.

A reporter for the Los Angeles *Times* interrupted me during an interview to assert, "I don't see anything wrong with values clarification. I spent a weekend attending a seminar in which I took the training myself." What she did not realize is that when she subjected herself to the training, her moral values were solidly in place; she was a wife and mother of two children, and she would not be adversely affected by the moral values of the group. Not so an elementary-school-age child or a secondary-level young person, whose moral values are not established and who is particularly susceptible to peer pressure.

By contrast, I am reminded of the two certificated California schoolteachers I met while teaching a Bible conference at Hume Lake Christian Camps. They had just resigned their secure positions with tenure as kindergarten teachers because they would not teach values clarification as their district demanded. For five years, after taking the values-clarification training, they were closely supervised in its use among kindergarten children. Both were expressly forbidden to teach their personal moral values.

As an illustration of values clarification, the wife shared with me the following story that had been recommended for use in their manual. According to a hypothetical situation, "Next Sunday is your mother's birthday. You have three quarters in your bank to buy her a present. What would you buy?" The class then discussed the kind of gift to purchase for a mother. The teacher injects, "Next Sunday is your mother's birthday and you have three dollars. What would you give her?" The class proceeds to discuss this possibility. Finally, the question is broached, "Next Sunday is your mother's birthday, but you have no money. What would you do?" After several suggestions, one youngster proposed, "I would take three dollars out of my mother's purse and buy her a present." At this point the class enters into a discussion on the merits of taking money out of mother's purse, concluding, "Since it's for mother's birthday anyway, it really isn't stealing." The teacher's conscience would not permit this subtle form of indoctrinating kindergarten children, creating a justification for stealing contrary to the principles of the Bible. The fact that she was expressly forbidden to inject the biblical principle made her situation intolerable.

The whole thrust of humanism is that whatever is good for the individual in a given situation—and doesn't hurt another—is permissible. This contradicts centuries of traditional moral values that have produced the greatest amount of good for the largest number of people in the history of the world. The Bible teaches that "when every man does that which is right in his own eyes," he destroys his culture. Read the book of Judges if you wish to find confirmation of that premise.

The familiar maxim "He who refuses to learn from history is destined to repeat it" is certainly apropos in values clarification, where history, tradition, and moral absolutes are forbidden; only the values of the group under discussion are important. I doubt that a group of thirty-two kindergarteners, without benefit of adult guidance, are qualified to make moral judgments and reach ethical conclusions that would keep them from repeating the mistakes of the past. In addition, immature group decisions will invariably be 180 degrees opposite of the values of those children's parents.

Education or Indoctrination?

The only way to convince you of the harmful effects of values clarification is to let you read for yourself the questions asked. The more we can circulate these devastatingly provocative questions, the sooner we will awaken concerned parents to their harmful influence. Although educators themselves are trying diligently to keep these questions out of the reach of parents, they are accessible and, in some cases, appear in teaching manuals.

Mel and Norma Gabler, of Longview, Texas, are acknowledged by both friend and foe to be the most informed authorities on textbook content in the United States today. After years of painstaking research of textbooks and school curricula, Mel Gabler makes the following analysis.

VALUES CLARIFICATION
(DOES IT BUILD OR DESTROY BASIC VALUES?)

For years, schools took a neutral stance on morals. Gradually, neutrality changed to attacks on moral standards, until student beliefs or values were under attack in both textbooks and school programs.

Then a seemingly wonderful solution appeared—a "values education" program which is sweeping through schools like wildfire. The descriptions of these programs delight the many parents who consider the teaching of morality a school responsibility. Students are to clarify, that is, evaluate their values by coming to their *own* conclusions based on the following seven criteria:

A VALUE MUST BE:

Step 1

Choosing: 1. *Freely chosen.* (Anything *taught* is authoritarian imposition, so cannot be a "true" value.)

2. *Chosen from alternatives.* (Variables must be considered with no indication from the teacher that any values are fixed or are of more importance than other values.)

3. *Chosen after careful consideration* of the consequences of each alternative. (How many children will know the consequences?)

Step 2

Prizing: 4. *Prized* and/or cherished.

5. *Publicly affirmed.* (Makes it difficult to back down.)

Step 3

Acting: 6. *Acted upon.* (Example: If the choice were that premarital sex is acceptable, find someone and practice it.)

7. *Acted upon regularly.* (To establish it firmly as the chosen behavior.)

To qualify as a "true" value, ALL seven criteria must be met!

Traditional values do NOT qualify if they have been taught, because students received those beliefs through "authoritarian indoctrination." They were not chosen of the students' own free will. Thus, values previously taught by the home, church or school are eliminated. Religious faith held by students is not valid since it cannot meet the criteria listed.

In their instructions to teachers, prominent proponents of Values Clarification say guided discussion is disastrous for the consideration of values such as honesty. With no absolute values considered, a seed of doubt about the firmness and validity of traditional values is planted each time a choice of alternatives is made.

Even proponents of Values Clarification concede that it is based entirely upon relativism or "situation ethics" (the philosophy that circumstances determine whether an action is right or wrong). Granted, some students may select absolute, moral positions; but since teachers are prohibited from favoring any moral stand, decisions will be heavily influenced by peer group knowledge and peer pressure. How many students will be able to stand firm in their religious faith while being constantly confronted by relativism in a public school classroom? In most instances there will be secular teachers and an intense atmosphere of "group consensus" against any individual student deviating from the norm of the class. At the very best they gradually, and usually unknowingly, receive an indoctrination in situation ethics. Thus, in practice, Values Clarification DESTROYS HOME TAUGHT VALUES.

Values Clarification programs are presented so favorably that few Christians realize they are based upon humanistic relativism, in direct opposition to the Judeo-Christian ethic. Values Clarification is supposed to allow each student to form his *own* values, but in practice the student merely *trades* his personal convictions for the norm of the group. Thus, it produces students with no fixed values, and they are set adrift in the sea of life as a raft without oars, sails or rudder.[1]

© 1981, The Mel GABLERs.

Do we really want values for the next generation to be established by immature eighth graders without the benefit of traditional morality? Such values, which would reduce centuries of cultural standards to the level of the jungle, are not even in the best interest of the teens themselves, not to mention their parents or the nation at large.

As Mel Gabler asks, "Who has the right to set values—the parents or the school system? Don't the parents have the right to teach the values they desire to be taught to their children without deliberate interference by the school system?"

In the March 1981 edition of *Educational Research Analysts Handbook No. 2,* "Values Clarification," a lengthy review by Dr. O. M. Wellman appeared (© 1981, The Mel GABLERs). He concluded that values clarification:

1. is an invasion of privacy
2. promotes situation ethics
3. associates good concepts with greed and hypocrisy
4. suggests and promotes immoral concepts (for example, abortion, homosexuality, and promiscuous sex are viewed as valid moral alternatives because they are presented in a positive fashion)[2]

Dr. Wellman further states, "The logical and inevitable result of this indoctrination is a further deterioration of moral standards. Parents must object and refuse to let their children participate."[3] The following list of questions is included by Dr. Wellman in his review of Sidney Simon's textbook to teachers, which explains how to conduct values-clarification training in our humanist-dominated schools. As you read through these questions, ask yourself if you want your children to freely discuss these subjects in an environment where religious absolutes and Christian presuppositions are expressly forbidden and where the "change agent" in charge of the discussion will probably either be a committed humanist or heavily indoctrinated with humanist, anti-moral principles. Imagine these questions being discussed, challenged, and debated in a classroom where one basic rule dominates: "There are no absolutes, no rights or wrongs."

How many of you:

2. go to church or temple regularly?
3. enjoy going to church or temple? (p. 41) ...
5. think there are times when cheating is justified? (p. 38) ...
18. think that at this point in your life you are a complete flop or failure (p. 42).
23. have ever had problems so bad you wished you could die so you wouldn't have to face them?
24. are in favor of having American police follow the example of the British "Bobbies"—no live ammunition?
25. would choose to die and go to heaven if it meant playing a harp all day?
41. think people should limit the size of their families to two children?
42. would favor a law to limit families to two children? (p. 43)
43. often think of death? (p. 44) ...
83. think there should be a law guaranteeing a minimum income? (p. 45)
88. would like to have different parents?
99. think capital punishment should be abolished?
105. think we ought to legalize "pot"?
106. think we ought to legalize abortion? (p. 46)[4]

For use with secondary students and adults (pp. 48–53):

1. feel free to discuss sex with your parents/children?
2. think giving grades in school inhibits meaningful learning?
3. approve of premarital sex for boys?
4. approve of premarital sex for girls? (p. 48)
7. think sex education instruction in the schools should include techniques for lovemaking, contraception?
10. think a suspected homosexual should be allowed to teach in the public schools?
13. would approve of a marriage between homosexuals being sanctioned by priest, minister or rabbi?
14. would approve of a young couple trying out marriage by living together for six months before actually getting married?
15. practice religion along with your parents? (p. 49)
25. would encourage legal abortion for an unwed daughter?
28. think homosexuals should be fired from government jobs?
29. read Playboy Magazine? (p. 50)
38. would approve of contract marriages in which the marriage would come up for renewal every few years?
41. would be upset if organized religion disappeared?
42. think the government should help support day care centers for working mothers?
49. would not hesitate to marry someone from a different religion? From another race? Ethnic group? (p. 51)
51. think that parents should teach their children to masturbate?
69. would approve of a couple using artificial insemination if the husband was sterile? (p. 52)
73. think we should legalize mercy killings?[5]

STRATEGY NUMBER 4—*Rank Order* (Pp. 58–93)
(Gives students practice in choosing and publicly affirming, explaining or defending choices)

Asks questions which have three (or four) alternative choices for responding. Students are to rank order the choices according to their own preferences. A sample of these questions follows:

25. If your parents were in constant conflict, which would you have them do?

—get divorced, and your father leave home

—stay together and hide their feelings for the sake of the children

—get divorced, and you live with your father (p. 66)

29. If you were a pacifist and you found out your friend supports certain wars, would you

    —discontinue the relationship

    —overlook the discrepancy in views

    —try to change his viewpoint

30. Which do you think is the most religious thing to do on a Sunday morning?

    —go to church to hear a very good preacher

    —listen to some classical music on the radio

    —have a big breakfast with the family (p. 67)

31. Which of the following measures should be taken to alleviate the population problem?

    —legalize abortion

    —limit each family to two children and sterilize the parents afterwards

    —distribute birth control information everywhere

    —trust people's common sense to limit the size of their families

32. Which would you rather do on a Sunday morning?

    —sleep late

    —play with a friend

    —watch TV[6]

How would you like your children to discuss these questions without traditional adult guidance:

7. A college student who lends his tuition money to a friend who has to obtain an abortion.

9. A father who runs his family with complete democracy—one man, one vote. Even the three-year-old has a vote on where to go for their vacation. (p. 106)

1. Violent protest as a method of bringing about change.

2. Modifying school curriculum to make it more relevant to the present society.

6. Greater federal financing for education.
9. National control to reduce pollution and *protect natural resources.* (p. 108)[7]

I cannot help responding to the phrase "protection of our natural resources." We have no greater natural resource than our children, and the last thing our children need is to have their young, impressionable minds exposed to the valueless values of humanism. Any parent who permits his child to be subjected to values clarification does so at his own risk.

Values Clarifiers Equal Change Agents

A Carter administration educrat, during a discussion on funding for government-controlled preschool day-care centers, made an astonishingly revealing statement: "One of the reasons we need to establish preschool day-care centers for children from three years up is because, in spite of the billions of dollars at our disposal and the thirteen years we have the children in our public schools, we are still not able to undo the harm done to them before they arrive in kindergarten." In context, "harm" refers to a belief in God, an absolute value system, patriotism, and respect for the authority of parenthood. There is no question in my mind, after examining school curricula, evaluating reports from Christian teachers who have been subjected to values-training seminars, hearing the reports of students in the classroom, reading National Educational Association literature, and studying the *Humanist Manifesto* (which clearly outlines humanist teachings), that humanist educrats are determined to preempt the moral values of parents and forcibly teach our nation's children the bankrupt values of humanism, whether or not parents like it.

I recommend Barbara Morris's spine-chilling book, *Change Agents in the Schools,* to every parent of public-school children. Any reader who doubts the veracity of what I am saying should get a copy of her book and read it. She has not overstated the case. (CHANGE AGENTS IN THE SCHOOLS is available from The Barbara M. Morris Report, P.O. Box 756, Upland, CA 91786 $9.95. CA residents add 6% tax.)

Morris reports a statement made at a New York State Education Department Conference in 1975 when Dr. R. Grey Bridge, a resident consultant at the Rand Corporation, showed his contempt for parents and their right to teach values to their children. He said, "When the kids come to us at age four, five, or six, they already have these beliefs set. We have to unwind them and start over, and even then, we get them only a few hours a day."[8]

Barbara Morris has done a superb job of researching the connection between Washington and the "change agent" philosophy of some public-school teachers and educrats. (Newsletter published by The Barbara M. Morris Report, P.O. Box 756, Upland, CA 91786 $20/10 issues.)

Change Agents: The Washington Connection

Much is made of education being controlled by local school boards that reflect the wishes of the local community. Local control may have existed at one time, but today it is a fantasy. Just about all of local education is controlled by the federal government through money funneled to government agencies such as the National Science Foundation (NSF) and the National Endowment for the Humanities (NEH). In turn, the NSF, NEH and other government agencies contract with change agent curriculum developers who produce curricula that win the approval of federal bureaucrats who control the purse strings. For instance, it was through a NSF contract with the Education Development Center that we now have the infamous *Man: A Course of Study* (MACOS) curriculum. A grant from NEH assisted development of the values-changing curriculum *Ethical Quest in a Democratic Society* currently being piloted in Washington state schools and slated for use nationwide. Another NEH-funded curriculum, developed by the Center For Global Perspectives is called *Global Perspectives: A Humanistic Influence On The Curriculum.* It is being piloted in several areas around the country preparatory to being used in schools nationwide. This program and others very much like it satisfy the *Humanist Manifesto* call for ". . . each person to become, in ideal as well as in practice, a citizen of a world community."

Federally funded change agent programs and curricula were ushered in soon after passage of the federal Elementary and Secondary Education Act (ESEA) in 1965. By 1969 the federal government had published *Pacesetters in Innovation,* a nearly two-inch thick volume of all innovative projects in operation in schools as of February,

1969. Here are a few examples of projects listed in *Pacesetters in Innovation* that deal with changing teachers and children:

Project ES 001 996: Describes how "experienced teachers from the model school will serve as change agents" through staff rotation.

Project ES 001 783: Describes teachers as "inhouse change agents" who participate in "a 5-day resident laboratory in human relations/sensitivity training . . ."

Project ES 002 010: Describes how workshops will be established to train selected teachers as change agents.

Project ES 002 230: Explains how emphasis will be placed on creating behavioral change in students through a combination of guidance counseling and occupational training.

It is interesting that resistance to change was anticipated, and that it would not be tolerated:

Project ES 002 230: "Forces which block the adoption of new ideas will be identified and ways to overcome these forces will be explored."

Other evidence of the schools functioning as change agents with the help of the federal government can be found in information offered by the Educational Resources Information Center (ERIC). This federally funded operation of the U.S. Office of Education provides materials to help educators function as change agents. For instance, it sells such documents as ED 056 345: *Humanism: The Counselor's Role as a Change Agent;* ED 058 664: *Change Agent Teams Changing Schools: Case Studies;* ED 054 513: *Emotional Arousal and Attitude Change During Simulation Games.*

In a document titled *Report To The President's Commission on School Finance,* the concern was expressed that the majority of our youth hold the same values as their parents and that this pattern must be altered. The report also stated that the use of "conventional wisdom as a basis for decision-making is a major impediment to educational improvement." For educational improvement, the report recommended ". . . that the change agent is the decision-maker about the innovation. That is, it is assumed that he decides what the adopter will change to." But there is concern expressed about willingness of people to change: ". . . people cannot be forced to change until they are psychologically ready."

To help make people psychologically ready for the change, U.S.

government grants have been given to universities for the training of change agents. In August, 1973, the U.S. Department of Health, Education and Welfare (HEW) awarded $5,900,000 to 21 institutions to train 500 educational personnel to become leaders of educational change.

It should be clearly understood that such "leaders of educational change" do not engage in value-free activity. Gerald Zaltman and Robert Duncan in *Strategies for Planned Change* challenged the "value-free" position as a myth. They said: "The issue becomes what values and therefore whose values are to be served by change. There is a natural tendency for the change agent to promulgate his values, and in such circumstances we must ask whether these values are representative of those possessed by the target system."

Zaltman and Duncan then asked the question parents ought to ask of every change agent educator: "Is the change agent really concerned about the welfare of the target system, or does the change activity satisfy his or her needs for power and control? If the latter motives are operating, this might cause the change agent to be more manipulative in dealing with the target system."

If you look at the scope of the change process in the schools, it is evident that the change agent is not "really concerned about the welfare of the target system". The "target system" is *the children.* Children are to be changed for a particular purpose with a particular goal in mind. When the federal government spends millions of dollars to train "leaders of educational change" it is obvious the purpose is not to perpetuate the status quo. The purpose is to satisfy the desire of the government to amass power and control in order to facilitate the Humanist new world order. And how could any of it be done without the government school curriculum?

Indeed, the curriculum—be it math or home economics, vocational training or guidance counseling—must be a tool for change. Therefore, curricula cannot be designed or developed by those who think in the "traditional mode" or who use "conventional wisdom." Funding goes only to those curriculum developers who do not block the adoption of new ideas, but in fact, facilitate change. ". . . A curriculum . . . whether it is a textbook, a complete set of materials and activities, or a whole school program—must have some ends in view. It must be constructed in relation to some purposes. Ideally, these should be formulated in terms of the change in students the curriculum is intended to bring about."

Increasingly, the degree and scope of change agent activity that goes on behind closed classroom doors will be decided in Washington, D.C., by a carefully chosen panel of 22 elite change agents. . . . 22 members of a Joint Dissemination Review Panel of the NDN—11 each from the U.S. Office of Education and the National Institute of Education "... are chosen by agency heads for their ability to analyze the effectiveness of education programs. . . ."

"Currently, 199 programs have passed the Panel. Of that number, 109 were funded for the 1977–78 school year . . ." At the time this is written, such programs are in 36 states.[9]

By this time, such programs could be established in every one of our fifty states. Think of it: twenty-two educrats making the decisions on the programs that schoolteachers and their change agents can use on your most precious possession, your children. I hope the Reagan administration will be able to curtail some of the aggressive humanist influence, but I would not count on it.

The only way it can be stopped is to have it condemned as unscientific, counterproductive educationally, morally harmful, and supportive of a nontheistic religious-belief system that is in violation of the Constitution of the United States.

As a result of well-researched books like that of Barbara Morris and the many newsletters that have sprung up from concerned citizens' groups across the country, we have heard an incredible outcry on the part of parents throughout the nation, and educators are beginning to feel the first wave of hostility, distrust, and disrespect that is destined to increase until they face the fact that it is not their job to dictate a moral-value system for our children, but God and society have given that responsibility to parents.

One mother of an eighth-grade girl in Georgia reported to my wife that she had alerted her child to the potential questions that could be asked on values clarification. Such questions have created vehement protests throughout the country from parents who consider them an invasion of privacy. One day the daughter, at her mother's instruction, ignored the teacher's demand to collect the questions at the close of the hour and brought them home from school. The next day, when the mother confronted both teacher and principal with the evidence, in both cases she received the same spontaneous response: "You have no right to hold a copy of those questions."

What arrogant educratic nonsense! That kind of mentality is doing more to fill the classrooms of our Christian schools today than anything else. Parents have not yet surrendered the control of forming the attitudes and values of their children to the public schools. Unless educators wake up to that fact and return to the time-honored tradition of schools being supportive of the family, an extension of the home, and a reflection of the moral values of the community, the Christian-school movement will reach its goal of training one-half of the nation's youth by the year 1990.

The Three Categories of Learning

Modern education can be divided into three major sections:

1. Cognitive: refers to thinking/reasoning skills and involves training in the basics of reading, writing, spelling, math, grammar, history, geography, etc.
2. Psycho-Motor (physical education): includes every sport from sandbox to college football.
3. Affective: refers to feelings, emotions. This category was traditionally left to the family and church. In recent years educators have invaded our children's emotional lives with a blitzkrieg worse than Hitler's invasion of Poland.

Affective education at first confined itself to the arts: theater, dance, music, art. Today, however, it may include massive doses of explicit sex education, values clarification, psychodrama, sensitivity training, role playing, death and dying, global education, survival education, and almost any new fad that permits its humanist educators to encroach upon the emotional lives of our children in an effort to change them. Educators talk incessantly about *self-concept, attitudinal change,* and *self-actualization.* In reality, they are experimenting with a dangerous form of brainwashing that is condemned by some psychiatrists because the sensitivity training and group-therapy techniques used are much too powerful for nonmedically or nonpsychologically trained "experts." A few academic courses hardly qualify a classroom teacher to direct such sessions with a captive audience: our children.

Only a few years ago parents were concerned that sports were getting out of hand and that classroom time for learning cognitive skills (basics) was being sharply reduced. Presently, in some schools, sports and affective learning are making eighth-grade readers out of twelfth graders. Admittedly, sports and courses that stress affective learning are more exciting to the students than reading or math. So what's new about that? Fun and games have always been more interesting than hard work. But more than 85 percent of the parents in this country send their children to school to learn cognitive skills—information that will help them later in life. Besides, dumping adult emotional situations on children can be harmful to their normal emotional adjustment. I predict that, in the decades to come, these new techniques will fill psychiatrists' offices with their victims.

I have consistently observed that schools which major in the cognitive skills, maintain a balanced sports program, and have little or no time for the new affective-learning programs are not riddled with parental conflicts. The schools with humanist educrat superintendents or principals determined to jam these indoctrination techniques down the minds of their charges are generating the conflicts.

The two courses that generate the greatest amount of heat are explicit sex education and values clarification, for they strike at the heart of a person: his sexuality, emotions, ethics, and values. A person's control of these areas will determine his character, and a person's character makes him what he is.

Some Experts Disagree

All "authorities" do not favor values clarification, and many consider it downright harmful. Dr. Rhoda Lorand, a highly respected clinical psychologist and professor in the graduate school at Long Island University, has been an outspoken antagonist of values clarification and sex education, citing both as being harmful to our nation's schoolchildren. In a newspaper article she is quoted by editor Dr. Murray Morris:

> Dr. Lorand is not only concerned about the damage being done by sex education, but also about the "self-awareness fad" and the "values clarification fad."
> Values clarification, she explains, is "group discussions about feelings about moral issues and character traits . . ." "These discussions persist until the child, as many parents can attest, is totally confused

and his belief in the moral absolutes of the Judeo-Christian ethic weakened, if not indeed extinguished."

In a review of the Social Studies series, *Dimensions of Personality,* using the textbooks for the fourth, fifth and sixth grades from an Ohio school, she explains that both values clarification and self-awareness are involved.

(This same series of textbooks has been found in a dozen other states that I have visited—including my own. Editor)

The series of books "reveals throughout an acceptance of crude, cruel, selfish primitive behavior—even lawless behavior if it is a requirement for group behavior. This directly subverts the teachings of the average sensible, devoted parent, and alienates the child from them."

She goes on to explain the attacks on parent-child relationships, and concludes that Dimensions of Personality textbooks, "clearly regards parents as destructive to their children and views the class teacher as the healer who will undo the damage allegedly inflicted on the children by their parents. These courses obviously aim to make the teacher the most important person in the child's life."[10]

This position was also highlighted by Dr. Charles Macmurdo, PhD, the research chairman of Concerned Citizens and Taxpayers for Decent School Books, who headed a drive of parents that forced values clarification out of a Baton Rouge, Louisiana, school. He explained that the course:

> "Tends to alienate children from parents by open discussions in the classroom of the faults and shortcomings of parents, thereby aiding and abetting in the classmates and teachers, even to the point of confessing knowledge of illegal actions by classmates and themselves as well.
>
> "Values clarification interferes with the moral responsibility of parents to God and their legal responsibility to the State for the actions of their children."
>
> Pointing out that the values clarification programs can actually damage the mind of children, Dr. Macmurdo said, "Techniques involved in mind manipulations constitute risky business regardless of who does the manipulating."[11]

Dr. Macmurdo felt so strongly about this that he flew to Great Neck, New York, to help parents there stop this perniciously evil teaching method. He insisted:

". . . values shouldn't be dealt with in the school, but should be left alone for the church and home. . . ."

"If permitted to spread unchecked, values clarification will end up weakening the moral fiber of youth, eroding family solidarity, and even jeopardizing the future of America as the land of the free and home of the brave. . . ."[12]

In 1978 Senator Sam Hayakawa read into the Congressional Record his objection to values clarification. Coming from a PhD educator with fifteen years experience as a college professor before his election to the United States Senate, it is particularly significant.

"To inquire into the sexual attitudes and beliefs of 8-year-olds, to probe into their psychic and emotional problems, real or imagined, rather than into the level of their intellectual achievements—these are serious invasions of privacy," said Senator Hayakawa. "And messing around with the psyches of young people does not stop with testing and inquiries. There are exercises in psycho-drama, role-playing, touch therapy, encounter groups, and other psychological games that have no academic significance whatsoever. . . .

"Teacher institutes buzz with talk of neurosis, resistance, adjustment, maladjustment, attitudinal change," he said. Then he concluded that this type of thing doesn't belong in the classroom, but with the child's family, physician or psychiatrist.[13]

Do you get the impression that many humanist educrats who come up with these moral modification techniques are sometimes more interested in changing the values of the next generation than they are in educating them? Sometimes I feel they are trying to create a valueless human robot who can be easily fomented into an "anything goes" revolution.

Even some educators are beginning to voice their concerns relative to the harmful effects of values clarification on our nation's children. Shortly after a Warsaw, Indiana, school board threw it out completely, the Minnesota commissioner of education, Howard Casey, was reported as saying:

"For the past 10–15 years we've been teaching the inquiry method of instruction. We've asked these young people to question, to experiment on their own, to develop an inquisitive mind . . . and now it's coming back to haunt us."

". . . On the other side are parents and schoolmen who are not quite ready for the type of product the schools have produced. We don't know how to handle what we've been instrumental in developing."[14]

All across the country parents and responsible educators are awakening to the realization that values clarification, one of the leading educational fads of the seventies, is having a harmful effect on our children. As they become aware of its dangers, they are alerting other parents and school officials. I hope this reaction will spread throughout the nation.

In the meantime, if your children attend public school, study the subject carefully and be watchful. Put your son or daughter on the alert, and have him or her bring home any questions of this nature to you, particularly if any of the following questions are asked:

Do you think there are times when cheating is justified?
Do you think we ought to legalize pot?
Do you think we ought to legalize abortion?
Do you approve of premarital sex for boys and girls?
Do you think a suspected homosexual should be allowed to teach in the public schools?
Do you think we should legalize mercy killings?

How They Bootleg It Into Your School District

The primary device for retaining values clarification in a district or school is to emphasize its totally "local" identity. Because of vigorous parental protest, particularly against the Simon-Kolberg method, superintendents and principals have developed an incredibly subtle method for avoiding the heat while maintaining the program.

They will quietly send one or two liberal or outright humanistic teachers to a Sidney Simon or Lawrence Kolberg values-clarification seminar, then appoint a special values-clarification-curriculum commissioner "from within our own district." Of course, the seminar grads serve on the commission and can easily bootleg in the national program by rearranging the questions, course structure, and artwork. By putting the lessons in looseleaf form, they can run them off on a duplicator or the school's small printing press. Consequently, the school or district loudly proclaims its "local program of values clarification—using local resources." For some strange reason, from California to Florida, these "local" materials reflect a basic sameness that includes such concepts as, "There are no rights and wrongs," and, "There is no right answer." Methodology stresses role playing, group decision making, and so forth.

When confronted, local educators will usually respond, "Yes, we use this technique, but why not? Many school systems do. It is a state-evaluated, government-funded program approved by the best educators and universities in the country" (they might add the NEA, Aspen Institute, Department of Education, and so on). How intimidating to a mere parent! When will we awaken to the fact that a humanist educrat will approve anything he thinks will advance the cause of humanism in the next generation of voters.

Parents may be fighting a "local" values-clarification program, but it will always teach a flexible or situational moral code, if it teaches any morals at all. And the refrain is inevitable: "There are no right and wrong answers." That is intellectual dishonesty! If your child is standing on the Golden Gate Bridge, trying to decide whether to jump or walk to the other side, is it true that there are "no right or wrong answers"? There is only one right answer, and we don't pay taxes to let children be taught to the contrary.

Man: A Course of Study

Known as MACOS and designed, in 1972, at a cost of $6.5 million by the humanist-controlled National Science Foundation, *Man: a Course of Study* is probably the most deplorable illustration of humanist educrat reasoning in the history of education.

MACOS is a values-clarification technique attached to an almost extinct tribe (twelve persons) of Eskimos who are not even representative of the Eskimo people. The twelve pitiful people are threatened with hardships of life, caused by their total lack of moral values.

This course, which has caused furor all over the country, is not used in every district because it has so little relevance to anything in education. With over 4 billion people on earth, from over 137 countries, why spend so much fifth-grade time on twelve obscure and unrepresentative people? Parental reaction has so fiercely objected to the dehumanizing method of teaching and the colossal waste of educational time in the crucial fifth grade that it has cost some educrats their jobs. Parts of Myrtle Creek, Oregon, deemed the course so gruesome that their protests resulted in the firing of the superintendent. The course was discarded.

Hear Mrs. Gabler

Norma Gabler and her husband, Mel, have probably done more to halt the spread of humanism in our school textbooks than anyone else in America. Consider Mrs. Gabler's studied appraisal of the MACOS series.

> There has been relatively little opposition to this course (MACOS) from parents because the booklets never leave the classroom.
> If parents had examined the approximately 30 booklets, nine teacher guides, games and films as carefully as I have, they would have found:
> WIFE SWAPPING—From page 117 of "Talks to Teachers" we see— "Husbands have a very free hand in their married life and it is considered to be quite in order for them to have intercourse with any woman whenever there is opportunity."
> To trade women as mere property is certainly not representative of the importance of women. Most persons would consider such actions as lewd, promiscuous and obscene.
> This certainly would not be appropriate for a ten-year-old child.
> To further reveal the "importance" this series attaches to women, we quote: "For it is solely economy that lies behind the custom that girls are killed at birth, if they have not already been promised to a family where there is a son who someday is to have a wife ... they encourage the number of births ... when it is a girl that is born ... either by killing it or giving it away immediately. ..." (Page 99 of "Talks to Teachers.")
> "MARRYING OF ANIMALS, THE MANY WIVES OF KINOK" is a student booklet which tells of a Netsilik hero who travels from village to village, taking to wife animals, including a detailed account of his wolf wife's killing and skinning her own daughter so that she might have her son-in-law as a husband.
> "Kiviok has learned about the way of animals by taking to wife many animals in human form. ... He is hurt by the unfaithfulness of his wives, his human wife and his goose-wife. He loves his wolf-wife

and mourns her death; he travels far to recover his fox-wife and his goose-wife and children . . ." (Page 90 of "Talks to Teachers.")

CANNIBALISM—There is a detailed account of a man eating his wife and then collecting her bones in a heap by his bed.

This story is followed by one of a man eating his own little brother, first eating the frost-bitten feet of the living brother, then eating all of him.

Cannibalism and murder are included on pages 97 to 99 of "Talks to Teachers."

LEAVING OLD PEOPLE TO DIE—A great amount of emphasis is placed on this, including having children role-play leaving grandparents to die. They may also listen to records and read poems and stories about this practice which is covered in not one, but two student booklets, plus the teachers' guide.

"I took the old woman out on the ice today."

"It was his own mother that he had driven out and set down at sea to freeze to death."

It is suggested that some children might enjoy reading the poem "Old Kigtak" who was left to die. (Pages 18–21, Teachers Guide, "The Netsilik Eskimos on the Sea Ice.")

How many readers would consider this treatment "humane"?

Why should so much time, two full days, be spent impressing on young minds that such treatment is an Eskimo practice?

(One school official in Oregon who objects to MACOS in his school said, "They, the teachers, want you to accept these things that are taught in MACOS.")

Much of the MACOS course is based on the finding of an early explorer, Knud Rassmussen, who found:

"I made exhaustive enquiries as to the treatment of the aged and the only case of heartlessness that I came across was that of a woman by the name of Kigtak." (Page 101, "Talks to Teachers.")

FILMS—No, the films do not show "cannibalism, murder or wife-swapping." This is to be found in the booklets and teachers' guides. The films do include 4½ hours of bloody gore, showing the stoning to death of a bird tied by one leg, the braiding of bloody guts, etc., with no narration.

How many parents have been allowed to examine all the teachers' guides?

Is it strange that the contents of the nine teachers' guides are seldom quoted and almost never available for parental inspection?

Some of the booklets in this course are benign and these are the only ones parents can expect to examine.

If this depraved course, filled with violence and death, is "one of the best series to be developed for use in our schools," parents had better become concerned about our nation's future, which is our children.[15]

Consider a Teacher's Testimony

Sheilah Burgers, a teacher in Sheffield, Massachusetts, taught the fifth-grade MACOS course for one year. Read her personal appraisal:

"I felt that MACOS not only restricted academic freedom but also inhibited the development of my students by presenting a negative, one-sided and dishonest picture of man. In short, MACOS is a brainwash—clever, well-executed and lethal."

Mrs. Burgers said she reviewed the 31 books, reviewed the 21 films many times, read the nine teacher manuals and taught the course to 75 fifth graders. She said:

"The method of teaching is inquiry. The teachers ask questions; the students find answers. This has been a valid method since Socrates, but Jerome Bruner and his friends have developed a new twist. The teacher is not permitted to initiate the questions, all questions come from manuals—and the manuals must be followed exactly.

"All answers are found in course books and films. Outside sources cannot be used because material concerning the course content (the social structure of the herring gull, salmon, baboon, and the Netsilik Eskimo) is understandably non-existent at the fifth-grade level. Input and output are thereby totally controlled.

"Books cannot leave the classroom. Except for projects, homework is discouraged. Manuals are kept at school for professional use only. Adult intervention therefore is minimal.

"How are the children controlled?

"Bruner knows psychology well. Children are at their most passive, and therefore most receptive, at 10 and 11. They like games, films, role-playing; they like animals and they not only empathize, they identify with them. In a matter of days, they speak fluent baboon.

"They readily learn that the physically strong survive at the expense of the weak. And if they do not learn this from hours of filmed violence, which ranges from the mating rites of herring gulls to the drinking of fresh caribou blood by the Eskimos, they learn by role-playing and games.

"Hunt the Seal is a stimulation game. It takes a week to play. The victor must procure enough seals to insure his own survival. He can do this only by 'starving' his co-players. The price of survival is killing. The lesson is reinforced by the story of the old woman who was left on the ice to die because she could not contribute to her society.

"The book word for this is 'senilicide,' a tough word for fifth-graders, but they got it. They approved and defended abandonment of the old woman.

"At this point I deviated from the manual and asked one of the children what he would call this act in terms of his own culture. He gulped and answered, 'murder'.

"I was reprimanded for infusing irrelevant questions into the program.

"Defenders of MACOS insist that the teaching materials give children an opportunity to compare different life styles, to become tolerant of other moral values. The defenders never mention that 10-year-olds have not studied Western civilization, and have no formal training in the history, technology, or social structure of their own world.

"The only moral values children in MACOS are taught are the moral values of a primitive, nearly extinct tribe—and those of the baboon."[16]

Any nonhumanist can see that the Netsiliks are almost extinct because of their life-style. One cannot violate traditional moral values indefinitely without bearing the consequences. But that fact is not permitted in this values-clarification specialty.

I find it ominous that the course is still being taught in some of our schools. I can understand how, back in 1972, because of their respect for the National Science Foundation, educators accepted their recommendation and used the materials. But with all the public outcry and printed exposure of it as a not-so-subtle attack on the family, moral values, and a means of promoting infanticide, euthanasia (killing off the elderly), and other revolting subjects (even cannibalism), I cannot understand why they are still using it. Of course, it *is* an effective way of imposing humanist values on the children of traditional-valued parents, millions of whom are Christians.

My call to an official in the Education Department in Washington, to determine if it was still being taught as late as 1982, brought this response: "Yes, in many districts throughout the nation."

I don't know about you, but I find that frightening.

The Harm of Values Clarification

Values clarification is an ingeniously evil technique of applying peer pressure to questions, selected by atheistic humanist educators, that are usually far too advanced for the group. When no moral absolutes are permitted in a discussion, the group usually comes to the lowest-common-denominator value, just as the educrats intended. This would ultimately create a value-free society—a very immoral society that will produce an anarchical, lawless culture.

The humanist educrats who are pushing values clarification throughout America seem oblivious to the fact that this public-school fad of the seventies has ignited a greater outcry from concerned parents than any other subject except explicit sex education. A much more accurate term for values clarification would be *morals modification,* because that is exactly what it is: the most poisonous technique ever devised for turning 43 million schoolchildren away from the traditional moral values of their parents and country.

Without values, an individual does not build character, which is more important than knowledge because what we are determines how we use what we know. A sterling example of people who possessed great knowledge and power but lacked character were the humanist psychiatrists of the Third Reich, back in the late thirties—men who conditioned the German people for the genocide of the Jews by practicing euthanasia. They decided that some of the elderly were no longer useful, so their lives could be forfeited. Behavior modifiers and humanistic psychologists, the inventors of values clarification, hold many of the same secular humanist beliefs about God, man, evolution, morals, economy, and world order that were advocated by the Nazi educators. The major difference is that Hitler's psychiatrists were commissioned under the authority of an evil state government. Our humanist educrats are not—yet!

Jo-Ann K. Abrigg, the late founder of the Committee for Positive Education, was educated in psychology at DePauw University. Because of her background and training, she was able to perceive the harmful effects of both behavior modification and values clarification as taught in our public schools. Before her death from cancer, she waged a tireless campaign to expose the dangers of this Frankensteinian program of reducing our nation's youth to moral neutrals who could easily be manipulated by the humanist elite—or Big Brother.

In a classic warning delivered in a speech to concerned parents and educators, she cautioned:

And indeed it is an experiment—using psychological techniques such as role playing, role reversal, soliloquy, simulation games, reality therapy, group dynamics, encounter group, magic circles, sensitivity training in many varied forms, but always with the underlying purpose of thought reform and "behavior changing." These techniques, as well as "Diaries" and "Daily Journals," are incorporated into many different courses—whether it be reading, social studies, sex education, drug education, home economics, family life programs, supplementary reading materials, films, the new "parenting" programs, or any number of so-called human development programs. But MOST significant, and MOST important about these techniques is this: All of these techniques were designed and utilized originally by licensed psychologists and psychiatrists treating emotionally disturbed patients in the controlled situation of mental clinics and hospitals. Now we find them being used in classrooms by teachers playing the role of amateur psychologist on normal healthy well-adjusted American children, who have never been diagnosed as in need of psychological help. . . . even Dr. Maslow himself back in 1965, in commenting on his view of human nature warned, "I of all people would know just how shaky this foundation is as a final foundation. My work on motivations came from the clinic, from a study of neurotic people . . . I am quite willing to concede this . . . because I'm a little worried about this stuff which I consider tentative being swallowed whole by all sorts of enthusiastic people." But—enthusiastic the humanistic educationists are, and enthusiastic are those in the various Departments of Education, who continue to throw unlimited federal, state and local tax dollars into these programs—as with great enthusiasm they lead American children from one humanistic program to another.[17]

Some Christian Colleges Teach Values Clarification, Too!

I spoke to one woman who went to a leading Christian college on the West Coast, where she became a certified schoolteacher. Her course of study included instruction in values clarification as a new teaching technique. During her first year of public-school teaching, on the eighth-grade level, she realized how humanistic it was.

"While in college," she said, "I was impressed with the idea that we could come to our own conclusions, make up our own minds, and determine our own values—as if there were no moral absolutes. As a twenty-year-old Christian raised in a good Bible-teaching church, one who had memorized hundreds of Scriptures, I was able with some degree of moral awareness to discuss abortion, teenage sex, unwed pregnancy, euthanasia, infanticide, and other moral issues. But when my eighth graders began the same discussion, they came to much different conclusions than we did while students in a Christian college. And to top it off, I was handcuffed! I was forbidden to 'moralize' or present 'moral absolutes.' Eighth graders without moral absolutes have no business discussing such adult subjects unless the public schools intend to inculcate the traditional moral absolutes that are held by the majority of American people."

When humanist educators declare, "There are no right and wrong answers," they are falsely assuming that moral absolutes do not exist. And that is the burning issue of our day: whether there is a God who has imparted moral absolutes to live by, or whether He is a myth, a figment of man's irrationality. Since almighty God *does* exist and *has* communicated His principles to mankind, I have a hard time understanding why Christian colleges introduce values clarification, a teaching technique invented by humanists, who are convinced that God and moral absolutes are defunct. But it does illustrate how easily Christians can become humanized in the pursuit of graduate degrees.

William Glasser, Sidney Simon, and Lawrence Kolberg have simply parroted the serpent's words to Eve, "Hath God said?" That is devilish! There *are* right and wrong answers. It is either wrong to kill, steal, lie, and commit adultery, or it isn't; and Christian teachers need to be more aggressive than ever in teaching these moral absolutes in Christian schools. Our humanist educrats implicitly deny such absolutes, but Christians have a right to expect better teaching at Christian colleges.

The Battle for the Twenty-first Century

Betty Friedan, the Humanist of the Year Award winner in 1975, looked into a TV camera one night and announced, "I have dedicated my life to making America a humanist nation." And she is dead serious! In fact, she could have added "by the twenty-first century," for that is the stated target in the *Humanist Manifesto* ("The next century can be and should be the humanistic century").

Both humanist manifestos serve together as the firm foundation for values clarification, which in reality becomes moral modification. According to *Humanist Manifesto I:*

> Religious humanists regard the universe as self-existing and not created. . . . We are convinced that the time has passed for theism, deism, modernism, and the several varieties of new thought. . . . Religious humanism considers the complete realization of human personality to be the end of man's life and seeks its development in the here and now. . . . Humanists are firmly convinced that the existing acquisitive and profit-motivated society has shown itself to be inadequate and that a radical change in methods, controls, and motives must be instituted. . . .[18]

More explicit is *Humanist Manifesto II,* which states "that traditional. . . . religions that place revelation, God, ritual, or creed above human needs and experience do a disservice to the human species. . . . Ethics stems from human need and interest."[19]

Most people resent it when I insist that we are in a titanic battle for control of our culture, a battle that will rage between now and the next century. America will either return to the traditional moral values upon which it was founded or become the value-free, anarchical society that the humanists are trying to make it.

So far the humanists are winning—not because they have a superior ideology and certainly not because they represent a significant percentage of the population, but because the greatest army, the Christians and adherents to traditional moral values, have been sound asleep. Most of our people don't even know a war is being waged, and when they hear of it, they refuse to accept it as a fact.

Fortunately, our people are beginning to awaken from their century-old slumber, and the humanists are running scared because they are fearful that we will expel their humanistic doctrine from public education, which will cut off their source of support and virtually destroy their religious power in this country. Their greatest weapon in this ideological battle is the public school, for that is the one institution over which they exercise nearly absolute control. In my opinion, values clarification is the most effective weapon of the entire humanist arsenal for changing the moral values of today's children, who will be the adults of the twenty-first century. We simply must have values clarification in its many forms—psychodrama, role playing, group dynamics, sensitivity training, peer pressure, and so on—expelled from our public schools.

Death Education

> Promises of immortal salvation or fear of eternal damnation are both illusory and harmful. They distract humans from present concerns, from self-actualization.... There is no credible evidence that life survives the death of the body.
> We strive for the good life, here and now.
> ... the individual must experience a full range of civil liberties....
> It... includes a recognition of an individual's right to die with dignity, euthanasia, and the right to suicide.[1]
>
> *Humanist Manifesto II*

In pursuit of her California teaching credential, my daughter recently took practice teaching at one of our local high schools. The course assigned? Death and Dying.

Death and dying? What does that have to do with a traditional education? Nothing! But it has everything to do with inculcating a humanistic point of view in our young. Don't be surprised if that does not make any sense to you, because one has to think like a humanist to understand him.

Just suppose you were a humanistic educrat determined to make humanists out of those children in your charge. You have successfully launched the most vicious double-barreled attack in the history of mankind on a generation of young people's morals in your sex-education and values-clarification courses. Unfortunately, all your young pupils were not willing to respond like the sexual animals you taught them they were. For instance, some evidently retained a natural fear of death and Judgment Day that follows the sowing of wild oats (in the manner suggested by sexologists). What better way to instigate an "eat, drink, and be merry, for tomorrow we die" philosophy than to give those students a desensitizing course in death, which explained away all their fears? Preposterous? Don't count on it, for you will have a difficult time devising any other "logical" reason for our schools— presently doing an inadequate job of teaching the basics—to take up valuable time delving into the grim subject of death.

Asking Religious Questions

Do you want a humanist teacher, one who rejects all absolutes and may be hostile toward a belief in God, the Bible, Jesus Christ, salvation by faith, and many other truths you hold dear, leading your child in a discussion of the following questions:

Do you believe in life after death?
Do you believe in heaven or hell?
Do you often think about your own death? How often?
When you think of your own death, how do you feel?
Have you seriously contemplated committing suicide? How often?
Suppose you were to commit suicide: what method would you most likely use?

These and other questions are cleverly utilized by humanistic missionaries (masquerading as schoolteachers) on our captive children in the seventh to the twelfth grades; the questions serve as springboards to teaching their anti-Christian concepts in our public schools. They are nothing more than a devious means to indoctrinate our youth with their anti-God religion. And they have the audacity to call it education. Score humanistic religion, ten; literature, grammar and history, zero. This may be an effective way to graduate a nation of undereducated atheists who have difficulty reading, writing, and earning a living, but who will know authoritatively that there is no God, no soul, no life after death, and there are no moral absolutes because their "teachers" taught them so. I don't pay property and income taxes to subsidize these heretical teachings of the religion of humanism. And I don't think you do either.

This entire issue exposes the Supreme Court's 15 December 1981 reasoning on the prohibition of high-school young people from using school property for prayer meetings as nothing more than religious bigotry in favor of the religion of humanism. For even though the high court ruled that colleges are available for student groups, high schools are excepted because "a high school is not a forum where religious views can be freely aired." In light of that ruling, since the Supreme Court ruled in 1963 (in *Torcaso* v. *Watkins*) that humanism is a religion, how can they permit death-and-dying instruction that is nothing more than a not-so-subtle attack on the religious beliefs of our youth and an authoritative indoctrination in the religion of humanism?

Needed: a New ACLU

America needs an American Christian Liberties Union as a counterpart to the American Civil Liberties Union, which in my opinion has become the most harmful organization in American history. We need a group of 2,000 attorneys who will become aggressive in the defense of our traditional moral values and freedom. To do so, they will be obliged to volunteer their services to defend religious liberty—even in education.

Christian attorneys need to be more aggressive in defending Christianity and religious freedom against the bigoted attacks of atheists and other secular humanists. It has long struck me as strange that most of the aggressive attorneys in America represent the ACLU. These anti-Christian zealots have for years willingly leaped into action at the slightest provocation to remove Christmas carols, Bible reading, prayer, and moral teaching from our public schools. Now they are on a campaign to remove all religious symbols from public places, including crosses from our hillsides.

Very few Christian attorneys (William Ball, John Whiteland, and some others excepted) will freely defend the civil and religious rights of the majority. That is one reason why we are consistently losing our rights. In one Christian-school case with which I am familiar, ACLU attorneys volunteered their services to serve their master, while Christian attorneys charged $125.00 an hour to serve theirs. That is not the way wars are won.

Needed: Aggressive Christian Attorneys

We need to activate the thousands of Christian attorneys in this country to defend Christians every time some blatant atheist uses our government-controlled schools to attack the religious beliefs of the majority of our nation's taxpayers.

The following letter came from a sophomore student at Michigan State University:

> Within my first two days of Humanities 201 my professor introduced himself and told us what his course was to cover and what to expect throughout the term. Then, at the end of class, he warned us that we may not like him as a professor if our favorite reading material is the Bible or the Koran, or any of those other books that those lunatics read. The next day in class he went through the whole day elaborating on the beliefs of our "primitive" ancestors and the credence they gave to the "mythical" creation of the universe and their "superstitious" practices of worshiping God. He also taught about the fact that some people do this in our times, and that is how we get our sickly "born agains" that we have around today. Christians, Moslems, and Jews have no reason to live, because they are merely waiting for death to take them to their place of eternity.

There are about 3,000 such colleges in the country, most receiving public subsidy through the taxes of people, 94 percent of whom, according to George Gallup, do not agree with this "public servant." God only knows how many of them teach our youth such blasphemous ideas. On the other hand, Josh McDowell has publicly stated that he is forbidden to use the name of Jesus Christ when speaking on our college campuses.

The number-one need in education today is for some sharp Christian attorneys to file a lawsuit against the humanistic religion being taught in our tax-supported schools. The case should advance to the Supreme Court and finally expel humanism from our public schools. That would put an end to our present death-and-dying course.

Where are our Christian attorneys whose silence permits such blatant attacks on their Lord to continue and spread? Will not their children also inherit the next generation? In the words of Dr. Francis Schaeffer, if the Christian attorneys who have remained silent continue their silence, "Will their children and grandchildren rise up to call them blessed?" I doubt it.

One attorney pointed out that the primary battle for the eighties and nineties will not be between Communism and anti-Communism or socialism and antisocialism, but between secular humanism and Christianity. Both cannot coexist indefinitely. One must control the other. For the first 150 years, Christianity's moral values controlled secular humanism. During the past 50 years that has gradually changed until secular humanism has become a 65 percent or more dominating force, controlling Christianity. The future belongs to those who will fight the hardest for their values.

It Is Sweeping the Country

Ever since the school year of 1976–77, death education has been springing up all over the country. How do we know? By the spontaneous outcry from concerned parents who recognized this morbid fascination with death as a dangerous attack on our traditional moral and religious values.

Death education is becoming a big thing in many schools across the nation. The reason given by educators is the same as the reason for sex education. "We have to include it in school because the parents are not teaching it at home."

True, few parents are teaching explicit sex, promoting homosexuals or conducting seminars on DEATH at home. It is because they know better.

In Oregon, Washington and Wisconsin, there is a program that is now in its third year in many schools. It is called "Health Education Curriculum Guide" and is signed by the state superintendent of schools in each of these three states.

In the manual published for this "guide" are suggestions to have the children role-play suicides, have the students visit a funeral home, and take a survey of the class on specialty arrangements for funerals, and tell how they think people close to them would handle their own funeral.

In Roseburg, there is an ad hoc committee studying the curriculum. They have been told by a school health coordinator that he would like to include death education. Some "good" death education courses are available and are being taught at high school level elsewhere, said the school official. A member of the committee, an employee of the county health department, expressed hope that death education would be included in the Roseburg school curriculum.

Both suicide and death are on the list of topics approved by the Roseburg ad hoc committee and given to teachers for inclusion in the Roseburg curriculum.

School officials setting up the ad hoc committees to "study" the curriculum usually weight the committees in favor of the programs they have in mind, and frequently guide the direction and conclusions of the meetings. In this way, they insist that the public is demanding death education, anti-religious programs, sex education, and other programs attacking values from the home and church.

To get a good start in Roseburg, second and third graders will study about the death of animals in their mental health course, according to the topical outline prepared by teachers. Human death will doubtlessly be studied by fourth, fifth and sixth graders under the *Family* and *Death* class titles now prepared for Roseburg.

At one Midwestern workshop for teachers, these death questions were provided:

How often do you think about your own death?

If you could choose, when would you die? (Questions of suicide come later.)

When you think of your own death, how do you feel?

How do you feel about having an autopsy done on your body?

How often have you been in a situation in which you seriously thought you might die?

For whom and what might you be willing to sacrifice your life?

For whom or what might you be willing to kill another person?

Then in the same seminar came these questions on suicide:

How often have you seriously contemplated committing suicide?

Have you actually attempted suicide?

Whom have you known who has committed suicide?[2]

Also included were those questions on suicide that my daughter found in our California high school.

Suppose you were to commit suicide, what methods would you most likely use?

Suppose you were to commit suicide, what reason would most motivate you to do it?

Suppose you were ever to commit suicide, would you leave a suicide note?

To what extent do you believe that suicide should be prevented?
What kind of funeral would you prefer?

Because death courses are so popular in school districts across the
nation, many textbook publishers have put out books on death
courses—assisted by such groups as Planned Parenthood, the Euthanasia Education Council, the Cremation Association of
America, and the National Funeral Directors Association.[3]

The Chicago *Tribune* also registered concern for the problem in an
Amherst, Massachusetts, school.

Until very recently, children received no classroom instruction
about death. Now death is the latest "hot topic" in many schools.
Scores of high schools are scheduling seminars and even semester
courses on the subject, with such names as "death education," "death
and old age" and "philosophy of death."

Students in the 18-week course at Amherst Regional High School
are told: "We will have some speakers from the community whose
work in some way involves death—a doctor, funeral director, lawyer,
clergymen—so as to help answer technical or philosophical questions.
Also, we plan to visit a cemetery and a funeral home to further en-
hance your understanding of societal values and practices."

In a report to the National Education Association, Richard O. Ulin,
an education professor at the University of Massachusetts, said,
"Death has made its debut in education."[4]

When confronted with the alarming suicide rate that is reaching
down even into our junior high schools, one death-education teacher,
typical of humanists in education, denied that such teaching was increasing youthful suicides.

"Certainly, third-graders are not ready to debate the pros and cons
of euthanasia or abortion, but they are ready to begin thinking about
when, if ever, is it right for one person to take another's life," he said.

A teacher has no more reason to avoid discussing suicide with students out of fear that it may influence them to commit suicide than he
or she has to avoid discussing murder, rape, violence, theft or income-
tax evasion, according to Ulin.

"What is needed is to remove it from the taboo list so they can find
out what the data show, recognize their own current attitudes toward

it, wrestle with other viewpoints and then establish their own personal and rational position," he said.[5]

Anyone who thinks third graders are old enough to decide if "it's right for one person to take another's life" is incompetent to teach in our schools. Yet this educator is a teacher of death-education teachers.

Howard County, Maryland—which many federal politicians and bureaucrats make their home—erupted over this issue, which had invaded their schools three years before. Calling the program a " 'hop on the bandwagon' educational fad," a group of citizens pressed such a complaint that the school board forbade that it be taught in compulsory courses such as Contemporary Issues; it must be limited to an elective course.

> Since death anxiety may rise as a result of death education, it would seem that students and parents should have some choice about the contents of a required course. Any student or parent of a teenager knows that leaving the room during the unit is not a viable alternative—the ridicule in the lunchroom is too great.[6]

The Funeral-Home Field Trip

Field trips have long been a part of the educational process whenever they can be financed and justified as a contribution to educational growth. (They even had them when I was in school.) Field trips to a local funeral home, like the questionnaire my daughter received, are a nearly universal feature of death-education courses all over the country. Isn't that in itself instructive? It necessitates a central planning agency producing a basic curriculum for our 16,160 "neighborhood schools." Since the course always espouses the concepts of secular humanism, we can be sure that some high priests of humanism were its originators. Our neighborhood "teachers" (or "change agents," as some call them) serve as missionaries of the humanist religion in our so-called public schools.

Be sure of this: death education cannot be taught without involving religious doctrine. The course cannot be neutral. It will either communicate the theistic doctrine of traditional religion or the nontheistic doctrine of the humanist religion. Since our humanist educrats have censored theistic religion from the classroom, we know whose religion is being taught—and at our expense.

UPI reporter Dan Chiszar went along on one of these field trips in Greeley, Colorado. His account of the funeral director's tour for the sixth and seventh graders of the Chappelow Middle School is most enlightening.

"I'm a licensed funeral director," Bob Hansberry was saying at the podium. . . . "Embalming is a process of disinfection, preservation and restoration," said Hansberry. "Decomposition starts immediately after death. In restoration, we try to make the body as lifelike as possible. We try to give the family—in an old mortuary term—a good memory picture. . . .

"Follow me downstairs to the embalming room," said Hansberry.

"Yeah," the kids said again.

"I'm not going in there," said a boy with glasses.

"Chicken," said his friend.

In front of another door, Hansberry again offered the kids a chance to sit it out. No takers.

"This is our preparation room," he said inside the clinical-looking chamber. "We can embalm two bodies at the same time. The tables are stainless steel. This is our embalming machine; it's a stainless steel tank and a pump. The blocks are for holding the head in position. After death, there is no muscle tone. The body is limp, and it has to be held in position."

The kids stared, and several girls clutched their large plastic combs with both hands. Someone accidently kicked a trash container, and the children started.

Hansberry held up a brown plastic container.

"This is 15 percent formaldehyde. We dilute it with eight ounces to a gallon of water. That makes it 1½ percent formaldehyde solution. We use the same circulation system the body normally uses."

He pointed to his neck. "We inject into the carotid the embalming fluid. This goes around the body and comes out the jugular vein. There are six points where we shoot into the body. A good embalmer hopes he won't have to shoot more than one point, but sometimes you do."

A blonde girl, Tammy Warehime, 14, noticed a block and tackle affixed to the ceiling. "What's that for?" she asked.

"That's for very heavy bodies," answered Hansberry.[7]

Is that why you send your children to school, especially your sixth and seventh graders?

I will never forget the nightmares my grandfather's death caused me. For weeks I awoke, terrified by the memory of his red Shriner's vest, when I saw his body laid out. Children should never be subjected to such sights, unless it is absolutely necessary. Who is going to get up at night to contend with the nightmares and horrible dreams of these young people? The schoolteachers? Of course not! The humanist educrats who conceived this diabolical attack on the minds of our youth? Of course not! The parents will get up and try to soothe them after fearful dreams—the same people who are forced to pay their taxes and send their children to school so humanists can try to bend their minds. Isn't it time we put a stop to such incompetence in the name of education?

Death Education Is a Violation of Parents' Rights

As long as humanistic educrats believe that children are wards of the state and that they, the elite who control our government schools, are the only ones qualified to administrate the education of our 43 million public-school children, parents' rights will continue to be trampled underfoot. This was the same problem the good citizens of Hitler's Germany confronted with the education of their youth. The Nazi humanists had no regard for the rights of the parents. We must elect school-board members who:

1. recognize humanism as a dangerous religion
2. recognize that children belong to parents
3. realize that schools should be "servants" of the community, not masters
4. commit themselves to raising the standard of learning with a special emphasis on reading, math, spelling, writing, science, geography, good literature, true American history and the merits of free enterprise

Until we do, we will continue to see an elite minority abuse the children of the majority.

Why Do They Do It?

Once you understand what a humanist believes and how he envisions the future, you become suspicious of everything he does—particularly when he introduces an unpopular subject like sex education, values clarification, or death education, in spite of parental opposition. Humanists don't like controversy anymore than the rest of us, and they certainly know their schools are in trouble. Yet they weather the storm of spontaneous protest on these subjects all over the country. Why? Because they think they are in sufficient control that we cannot stop them, and they have ulterior reasons that are so important to them that they will endure the "heat." Indoctrinating our young with humanist beliefs is of paramount importance to them.

What They *Say* Is Not What We *Get*

They *say* that they teach death education because parents do not adequately prepare a child to face death. They *say* it will help to lessen suicide, because it will confront young people with the reality of death. The facts are as convincing as the alarming increase in teenage pregnancy and VD that their sex education courses have produced. Remember, they were sold to us on the same premise: it would correct these problems. The truth is, parents don't want amoral and anti-Christian humanists teaching their children about either explicit sex or death.

I have conducted over five hundred funerals and have attended thousands of people of all ages at the time of death. Apart from a personal faith in God, through His Son, Jesus Christ, it is impossible to prepare for death. I have heard one consistent message from loved ones: "Even when you know death is inevitable, you aren't prepared when it strikes."

Death is painful! And no amount of advanced education is going to make it easy. In fact, it shouldn't be easy. The more you love someone, the more painful his or her death will be. All the death-education courses dreamed up by humanists will not change that—unless, of course, they really do succeed in convincing our youth that they are animals. Then our loved ones will die like brute beasts, and we can walk away in search of "another relationship," as if nothing happened. But I wouldn't count on it. Remember, we are humans, not animals.

Besides, God has given human beings an amazing ability to cope with the trials and struggles of life, including the ability to face death bravely. But that ability does not really surface until adulthood. Coping with death requires maturity. God has given children two parents and a family to help when death strikes before maturity, and this composite works, unless the humanistic educrats have undermined the child's confidence in his parents. How do I know? Because it did for me. My mother's love, together with the comfort of other "family," including neighbors and church friends, helped me weather the emotional strain of my father's death three weeks before my tenth birthday. Of course, that was long before death education.

Five Excellent Reasons Humanists Teach Death Education

We probably could cite more than four reasons why humanistic educrats have injected death education into our nation's school system, but these will demonstrate how dangerous the program is and what they are *really* trying to do.

1. Death education is an excellent way to attack the traditional belief in God, salvation, life after death, and other truths held dear by Christians and others who believe in the supernatural.

When we understand that a humanist is just as religious as a Christian, though in a completely opposite direction, we will recognize that death education is tailor-made to introduce many important religious issues but supply *only* humanistic answers. After all, "We can't teach Christianity in the public school." Then why is it just and right to teach the religion of humanism in school? Because we don't label it a religion or acknowledge it as the most dangerous religion in the world. A humanistic education provides not only inadequate preparation for life, but inadequate preparation for a confrontation with death. Remember, humanists have no answers.

A typical teaching procedure in death education, and the one used in the high school where my daughter observed, is to pass out a questionnaire with questions similar to those already cited. Then a discussion can be launched with regard to any subject of the teacher's choosing. In my daughter's class the teacher asked, "How many of you believe in heaven? in hell?" She then proceeded to ridicule those who raised their hands. Predictably, the class was intimidated so that on future questions the students voted like a group of atheists. Had it not been for one courageous believer who refused to be browbeaten by an educational bully, the entire course would have resulted in humanistic brainwashing.

Incidentally, if you consider the use of the word *brainwashing* too strong or unfair, listen to one of the founders of death education. Dr. Daniel Leviton recognized the potential for brainwashing created by this course when he advised:

> "A short note of caution: A great need exists to prevent death education from becoming a brainwashing process designed to condition people to accept death with equanimity for ignoble reasons. 'To die for the glory of the State,' has a familiar and frightening ring to it."[8]

Adolph Hitler wasn't the only one who saw the potential for such brainwashing. Liberal humanist minister Jim Jones and his Guyanan tragedy illustrates its uncanny effectiveness.

A better method of introducing religious subjects under the guise of "academics" could hardly be devised than death education. This subject quite naturally gives rise to discussion about the deity of Christ, judgment after death, the soul, eternity, and so on. But at this juncture be extremely wary: it is almost impossible to be neutral on such subjects, and humanists are not noted for maintaining their neutrality where God and Jesus Christ are concerned.

Thus death education is an ideal context in which to introduce the doctrines that are dear to humanists: "no Deity will save us," "there is no life after death," "you will not have to face eternal judgment," and so on.

2. This subject offers an excellent means of preparing young people to live like nihilistic hedonists.

In an article critical of four school board members in East Liverpool, Ohio, for voting death education into their schools, Margaret Walker summed up her case with a historical reference.

The point is that the philosophy held out here is Nihilism, which began in 19th and 20th century Russia. It maintains that conditions in the world are so bad as to make destruction desirable for its own sake (a salty dose for teenagers). It holds that only the useful is the good (one of the big arguments for euthanasia). It rejects religion, tradition, parental and church authority.[9]

As we have already seen, the best way to get hot-blooded young people to live like sexual animals is to tell them what to do and how to do it, then provide them with contraceptives and ridicule or explain away all the moral values of their parents. If that doesn't work, it is time to announce that there is no life after death, Judgment Day is a myth, and no God up in the sky can teach what is right or wrong. Would anyone be surprised that some would immediately proceed to sow their wild oats—*if* the death and sex educrats are right? But if they are not, what then?

Humanists will have to take full responsibility for actions which result from their teachings. Unfortunately, so will their student victims—unless they hear the good news that God loves mankind and is willing to forgive *all* their sins through faith in His Son Jesus Christ (*see* John 3:16, 36; 1 John 1:9; and John 5:24). Remember, teaching that deals with cosmic values (the existence of God, the nature of life and death, and life after death) will generate life-affecting responses. The teacher is ultimately accountable for his attitudes and precepts.

3. Death education is excellent training in the commission of suicide—and how to do it right the first time.

A depressed woman came in for counseling, with both wrists bandaged. At my request she exposed enough for me to see my first case of "slashed wrists." That woman is alive today because she had never taken a modern course in death education. She had never been taught that there were four methods far more effective for taking her own life.

If you find that a rather severe indictment of our humanists in education, then read the questions taken from a *junior-high-school* questionnaire, containing seventy-five problems, entitled "Youth and Death":

How do you estimate your lifetime probability of committing suicide?

> Suppose that you were to commit suicide, what reason would most motivate you to do it?
>
> Suppose you were to commit suicide, what method would you be most likely to use?
>
> Suppose you were ever to commit suicide, would you leave a suicide note?
>
> To what extent do you believe that suicide should be prevented? What efforts do you believe ought to be made to keep a seriously ill person alive?[10]

Can you imagine a worse subject to bring up to emotionally unstable youth barely into the second decade of life? This would be particularly true if they were already unhappy due to the divorce of their parents or other domestic problems. Add to that the unstable world scene, economic instability, terrorists, crime, the threat of war—some problems we did not know existed when we were their age. Frankly, I am surprised that this course of "instruction" hasn't created ten times as much furor among parents as it has.

Hardly anyone took him seriously in 1974 when Nobel laureate Dr. Max Delbruck stated:

> I would suggest that our society provide "suicide education" as it now provides birth control information. . . . Society must have free access to information about forms of suicide that are not too repulsive.[11]

After four years of allowing humanistically styled death education to stalk our junior- and senior-high-school classrooms, we must take another serious look. No one in his right mind would ever propose that our humanist educrats are attempting to encourage our youth to commit suicide, particularly with the hostile liberal press ready to defend anything their fellow humanists in education do. But if the course accomplishes the same thing, what difference does it make whether or not they planned it? The results are the same.

Barbara Morris writes:

> Suicide is the leading cause of death among persons between the ages of 13 and 19, and the rate is rising among children as young as 6

years of age. Why? A review of newspaper reports provides an alarming answer. One account quoted a counselor who explained that youngsters take their own lives because:

". . . they possess a tremendous amount of freedom to experiment with drugs, sex or alternatives to their parents' values, while they frequently lack the wisdom to make wise choices."[12]

What neither writer mentions is that the guilt caused by sexual promiscuity, particularly among those whose adoption of their public-school's brand of amorality is contrary to the moral teachings of their parents and church, produces great depression. At such a time of psychic pain, any emotionally distraught teen may commit suicide. Who does the public school blame? Parents, of course! They obviously didn't provide their teen with "adequate support systems." In reality, parents should primarily be blamed for remaining silent in the face of such vicious attacks on their child's mind—by "educators."

Humanist educrats will not stop at death education, suicide education, explicit sex education, drug education, or any other fad that strikes their fancy. They must be halted in their tracks—at the ballot box.

Of one thing you can be sure: sooner or later some tragic teen suicide will ignite grief-stricken parents, and they will mount a charge that will expel death education from the schools. But that's the price we will be forced to pay for humanistic thinking in education.

Is Fear of Death Good or Bad?

Originally death education was sold to school boards and jammed down the throats of parents and the public on the premise that it would remove the fear of death. Barbara Morris quotes several students' attitudes after finishing the course, suggesting that death educators had achieved their goal.

"When the students come out of the course they certainly look at life a little differently. The *uncomfortable feelings* we have when the subject of death comes up can be removed."

"I think the best part was the open discussions we had in which we shared our fears about death. After discussing it with others, *death didn't seem like such a terrible happening.*"

"Through the course ... students ... understand their own preju-
dices and feelings toward death and dying ... *dying* ... may not necessarily be a bad thing."[13]

Parent, do you *want* the removal of the natural fear of death in normal human beings? (This used to be recognized as part of the first law
of life: self-preservation!) No wonder our newspapers are reflecting
alarm at the increase in teenage suicide. Dr. Zigfrids Stelmachers
points out, "If people were taught not to fear death, the suicide rates
would probably increase because most people who have considered
suicide decided against it because of their fear of dying."[14]

You may have severe difficulty admitting that professional, dedicated educators would do this to our children. You are right. Most
educators are not humanists, but there are enough in both classrooms
and key administrative positions to pressure for this new (four- or
five-year-old) technique for mind destruction, unless informed and
committed superintendents, principals, and board members have kept
it out. Most Americans forget that humanists believe in the civil right
of every individual to commit suicide. The *Humanist Manifesto* overtly
states that.

As a Christian I view the removal of the fear of death as not only
potentially fatal to an otherwise long life, but eternally dangerous.
Many people have accepted Christ as the means of forgiveness for
their sins because of a healthy fear of death. In fact, one of the changes
in many new converts after their salvation is a loss of the fear of death,
because they no longer must fear accounting for their sins to a righ-
teous God.

Is it good to lose one's natural fear of death? I'll leave that to you.
But a loss of the fear of death may well result in a loss of a proper sense
of awe before God, which Scripture identifies as "the beginning of
wisdom."

4. Death Education could become excellent training for euthanasia.

In Dr. Francis Schaeffer's great books that expose the dangers of
humanism, he declares that abortion is only the tip of the humanistic
iceberg.[15] Once that becomes commonplace (and after 10 million abortions, it is now gruesomely common), they plan to advocate infanticide
(killing babies born physically or mentally impaired), and then euthanasia.

Euthanasia primarily involves the killing off of the elderly who no longer can experience "a life worth living." Who makes that decision? The loved ones at first, but when mercy killing is socially acceptable, the state will make that decision. The state? Yes, the humanistic bureaucrats who run the state. Sound frightening? It should.

"But that's preposterous," you say? Consider these stories taken from death-education materials.

MILLION-DOLLAR STORY

You and I are alone in this room. Sitting on the desk before me is one million dollars in American currency. The bills are not numbered . . . nor does anyone have the serial numbers. I am going to ask you to perform an act. If you are willing, the money will all be yours—tax free. No one will ever know of this. I will never see you again, nor will I ask for further favors. The only thing you must do to earn this money is to push a button on the desk.

If you push the button what will happen? At this moment in Brazil there is an Indian who is a member of a tribe who still exists in a Stone Age culture. He is 29 years old. Life expectancy in his tribe is 30 years. He has been abandoned by his tribe since a large part of his body is an open cancerous sore in the terminal stages. He has about 2 weeks to live. His pain is unbearable and he has no access to pain killers. He will not be discovered by others until he is dead. If you push the button, he will be released from his pain since there is a charge of dynamite beneath him that will be discharged when the button is pushed. What is your decision?[16]

The game below has been denounced before the Congress of the United States, yet it continues to be played across America:

FALL-OUT-SHELTER GAME

The class is divided into "committees" and told that an atomic attack is about to occur. Citizens congregate at a bomb shelter. There are 10 people trying to get in the shelter, but it will only accommodate 6. "Your committee should select 6 of 10 possibilities."

Among those described is a pregnant teenager, a female doctor who has had a hysterectomy, a 75-yr.-old man, a retired prostitute, 20-yr.-old black militant with no particular skills, 45-yr.-old creative male violinist who's suspected of being homosexual, expoliceman thrown off force for brutality, an architect 37 yrs. old who is an ex-con convicted of pushing narcotics, 25-yr.-old law student who won't go without his wife—wife has a fatal disease and won't go without her husband.[17]

A book of essays on population, entitled *Population & Survival,* includes this essay, entitled: "An International Morality Lottery."

INTERNATIONAL LOTTERY

The author suggests creation of an extermination lottery. Each "Earth Inhabitant" from 30 to 40 would be in the lottery pool, and each year five percent of the people in the pool would be exterminated. One selected for extermination could evade his fate by substituting one of his children for himself. This would actually be encouraged because it would terminate a life BEFORE IT COULD REPRODUCE. The lottery agency would be staffed by nothing less than "the highest dignitaries in church and government.[18]

What church and government could possibly be staffing such a lottery agency? The Unitarian or liberal church and their fellow humanists in government, of course. When that day comes, this will no longer be America!

What They Are Really After

An eighth grader in the Peoria public schools, after a tour of a local mortuary, asked his teacher, "Why did we go there? That place gives me the creeps!" The answer he received gives insight that I have long suspected but was reluctant to put into print. "By seeing how really peaceful people are in death, you will realize that euthanasia isn't so bad after all." That is one of the most frightening admissions I have ever heard a humanist make.

Euthanasia is the officially approved plan of the humanists to remove from the earth all those "whose life is not really worth living." Propagators of euthanasia start by "educating" 43 million future voters that under certain circumstances "mercy killings are beneficial." When a teenager sees a dead person laid out at the local mortuary, lying peaceful in death, it is easier for him to conclude someday that grandma would be better off if they put her to sleep—mercifully, of course. The fact that many elderly grandparents have lived through illnesses, regained their health, and enjoyed one more decade of life is not evaluated by these humanist messiahs.

Once euthanasia has become an accepted norm, the next step will be to rid society of the "undesirables." This would include the helpless, mental incompetents, and those who oppose "progress"—like Christians and other traditional moral activists who do not approve of homosexuality and radical feminism or do not agree with antimoral humanists.

Impossible? Not at all. If the humanists rise to power in education, government, and the media during the next twenty years as they have in the past two decades, they will succeed in making America a humanist nation by the year 2000. And be sure of this: euthanasia is an official part of the humanist plan for America's future.

"That's Scary!"

"Sure it's scary," I told a minister when he heard me speak on this subject. But we have a precedent in recent history with which to demonstrate the viciousness of the humanist mind. Dr. Francis Schaeffer, hardly an extremist, notes in his classic book *Whatever Happened to the Human Race?* that the humanists of Germany were active promoters of euthanasia *before* they started killing the 6 million Jews.

Recent history has something to teach us about where we are. We think historians are becoming aware that a great number of the abnormal behavior patterns of man were concentrated in the Nazi experience. Richard L. Rubenstein, in his book *The Cunning of History: Mass Death and the American Future,* speaks of the Holocaust in this way: "The destruction process required the cooperation of every sector of German society. The bureaucrats drew the definitions and decrees, the churches gave evidence of Aryan descent, the postal authorities carried the messages of definition, expropriation, denaturalization and deportation. A place [of execution was] made available to the Gestapo and the SS by the Wehrmacht. To repeat, the operation required and received the participation of every major social and political and religious institution of the German Reich."

The important thing to remember is that the medical profession took a leading part in the planning of abortion and euthanasia. It seems likely that had it not been for the example and active role played by German physicians in the practice of euthanasia, Hitler's progress in the extermination programs would have been slowed if not stopped. The medical profession went along with Nazism in discouragingly large numbers. More than a few participated in the terror, genocide, extermination programs, and active and barbaric experimentation on the unfortunate minorities in the Nazi grip.[19]

Dr. Schaeffer adds that in the mid-forties a Boston psychiatrist, Leo Alexander, "was consultant to the Secretary of War and on duty with the office of Chief of Counsel for War Crimes in Nuremberg." In a paper entitled "Medical Science Under Dictatorship," he noted that the philosophical core of Nazi totalitarianism was Hegelian "rational utility," which supplanted all moral and religious values.[20]

> Medical science in Nazi Germany collaborated with this Hegelian trend particularly in the following enterprises: the mass extermination of the chronically sick in the interest of saving "useless" expenses to the community as a whole; the mass extermination of those considered socially disturbing or racially and ideologically unwanted; the individual, inconspicuous extermination of those considered disloyal within the ruling group; and the ruthless use of "human experimental material" for medico-military research....
>
> It started with the acceptance of the attitude basic in the euthanasia movement, that there is such a thing as life not worthy to be lived....[21]

The initial directive for euthanasia came from Hitler on 1 September 1939.

> All state institutions were required to report on patients who had been ill for five years or more or who were unable to work, by filling out questionnaires giving name, race, marital status, nationality, next of kin, whether regularly visited and by whom, who bore the financial responsibility and so forth. The decision regarding which patients should be killed was made entirely on the basis of this brief information by expert consultants, most of whom were professors of psychiatry in the key universities. These consultants never saw the patients themselves.[22]

It is only a step from acceptance of euthanasia to government control of euthanasia. Dr. Schaeffer is suggesting a frightening concept.

The day may come when a doctor or orderly comes to an elderly patient with the offer of a pill, and the senior citizen will not know
whether it is a death pill or a life pill. When one cannot trust the man
or woman in the long white coat, whom can he trust?

Dr. Schaeffer found disturbing evidence for his suspicions in the
media.

> The Associated Press reports: DEBATE RAGES IN ENGLAND OVER
> "DEATH PILL FOR AGED." A British doctor, John Goundry, says that a
> "death pill" will be available and perhaps obligatory by the end of the
> century. He says that doctors should be able to give a "demise pill" to
> old people if they ask for it. He also says, "In the end I can see the
> state taking over and insisting on euthanasia."[23]

He adds:

> Swedish public-health physician Ragnar Toss wants to open a sui-
> cide clinic for the more than two thousand Swedes who kill themselves
> each year—"not to treat them but to help them do it." Dr. Toss, writ-
> ing in the respected Swedish Medical Journal of August 1977, says that
> this suggestion is related to the choice that women now have about
> abortions.
>   So you see, this is not just theory for the future. As people are con-
> fronted with the flow of ideas from arbitrary abortion to infanticide to
> euthanasia, "death by someone's choice" becomes increasingly think-
> able. The case of a woman in Great Britain is an illustration of the
> drift to the thinkableness of abortion/infanticide/euthanasia—all part
> of the natural trend toward the loss of humanness. . . . [She] urged her
> mother in a nursing home to take an overdose of sleeping pills that she
> had brought her. The mother, showing attitudes rooted in Christian-
> ity, resisted: "A dog hasn't got a soul. I'm so afraid of being punished
> after. It's a mortal sin." The daughter gave the answer which the ero-
> sion of the Christian base and the consequent loss of humanness
> would naturally produce: "People are doing it left, right and center.
> It's not a sin anymore—it's nothing nowadays."
>   Of course, if a human being is not made in the image of God, why
> shouldn't the malformed young and the elderly be put out of the way
> for the good of society—once society and the courts separate life and
> personhood? "Right" or "wrong" is then only a matter of what the
> majority thinks at that given moment, or what the courts judge is for
> the benefit of society at that moment. The next turn of the screw
> comes quickly, when a noble-sounding phrase like "the good of so-

ciety" is replaced by cold, hard economics. . . . [This woman's] case is apt in this regard. She was in debt and, had her attempt at euthanasia been successful, would have inherited a considerable sum from her mother's will.

According to a new report, the doctor in England who advocated the "death pill"—and said that he could see the state's insisting on euthanasia—also built his argument on economics. "[Dr. John] Goundry said hundreds of British hospitals have been taken over to house the aged sick and that hotels once serving the rich now house the old. The economics are devastating."[24]

American Versus German Humanists

Most Americans will protest, "But our people would never stoop to such atrocities. We could never become so heartless." Are you sure? Germans did not murder their elderly, the impaired, infants, and their undesirable countrymen because they were Germans, but because they were *humanists*. Some American humanists are fully capable of the same actions. Already over 10 million unborn children have been murdered in the name of abortion, thanks to humanistic thinkers on the Supreme Court. We are less than two decades away from infanticide and euthanasia, if we allow humanists to remain in control of our country.

It will take a generation of electing the right people—politicians who understand the dangers of humanism—to school boards, city councils, state assemblies, Congress, and the presidency in order to stop the humanists from their scheduled takeover of our country. The next two elections may well be the most important in our history!

15

Global Education

At least 90 percent of America's parents and taxpayers expect our nation's schools to teach our children to be patriotic, loyal citizens and to inform our future voters that the free-enterprise system has produced the highest standard of living for the largest number of people in the world.

Nothing could be further from reality! Our humanist educrats, as committed international socialists, consistently brainwash our youth with the virtues of international socialism. Textbooks throughout the grades regularly implant the notion that capitalism is evil and government control or government ownership of industry is good.

Most parents have heard about the controversial social-studies text that spent six pages on Marilyn Monroe but only a scant paragraph on the father of our country, George Washington. A national outcry has eliminated that particular text from many of our schools, but the same educrats who authorized its use in the first place are still running the system.

In 1943 I was a student at Northwest High School in Detroit. During a free discussion in civics class I observed, "We are making a mistake to trust Russia as an ally. Communism will one day turn on us because it opposes everything America stands for." My teacher became enraged and threatened me with expulsion from the class if I ever again made such a statement.

In 1944 I entered the air force. When World War II had ground to a halt in Europe (1945), I was stationed in Germany, where we had to dynamite stockpiled P–51s, P–38s and P–47s so that our "ally," Russia, who was threatening to push on into Western Europe, would not capture and use them against us.

Postwar political and educational leaders began to suggest, however subtly at first, that American nationalism must be sacrificed to international unity. Myron C. Fagan, researcher and freedom advocate, gives insight regarding one crucial event in 1946.

> In his initial address before the first meeting of the United States National Commission of UNESCO, then Assistant Secretary of State Benton said:
> "We are at the beginning of a long process of breaking down the walls of national sovereignty. UNESCO must be the pioneer. The Department of State has fathered this national commission. Now you give it, for the first time, a collective brain to the whole nervous system of American science, culture, education and means of communication."[1]

In 1947 Dr. William G. Carr, then associate secretary of the Education Policies Commission of the National Education Association, delivered what the *NEA Journal* called a "magnificent address at the Cincinnati meeting." Excerpts from that speech will reveal just how long ago the one-world humanist educrats had recognized the power of the public school as a vehicle of indoctrination:

> The NEA sponsored a world conference of the teaching profession at Endicott, New York, in August 1946. With official representatives of national teachers associations from 28 nations present, that conference exceeded our brightest hopes for attendance and productivity. It drafted a Constitution for a World Organization of the Teaching Profession. That Constitution has already been formally approved by 14 of the national teachers associations. Its first regular meeting will be held in Glasgow [August 1947].
> This whole development would have been impossible without the NEA and the War and Peace Fund. Many individual teachers, educational groups, local education associations, and the really magnificent and generous help of some of the state associations have brought us to this point. This organization should become a mighty force in aiding UNESCO and in working with teachers in every part of the world for peace and mutual assistance.[2]

Dr. Carr had earlier stated:

> You were there by proxy when Unesco was established to give effect to those provisions. The Unesco program as developed in Paris last

November, includes many projects advocated by the representatives of the National Education Association. We urged particularly that Unesco emphasize the improvement of teaching international understanding, with full and adequate attention to the methods and problems of teachers at the elementary and secondary levels. Accepted without great enthusiasm at first, that idea is now being put into effect through the Unesco teachers seminar in Paris.[3]

This plea for "international understanding" may seem harmless on the surface, but as a patriotic American taxpayer, keep in mind that Alger Hiss, a convicted Communist spy, was the man most responsible for the charter of the United Nations and the institution of its educational department called UNESCO. He also selected most of the leaders back in those formative days of 1945–1950.

Dr. Carr described the plan in 1947. "During the past year, your NEA Committee on International Relations has been preparing, with the cooperation of two NEA departments, a detailed program for the teaching of international understanding."[4] He added:

As you teach about the United Nations, lay the ground for a stronger United Nations by developing in your students a sense of world community. The United Nations should be transformed into a limited world government. The psychological foundations for wider loyalties must be laid. Encourage, therefore, all kinds of international contacts, however slight, as long as they are cooperative and constructive. Teach about the various proposals that have been made for strengthening the United Nations and the establishment of world law. Teach those attitudes which will result ultimately in the creation of a world citizenship and world government.

Please note that I am *not* suggesting a campaign of schoolroom propaganda for some one particular plan of world government. I am suggesting the development of the attitudes, information, and ability which alone can make world citizenship possible. I am suggesting a careful study of textbooks and curriculums to eliminate the content which fosters prejudice [like nationalism and patriotism?].[5]

He was not naive as to the power of the professionals to whom he spoke, for he stated:

Our calling, too, has its special mission in the long-range strategy and day-by-day tactics of waging the peace. The teaching profession prepares the leaders of the future. The statesmen, the industrialists, the engineers, the lawyers, the newspapermen, the broadcasters, and all the leaders of tomorrow are in school today. Equally important, education prepares the common man to cope with uncommon problems as he seeks to maintain a peaceful world. The other parts of the armies that wage peace depend on us for the services of recruitment.[6]

These one-world educators are not confused about why they are here and what they are doing.

We cannot directly teach loyalty to a society that does not yet exist, but we can and should teach those skills and attitudes which will help to create a society in which world citizenship will be possible.[7]

Does it seem strange to you that thousands of young men have refused to register for the draft? And how do you respond to the "spontaneous" demonstrations against a strong national defense or anything that promotes American patriotism—demonstrations made up largely of the young, with a few older radicals, many from the teaching profession? None of this should surprise you. Educrats recognized over thirty-five years ago that the schools were the place to change the attitude of the next generation.

Does it seem peculiar that the higher up a person goes in education or the closer he is in age to the classroom, the more "international" his world view and the less likely he is to represent an America-first attitude? It shouldn't! We don't find carpenters, doctors, plumbers, and factory workers confused about Communist Russia's goals of world conquest—only our educrats. They have been brainwashed by the false humanistic notion that "man is basically good" for so long that they can actually turn their backs on the mass murder of over 35 million Russian people by their Communist dictators and gloss over the 67 million murders prescribed by Communist leaders in China. They ignore Castro's atrocities just ninety miles off our shores and have the audacity to teach our children that the only hope for world peace is for us to merge with these countries in a one-world order. History and common sense warn most of our people that we cannot merge with Communist countries without becoming their slaves. Unfortunately, our liberal humanist educrats either cannot or refuse to comprehend that.

In passing, I would like to observe that in the election of 1980, ten liberal United States Senators who had voted away the national-defense posture we once possessed were removed from office by an informed electorate. Since then several have reverted to teaching on college or university campuses, and others serve as popular itinerant lecturers. Why are they so welcome in higher education? Because they espouse the same political ideology of global education taught in those schools. Fortunately, that ideology is not shared by the majority in this country. When it is, our freedom will be lost.

Barbara Morris provides additional history and insight with regard to global education:

> *The Social Studies Professional* of November, 1977 stated:
> "Among the priorities for American education announced by newly appointed U.S. Commissioner of Education, Ernest J. Boyer, is global education . . . he immediately set up a U.S.O.E. Task Force on Global Education. . . ."
> The Task Force was to produce by June, 1978, recommendations on the aims, objectives and content of global education and the role of the federal government. The article also stated:
> ". . . global education as a priority . . . carries the personal endorsement of President Carter. Mr. Carter . . . is expected to make a significant move in the area of international education. . . ."
> President Carter has made many moves to advance globalism, but it has not only his endorsement but the benefit of federal funds. For instance, the federally funded National Endowment for the Humanities has awarded hundreds of thousands of dollars to the Center for Global Perspectives for the development of a program called *Global Perspectives: A Humanistic Influence on the Curriculum.*
> The grant proposal for this program, submitted to the National Endowment for funding declares that the program is based on the assumption that schools can "perform a corrective function" by ". . . helping students understand the changing world in which they will soon have citizenship responsibilities."[8]

Globalism in Our Textbooks

It would take an entire book to document the infiltration of globalism into our school textbooks. Such documentation is somewhat difficult in that, like values clarification, globalism is not confined to political science, social studies, or history. Instead, it is introduced wherever a globalist writer or teacher chooses to do so.

Mel and Norma Gabler have carefully researched the field, and here are some of their findings on this infusion of internationalism.

1. A 1979 Prentice-Hall textbook entitled *American Government: Comparing Political Experiences,* states, "The Future of Global Political Systems—You have seen how politics, economics, and the search for justice are all woven together in the fabric of global political systems. . . . Because of increased interdependence, some people predict one increasingly integrated system for global politics.

"A third alternative future would occur if the global political system moved in some entirely new direction, in other words if the entire global system changed. What if national and multinational corporations faded out of existence, to be replaced by one single international conglomerate? . . .

2. In *United States Government: The People Decide* (Science Research Associates, 1979) we read: "We now live in an age in which we must recognize that our interdependence extends beyond boundaries, from the local to the global community." (p. iii, lines 6–7)

3. *Introduction to the Behavioral Sciences* (Holt, Rinehart & Winston, 1969) states, "For these students, the problem is not political or social, but aesthetic; American society is ugly, trashy, cheap, and commercial; it is dehumanizing; its middle-class values are seen as arbitrary, materialistic, narrow, and hypocritical. . . ." (p. 159, par. 4)

4. In *Perspective in U.S. History* (Field Educational Publications) for high schools, the Gablers cite the following:

FREE ENTERPRISE ATTACKED

p. 518–19, ". . . challenged the belief that individual initiative, decentralized decision making, and free enterprise, backed at all points by the profit motive, constitute the best base on which to build a political and economic system that can provide a decent life for all its citizens."

PATRIOTISM DECRIED AS IMPERIALISM

p. 466, "Whenever possible, America aided revolution abroad and attempted to help rid the world of kings. . . ."

p. 492, 93, 94, 94, picture and caption on p. 249—The United States is branded as an imperialistic Nation while Russia which has taken over a tremendous amount of land and people is not called imperialistic. Why?

CAPITALISM MADE TO APPEAR EVIL

p. 519, col. 1, "Some critics argued that capitalism was evil because the vast wealth it produced was concentrated in the hands of a few." [This is not true of the free-enterprise system, which gives more people benefits than any other system—everyone has the opportunity to advance.]

ONE-WORLD SOCIALISTIC GOVERNMENT CONDONED

p. 34—Teacher's Manual, for discussion, "... One group, the United World Federalists, argues that young people should be educated to be 'world citizens' as one means of eliminating the narrowing and confining aims of intense nationalism. How do you react to this?" [Implies that nationalism, rather than international socialism, is to be feared.]

SOCIALISM LAUDED—GREAT AMERICANS BELITTLED

pp. 521, 23, "By 1936 the depression was seven years old, and conditions were steadily worsening. Only one bright spot stood out in the gloom. The collectivist economy of the Soviet Union ... stood without unemployment, unusual hunger, or sign of disease ... Is it any wonder that some ... joined the American Communist Party ...?"

(Chavey, Hughes)

Views of activists and pseudo-intellectuals who proclaimed atheism and communism (p. 574, 92) are lauded, while such men as Teddy Roosevelt, Booker T. Washington, and Douglas MacArthur have their faults magnified throughout the book. (p. 47, p. 566, p. 232)[9]

The preceding quote caught my eye because in 1977 my wife and I spent five days in Moscow. If ever socialism should have worked, Soviet Russia is the place. The Communists imposed socialism on their country in 1917; now, more than sixty years later, it is an abysmal failure. Even some of their satellites that do not practice total socialism are in better economic condition than Russia. It takes seven years' salary for the average Soviet worker to buy a car, and then it is so poorly made that he has no assurance it will last seven more years.

That is "a bright spot"? Only to a global educator who is so determined to teach his charges internationalism that he blinds himself to life in the real world. So again we must ask: are such people "qualified" to teach the children of the American people?

In reviewing history texts for the Texas State Textbook Committee, Norma Gabler pointed to a section on the Soviet Union which contained the following passage:

(From an interview with a woman taxi driver): "What baffles me," she continued, "is how you people over there put up with capitalism.

You're so progressive in other ways. You could overthrow it if you really tried. You just have to follow our example—no! You can do it a lot better than our example. And with all your wealth and learning—just think what a magnificent life you'll have."

"What's so wrong with capitalism?"

"What's wrong with capitalism? It's contrary to human nature, that's what's wrong with it. We know the West is rich, really rich. That you live far better than we, that everyone has a car. But I wouldn't swap for anything. Not so much because of the exploitation and lack of freedom and all that, but the feeling it gives you. You know the country doesn't belong to you. You exist to do the work of the capitalists. And besides, capitalism eats a person and cripples him psychologically. It's an evil thing."

"What is it that cripples people?" I asked.

"Private property. You know what private property means. It means jealousy and greed and hate. Your neighbor gets rich for no reason on dividends; you feel insulted and bitter. Is he better than you? Not a bit! Then why should he have more? Because he's crafty and cruel, or dishonest or lucky. You might work twice as hard and give society twice as much—and get a tenth in reward. Why? Because he or his father owns shares of stock. It's not decent or fair—not human. No thank you, that's not for me."[10]

The Fight for Freedom Goes On

Don Mantooth, editor of *The Mantooth Report,* uncovered the globalists' design in the state of Indiana. He wrote:

You will find this hard to believe! Indiana's Superintendent of Public Instruction, Dr. Harold Negley, a man elected, and reelected, by hard-working, patriotic, red-blooded Americans to this high state office, has quietly slipped in a program that threatens to eventually subvert all Indiana schools into centers for indoctrinating innocent Hoosier school kids into a belief in world government and "global citizenship"!

This is NOT to be an extra subject—but is to be a total, global approach to education and is to be integrated into all grade levels—and all subject matters.

Last September, workshops were held in 10 Indiana cities to acquaint teachers with the program. . . .

These workshops were conducted by Jane W. Lowrie, State Social Studies Consultant, working out of the department's Division of Curriculum. Lowrie was a co-director in developing the project and the teaching activities packet that was distributed to teachers.

While the teaching packet reveals a lot about the antinationalistic slant of the program, it is in the recommended bibliography and background reading that tells the whole story.

Teaching aids include materials from United Nation's organizations UNESCO, Foreign Policy Association, World Affairs Councils, Kettering Foundation, NEA, and all the many other traditional one-world promoting organizations that want to see America's nationalism and independence dead and buried.

These 10 Indiana school districts are to pilot the program and act as dissemination centers to infect neighboring school districts with the program.

The program is fueled by federal funds, of course—USOE Title VI–603–Citizens Education for Cultural Understanding.

To get a quick understanding of what's being planned, we have only to read "Schooling for a Global Age", a book edited by James M. Becker. He is director of the Mid-America Center for Global Perspectives in Education, housed at Indiana University in Bloomington, Indiana. Becker is lovingly referred to by the internationalist crowd as the "father of global education in the schools" [who believes that?]. . . .

Children are to become the first crop of 'planetary citizens'—they will be the collective of the 'world community', and their concern will be for 'human rights' and the 'injustices of the world' . . . they will work toward an 'equitable distribution of the wealth' and for the ending of private ownership of property, since, they have been told, it unfairly concentrates the wealth in the hands of a few . . . the principle cause of "social injustice". . . .

The whole plan behind "Global Perspectives in Education" of which Negley's "Indiana in the World" is a major part, is to turn all public schools into factories to assemble an entire generation of one-world socialist citizens under the central will of a world government body—such as the United Nations.[11]

I am not at all surprised that the originators of global education and many of its curriculum writers and advocates are secular humanists. They have duped some Christian teachers and no small number of patriotic Americans to promote it, but it is intrinsically humanistic, regardless of who teaches it.

One School-Board Member Fights Back

On 21 April 1980 the National School Boards Association held a convention in San Francisco. One of the school-board members who attended did not appreciate the one-world view it fostered, so he went home and wrote a critical appraisal of it. Somehow one of his copies was sent to me.

Speaking out against the session entitled "Global Education: How to Prepare Today's Kids for Tomorrow's World," taught by an advertising "expert," he wrote:

> We often wonder why school board members, administrators, and teachers tend to tune us out when we express concern about new curriculums being adopted in our public schools, curricula which we very definitely and quickly see as objectionable in our community; curriculums which we still have a right to be concerned about, since it is *our* children whose futures are at stake.
>
> If National Teachers and National Administrators Conventions are similar to the National School Boards Convention, especially pertaining to this particular session, the answer becomes obvious. [The expert] was a true professional in the application of values clarification, sensitivity training and group therapy. We, as members attending this session, were made to form "Magic Circles" where we learned that what we thought was right was actually wrong; we were fed information *only* which [the expert] deemed important; we even played "forced choice" games.
>
> I witnessed 250 school board members from the entire country leave the room believing that Global Education is the salvation of our country. . . .
>
> [The expert] did a masterful job of proving this at the meeting. The following quote was used by [him] to illustrate the need for "education for citizenship in an interdependent world." "The world we are living in is totally new. Since the world is totally new and since it has become so overnight, our ideas are obsolete or adolescent. In every aspect of our lives we are living without theory, or what is worse, we are living on the debris of outworn or disciplined theory. Our minds are like attics filled with abandoned and useless furniture. . . ."
>
> Although there was no question and answer time allotted during the session, after the session I asked [Mr. Expert] about the relationship of his program to that being promoted by The Aspen Institute for Humanistic Studies. He stated that many of the scholars presently working at the GPE. Inc. [Global Perspectives in Education] also wrote position papers for the Aspen Institute. He regarded them as the only great international thinkers of our time.
>
> A definition of Global Education was given during this session: "Global Education is preparing young people with the necessary

knowledge, attitudes and skills to be able to function effectively as responsible citizens in their own communities, the United States, and the evermore complex world that they must *interact* with."

It sounds great, but what is really the push behind Global Education? Who is really promoting Global Education?[12]

The school-board member was very informed about the Aspen Institute and went on to quote some interesting statements I had read in the January 1979 issue of the *Freeman Digest.* According to the Aspen Institute:

> Humanism is a supranatural, panhuman philosophy of universal relevance: It is the philosophic counterpart of world patriotism.
> —Education for citizenship in an interdependent world
> Earth to be managed by a consortium of the concerned.
> But the most important changes will be modification in attitudes which, in the nature of our pluralism, must first take place in the reasoning consciences of millions of individuals. The most important adjustment of all will be to blur, then erase, the psychic frontiers between "domestic affairs" and "international affairs."
> Global perspectives should be taught in elementary, secondary, and University school systems.
> The distinction between domestic and International is getting in the way of New World order.[13]

And that, mothers and fathers and fellow taxpayers, is what global education is really all about—the New World order!

The entire program prepares for the new world order of the humanist thinkers of the Aspen Institute and their fellow humanists in government, education, the media, and wherever Aspen has a sphere of influence needed by the humanists.

Does that sound familiar? It should—for two reasons.

(1) It reminds us of Plato's three classes of people:

a. The elite ruling class
b. The ever-present army
c. The masses

Whom do you think our humanist planners intend for the "elite ruling class"? Themselves, of course: they are the only ones "qualified."

(2) The New World order sounds like the book of Revelation and the religion of Antichrist. That will be the subject of another book in this series on secular humanism.

In the meantime, use whatever influence you have to stop this global brainwashing of the next generation's voters. Otherwise they may vote the humanist elite into the positions of power they crave, and you, as a nonhumanist, will be part of the controlled masses.

16

The Case for a Christian Education

As a young pastor of a Minneapolis suburban church thirty years ago, I was elected vice-president of the PTA in charge of programming. I have been a very interested observer of public education ever since.

The teacher-principal of that school and I worked closely together. She was a strong disciplinarian and a superb teacher. Her sixth-grade graduates were excellent readers and above average in academic achievement. Once each week she sent those students whose parents approved across the street to our church, where I taught their "release time" Bible class.

In spite of science texts being riddled with the study of evolution and some teachers who presented it as a "fact" (although thirty years later both the facts to prove it and the missing link are still missing), our children were not unduly hurt in their neighborhood public school. There was no explicit sex education, values clarification, drug education, death-and-dying course, socialism by the textbook load, or other direct attacks on our children's morals. Instead, character, self-discipline, consideration for learning, and good old hard work within the context of "the three Rs" were emphasized. Occasionally some humanist biology professor would attack the Christian faith with his "fact" of evolution, but our youth were not seriously influenced. In those days I was not interested in Christian schools.

All that has changed in just three decades. I am now convinced that most public schools are unfit to educate the children of Christian families. I know that is a controversial statement—and it was meant to be.

But I assure you, it was not said without careful and deliberate consideration.

For over twenty-five years I have been watching the California school system, in which every evil fad conjured up by the humanists has been instituted. When my daughter was in the ninth grade and my son was in the seventh, I began doing battle with the humanists in our local junior high. Many of the moral convictions and standards I taught my children were ridiculed, and they were subjected to humiliation and scorn by their peers. The vice-principal of that school, a committed humanist, determined to undermine the training of my children against my will. He seemed to delight in his daytime power over my treasured possessions.

After much prayer I called thirteen public-school teachers in the church for an informal meeting in our home. After I explained to them my concern that the battle for the minds of our young people was being lost on the junior-high through high-school level, they anonymously voted twelve to one in favor of our church sponsoring the first Christian high school in San Diego. An interesting sidelight of that memorable evening occurred ten years later. The one dissenter of that meeting came forward to admit, "I was the negative vote." Typical of a dedicated, conscientious teacher, she was trying diligently to salvage the sinking public school by serving as a quality teacher. Then she confessed, "I want you to know that I was wrong. This year I have begun teaching in our Christian school—and I love it!"

That year, 1965, our church started Christian High School of San Diego. Sixteen years later it is the largest Protestant Christian high school in the country. In 1970, together with Dr. Henry M. Morris and Dr. Arthur L. Peters, we founded Christian Heritage College, where Dr. Morris established the Institute for Creation Research. In 1974 the church bought a thirty-acre Catholic girls school and in 1978 a seventeen-acre military academy and started a second high school. During that time we established the Christian Unified School System of San Diego County. Today over 2,500 young people, kindergarten through college, are enjoying a Christian education.

My conviction in 1965 that the public school was unfit for educating the children of Christian families has only been confirmed with the passing of years and the deterioration of education in our country. Except for those rare communities (usually in rural areas or small cities) where Christian or aggressively traditional moralists control the school board or where a strong-willed superintendent or principal rejects the futile educational fads of the humanists, the schools are in a shambles. (Other exceptions include some of the basic schools or primary schools that deemphasize humanism and offer a return to quality education.)

Open classrooms, discovery learning, choose your own courses, schools without failure, ghetto English, and other humanist inventions have done to learning what explicit sex education had done to morality. It is time for Christians to wake up and face the fact that turning the innocent, impressionable minds of our children over to humanist educators is like subjecting them to the devil.

You have no more valuable possessions than your children! Their most important bodily organ is their mind. Why should Christians give them birth, feed, clothe, and house them, then turn their minds over to the enemies of the cause of Christ?

What Is the Beginning of Knowledge?

The fear of the Lord is the beginning of knowledge.

Proverbs 1:7

The reverential awe of the Lord is the beginning or foundation of wisdom. If the educational foundation is in error, the education itself will be in error. The only exception lies in areas like math, linguistics, meterology, and a few others where exacting material facts are required. But the more philosophical a course, the more vulnerable its conclusions to humanist error.

Why do you think all humanists with one accord vigorously oppose permitting little children to bow their heads and offer a voluntary prayer? How could an innocuous little prayer hurt anyone? It isn't the prayer they object to—it is the fact that the public schools would be acknowledging there is Someone up there to whom the children would be praying. Since these educational atheists control our schools, they will not permit it, unless forced by a constitutional amendment.

The following charts will illustrate the contrast between a purely secular education based on humanism and a Christian or traditionally moral education based on the Bible.

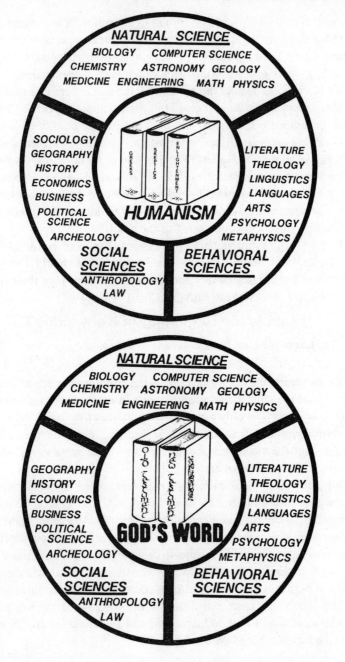

The three major divisions of education are basically the same for both humanists and Christians: natural science, social science, and humanities. But since the core is entirely different, the classroom teaching will be different. Humanists will approach these three divisions on the assumption that God does not exist; man is an evolved animal; there are no absolutes; man is autonomous, basically good, and self-reliant; and all citizens should be guaranteed economic success by government. A Christian teacher (unless brainwashed by humanist professors) will instruct from an entirely different set of assumptions—namely, God created man in His own image; man is morally responsible to and dependent on God, not his government, to provide for him; and the good life is found in serving God by helping his fellowman.

There is no possible way these two basic differences can be maintained without conflict. Humanistic theories are at war with Christian beliefs, and Christianity is at enmity with humanistic teachings (or should be). Unfortunately, some leaders of Christianity are still sound asleep because they do not realize the seriousness of the battle we are waging. Such individuals need to read Dr. Francis Schaeffer's three books—*How Should We Then Live? Whatever Happened to the Human Race?* (with C. Everett Koop) and *The Christian Manifesto*—as well as my two books on humanism, *The Battle for the Mind* and *The Battle for the Family.* Gradually our message is getting out, and thousands are awakening to the contrasting bases these two entirely opposite belief systems establish for education.

In the meantime, many of our Christian children are being destroyed in the classrooms of our public schools.

Humanist Course Emphasis

A humanist education not only contains instruction in the basic skills of learning, but demands a thorough indoctrination in humanistic theories, assumptions, presuppositions, and reasonings. That is as it should be. But I vehemently object when their religious interpretation of facts, life, science, history, and so on is paid for by taxes. If parents want a humanistic education for their children, that is their right. But they should pay for it in the same way we support our children's Christian education.

HUMANISTIC EDUCATION

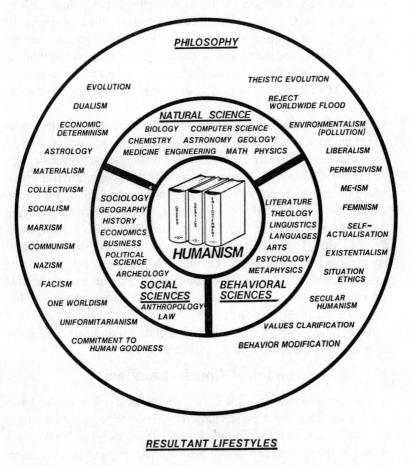

PHILOSOPHY

THEISTIC EVOLUTION

EVOLUTION

REJECT
WORLDWIDE FLOOD

DUALISM

ECONOMIC
DETERMINISM

ENVIRONMENTALISM
(POLLUTION)

ASTROLOGY

LIBERALISM

MATERIALISM

PERMISSIVISM

COLLECTIVISM

ME-ISM

SOCIALISM

FEMINISM

MARXISM

SELF-
ACTUALISATION

COMMUNISM

EXISTENTIALISM

NAZISM

SITUATION
ETHICS

FACISM

ONE WORLDISM

SECULAR
HUMANISM

UNIFORMITARIANISM

VALUES CLARIFICATION

COMMITMENT TO
HUMAN GOODNESS

BEHAVIOR MODIFICATION

NATURAL SCIENCE
BIOLOGY   COMPUTER SCIENCE
CHEMISTRY   ASTRONOMY GEOLOGY
MEDICINE ENGINEERING   MATH PHYSICS

SOCIOLOGY
GEOGRAPHY
HISTORY
ECONOMICS
BUSINESS
POLITICAL
SCIENCE
ARCHEOLOGY
**SOCIAL
SCIENCES**
ANTHROPOLOGY
LAW

GREEKS   SKEPTICS   ENLIGHTENMENT

HUMANISM

LITERATURE
THEOLOGY
LINGUISTICS
LANGUAGES
ARTS
PSYCHOLOGY
METAPHYSICS
**BEHAVIORAL
SCIENCES**

RESULTANT LIFESTYLES

Christian Education Course Emphasis

CHRISTIAN EDUCATION

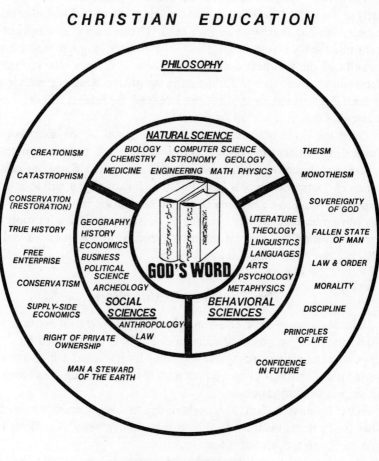

PHILOSOPHY

NATURAL SCIENCE
BIOLOGY   COMPUTER SCIENCE
CHEMISTRY   ASTRONOMY   GEOLOGY
MEDICINE   ENGINEERING   MATH   PHYSICS

CREATIONISM

CATASTROPHISM

CONSERVATION
(RESTORATION)

TRUE HISTORY

FREE
ENTERPRISE

CONSERVATISM

SUPPLY-SIDE
ECONOMICS

RIGHT OF PRIVATE
OWNERSHIP

MAN A STEWARD
OF THE EARTH

THEISM

MONOTHEISM

SOVEREIGNTY
OF GOD

FALLEN STATE
OF MAN

LAW & ORDER

MORALITY

DISCIPLINE

PRINCIPLES
OF LIFE

CONFIDENCE
IN FUTURE

GEOGRAPHY
HISTORY
ECONOMICS
BUSINESS
POLITICAL
SCIENCE
ARCHEOLOGY

GOD'S WORD

LITERATURE
THEOLOGY
LINGUISTICS
LANGUAGES
ARTS
PSYCHOLOGY
METAPHYSICS

SOCIAL
SCIENCES
ANTHROPOLOGY
LAW

BEHAVIORAL
SCIENCES

RESULTANT LIFESTYLES

A Christian education today usually spends more time on the basic skills of learning than does a humanistic education in our public schools. In addition it presents the facts of science, history, and so on, from a God-conscious base.

These two different kinds of education will be antithetical, particularly at the upper level of education. In first grade all children take beginning reading, but what do they read? The humanist, government-controlled schools rejected the McGuffy readers long ago and have substituted the mindless exercises of "Look, look, look—Jane, Jane, Jane—jump, jump, jump" for the more instructive "God is great, God is good." An examination of current look-and-say readers will demonstrate that it goes downhill from there.

Once the skills of reading, writing, math, and so on have been learned, the student in both kinds of education will be indoctrinated with the philosophy to which his school is committed. Since our government-controlled schools have rejected Christianity, a parent must expect his child to be exposed to purely humanistic instruction. Now do you understand why it is wrong to consider a public education a "free education"? It may be the most expensive involvement in your life, if it costs you your children.

The Results of Education

Education is not passive. If you believe that it is, you do not understand the affective power of education. Student rebels filmed on the evening news are just acting out what they have learned. Isn't it interesting that Christian colleges do not feature riots, building destruction, or violent demonstrations?

Why? Because students are taught differently. We instruct our youth that God commands them to submit to authority. Why? The Bible is our base, and that's what it teaches.

One's core beliefs will affect what he teaches or learns, and what he learns will influence his actions. Compare the next two diagrams, which produce totally different life-styles.

A Humanistic Education Causes
A Humanistic Life-style

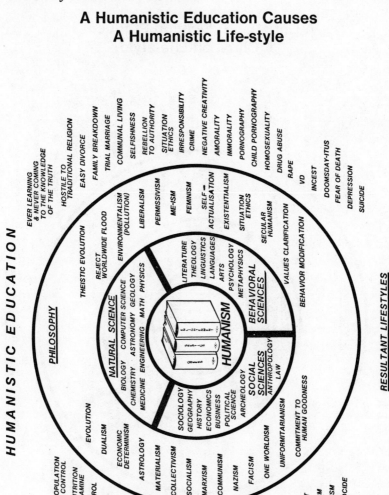

A Christian Education Produces
A Christian Life-style

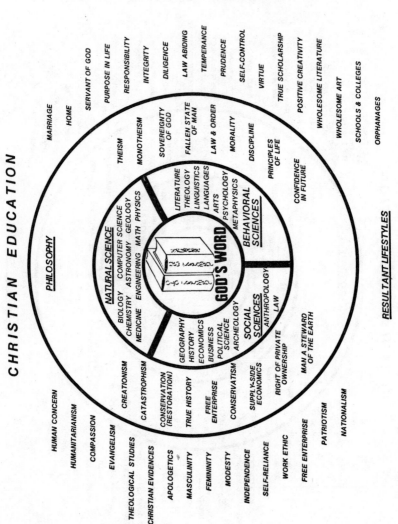

Now do you perceive why it is imperative to give children a Christian education from kindergarten through the university?

We cannot shield our children from evil. They see it on the street, on TV, in the neighborhood, and in the newspaper—almost everywhere. But should we immerse them in it from 8:00 A.M. to 3:00 P.M., 35 hours a week, at the most impressionable time of their lives?

Questions usually reveal the basic perceptiveness of people. When we inaugurated our high school, a mother inquired, "If I send my daughter to your school, will she get an accredited degree?" I countered, "With whom: God or man?" She eventually sent her daughter to the public school, where she became pregnant before graduation, married three months before the birth of her child, and divorced at nineteen. So much for her "accredited" high-school diploma. Ironically, our high school went on to become twice accredited, and the second time we received a six-year accreditation, the longest period conferred on a school. During the time our academic level has risen, the public-school level has decidedly tumbled. Don't say, "My school is different." Most Christian schools, large or small, offer a *better* education in the basics than can be found in the average humanistically controlled public school.

Admittedly, we don't teach horseback riding and basket weaving, and many Christian schools cannot develop a super sports program, but colleges all over America welcome Christian school graduates today. They know how to read, study, think, and work—abilities many humanist educators seem disinclined to stress. Our graduates do better on college entrance exams and, as noted in an earlier chapter, fewer of them have to take "bonehead" English.

If Christian schools are academically weak, why did the president of the San Diego Unified School District send his daughter to our Christian school? Or why during the accreditation process, when five educators thoroughly examined our school, did two of the three that were principals of large high schools confide to me, "I sent my daughter to a local Christian school"? Incidentally, both were from other cities.

We Christian educators cannot match the public school's facilities, money, or numbers of personnel, but they cannot equal us in two important areas. First, our teachers demonstrate an unusual sense of dedication. In fact, salaries are at times so low that they are forced to moonlight in order to maintain financial stability. But they *are* motivated. They see young people as the future leaders of tomorrow and prepare them to serve God. With that kind of motivation, it is no wonder we produce a superior education. Second, our students are free to learn. Young people enslaved by drugs, sex, booze, rock, and so on are not free to learn, for they are dominated by a mind-controlling obsession at the key time in their lives; since they do not know the truth as it is revealed in the Bible, they are not made free, for truth sets people free (John 8:32).

Christian parents often ask, "Shouldn't we send our children into public schools as witnesses, as missionaries to evangelize the lost?" If it weren't so tragic, that kind of reasoning would be humorous. Unfortunately, some ministers use that type of thinking as an excuse for not starting a Christian school, forgetting that they would never recommend a missionary to the church for support who didn't have at least four years of college, three years of seminary, and two years of internship. Only then is he qualified to penetrate some jungle and teach the gospel to natives who can't even read and write. Yet he wants to send fourteen- and fifteen-year-old children into the public zoo to do battle with the drug culture, anti-Christian humanistic professors who professionally destroy the faith of the young, and unbelievable peer pressure.

While some few young people can fight through such a conflicting educational program, most are scarred for life. During high school, they make some very important decisions.

The Five Major Decisions a Christian Makes

1. Where should I go to school after high school?
2. What shall be my vocation?
3. Whom shall I marry?
4. Where will I live?
5. Where will I go to church?

Most of these decisions are made between sixteen and twenty-four—the very years such a conflicting pattern of educational thought is freshest in a young person's mind. At that period in his life he needs

A Humanist Education for a Christian Is a Source of Conflict

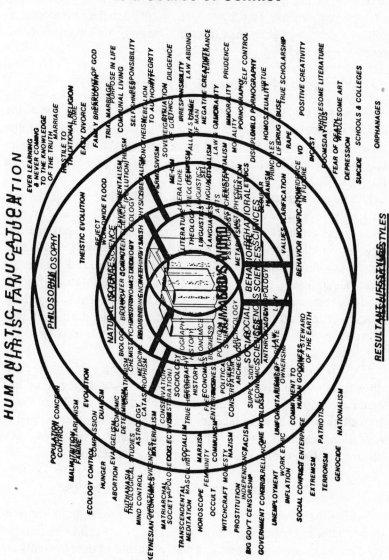

to be "of a sound mind," not confused by the subtle suggestions of humanistic thought. Admittedly, at thirty or so your son may get his head straightened out, five or ten years removed from the humanist-controlled classroom, but by then these five major commitments have already been made.

What Is a Christian Parent to Do?

Unless you live in one of those rare school districts that rejects the stifling domination of humanists, as a Christian parent you must first take your child out of the public school and send him to a Christian school. That may be impossible in your town, but seriously consider the possibility.

If there is a Christian school, get acquainted with it. If none is available, talk to your pastor. Every community can have a Christian school, and churches must accept their responsibility to start one. We have the buildings, the financial resources, the community respectability, the personnel, and, most of all, the mandate. Our Lord gave us the Great Commission, our divine mandate to educate (Matthew 28:20). God has commanded parents in both the Old Testament and the New Testament to train up their child. Christian parents during the past thirty years have seriously erred in remanding that instruction to the public school.

In the years to come, if Christian parents want their children to grow up with a love for God and develop a biblical world view, they had better recognize that our humanist-controlled schools will not do it. Instead, they will have to sacrifice tuition in order to assure a quality education (based on the Bible) for their children. But our young people are worth it, for they are the generation of tomorrow.

The Church and Christian Schools

During the seventies Christian schools have grown at an unprecedented rate, partly because Christians wanted their children protected from humanist indoctrination and partly because so many parents are concerned about low-quality education. If the current rate of four new schools a day continues, we will find 51 percent of our nation's children in Christian or private schools by 1990 or shortly thereafter. That schedule will, of course, be greatly accelerated if some form of tax credits can be approved by Congress during the next session.

Churches have been the principal sponsors of these schools because they view education as a part of their God-given mandate to teach. Our own church not only discerned the need, preschool through college, but also established a superintendent of Christian schools for our county. This man works with other churches and groups in an effort to assist them in starting schools, particularly in church facilities.

Some Christian schools use the ACE program of education out of Garland, Texas, pioneered by Dr. Donald Howard. ACE provides instruction, materials, and assistance for any church wishing to start a Christian school. Students are given cassettes, books, workbooks, and other superbly prepared materials, which, under the guidance of trained leaders, do an excellent job of teaching. We have enrolled many ACE graduates here at Christian Heritage College, and they do very well in our college, which maintains an above-average academic standard.

If you desire information about ACE, please write:

> Dr. Donald Howard
> ACE Headquarters
> P.O. Box 2205
> Garland, Texas   75041

Other schools, like Christian Unified Schools here in San Diego, are established on the conventional line of a master-teacher for each grade level. Again, leadership is the key, for we Christians have always placed such a premium on education and learning that most churches have enough qualified teachers within the congregation to establish a school. If not, certainly other churches can identify those who would be glad to leave the public schools in order to teach in a Christian environment. One year we received eighty-two applications for five teaching positions. There is usually no shortage of quality Christian teachers.

The primary educational problem is the scarcity of adequate Christian-school textbooks. Too many Christian schools have permitted humanism to slip into their classrooms through the use of secular textbooks, and not all teachers have been adequately informed to recognize it. Fortunately, a growing publishing program for the Christian-school market is producing thoroughly Christian materials. These would include:

Fleming H. Revell Company
Christian School Curriculum
184 Central Avenue
Old Tappan, NJ   07675

A Beka Books
5409 Rawson Lane
Box 18000
Pensacola, FL   32523

Mott Media
1000 E. Huron
P.O. Box 236
Milford, MI   48042

Christian Liberty Academy
203 E. McDonald Rd.
Prospect Heights, IL   60070

For further information about establishing a Christian school, write to Dr. Paul Kienel, of the Association of Christian Schools International, P.O. Box 4097, Whittier, California 90607. It is the largest Christian school association in the country, and they will be happy to assist you.

The Fight Ahead

Humanists don't give up easily, and the humanist educrats who have held a virtual stranglehold on public education for over fifty years certainly will not surrender without a fight. For example, right now they repeatedly refuse to permit public schools to close, even after enrollment drops so low that it is impossible to justify the tax money to keep them open. As they stir up parents and organize a so-called public outcry, the issue is never *quality education* but *jobs*. Whose job? Theirs, of course! When humanist educators stand in future unemployment lines, it may give them pause for thought to realize that they are the main reason for our child population dropping from 3.6 to 1.6 children per family during the past decade.

While humanists in education are fighting as if their religious domination of public education is at stake, their fellow humanists in the IRS are doing everything they can to help. Since 1979 the IRS has tried to lift the tax-deductible status of Christian schools if they did not establish racial quotas. Even as I write these lines, IRS agents are harassing Mississippi Christian schools over this very issue. One bizarre demand suggested that even the school board of the Christian school should reflect the racial balance of the community. How autocratic! In other words, big-brother humanist, not satisfied with his dictatorial powers in the public sector, demands the right to run even our Christian schools.

The hypocrisy in all this appears in the fact that many Communist and other liberal organizations enjoy a tax-deductible status. Are they expected to have racially balanced boards of directors? Of course not! Then why the double standard? Quite simply, to a humanist IRS agent, Christianity is more dangerous to America than Communism.

Most Christians today are not willing to permit people who think this way to be in charge of the education of their children. The Christian school provides them a welcome alternative.

The Future of Public Education (Or Is There Hope for the Public Schools?)

Everyone is interested in the future. Since education forms such an important part of American society, almost everyone is interested in the future of education—particularly the 98 percent of the population that does not work in education. Taxpayers are dissatisfied consumers who are registering serious concerns about the future of education in our country.

Is There Hope for Public Education?

Many taxpayers and concerned parents ask the reasonable question, "Is there hope for our public schools?" I would reply: not while the people who caused the problems are still in charge.

A normal person would logically conclude that the overlords of education should reevaluate their teaching techniques as they witness their students' tragic decline in reading ability, plunging SAT scores, and the increase in teenage pregnancy, VD, and teenage suicide. "Could it be," they should ask, "that we are doing something wrong?" Responsible educators have faced the fact that "progressive" or humanistic theories of education have gone awry, and they need to return to basics. To their credit, some have—experiencing a distinct improvement in discipline, learning, and achievement. But why have only a few districts responded to the wishes of more than 90 percent of our parents and returned to basic education?

You must understand that our public schools are not in their current sorry state, academically or morally, by accident! Humanist educrats have premeditatedly changed the intellectual philosophy of our schools from traditional morality to atheistic humanism. Since humanism destroys everything it touches, the present anti-intellectual and antimoral climate of our schools is the natural result.

The atheistic, amoral philosophies of John Dewey, George Counts, Horace Mann, Robert Owen, Jean Jacques Rousseau, Voltaire, and the Greek humanists before them has never produced a stable society *without totalitarianism!* In the name of "freedom, equality, and fraternity" their adherents eventually become subject to the iron grip of dictatorship. France and Russia are classic examples.

History shows that societies based on the philosophy of Moses, the prophets, Jesus Christ, and His apostles have enjoyed more freedom and prosperity for more people than any countries on record. America, Canada, and Great Britain before 1950 are prime examples.

Until the official philosophy of the public schools is changed, there is no hope of improving them. For the humanists who control the American schools from kindergarten through graduate school refuse to face the fact that their religious beliefs are destroying public education in our country. Since it is most difficult to remove these humanists from their present positions, the only way to improve public education is to cut off its unlimited access to money and find alternative sources of funding for our schools. Education is not the problem. Humanism is!

Four Necessary Changes

In order to salvage what is left of our once-great school system, four major transformations must take place.

1. The Religion of Secular Humanism Must Be Expelled From the Public Schools This anti-American and antifamily doctrine, which I have shown in these pages and in *Battle for the Mind* and *Battle for the Family* to be a religion, must be declared illegal and forbidden by the courts to be taught in our tax-supported schools. Surely, if Christianity is illegal to teach in school, the harmful ideology of humanism should be deemed equally illegal.

When one humanist educrat heard me say that, he asked, "If we stopped teaching humanism, what would we teach?" I responded, "How about reading, writing, math, geography, physics, and other subjects that provide a child with basic information and skills?"

2. Control of Public Education Must Be Taken From the Hands of Secular Humanists This will only occur when a sufficient number of parents and taxpayers recruit and campaign for informed antihumanists to run for the 16,160 school boards in America. It is too late to be passive about humanism! Until an educator recants his humanism, he is a liability on any school board. Once freed from humanistic members, school boards may proceed to replace brainwashed humanistic principals and superintendents with quality eductors accountable to the board for the educational level of their students.

Lack of accountability is one of the main reasons for the consistent deterioration of the educational level of our students. For example, school boards should require academic tests to be administered each September and again in June, so as to measure the progress students make each year. Teachers and principals could then be held accountable for an agreed-upon and reasonable improvement. The term *accountable* includes actions such as the cancellation of a teacher's contract, rejection of pay increases, or the demand that an instructor attend summer school in order to improve his teaching skills.

Dr. Max Rafferty, former superintendent of public instruction for the state of California, offered this suggestion in a tape-recorded speech in Washington, D.C.: "Give the top five percent of the districts' teachers who most increase the learning level of their students, according to their grade level, a thousand-dollar bonus for teaching next year." Where would the money come from? Dr. Rafferty replied, "Count the number of deputy superintendents, associate superintendents, assistant superintendents, administrative assistants, supervisors, and curriculum consultants—and fire them." Their $40,000 to $50,000 salaries would go a long way toward compensating the quality classroom teacher to whom it really belongs, for that is ultimately where teaching takes place.

Dr. Rafferty pointed out that even though he has been a public-school man all his life, he has noticed that private schools, lacking all the layers of administrative assistants demanded by the public schools, have a higher academic level and do a better job of teaching than the public schools.

Secretary of Education Terrel H. Bell, a professional educator throughout his vocational life and United States Commissioner of Education (1974–76), was interviewed recently by a national magazine. He offered several solutions for the problems of our public schools.

Q. Mr. Secretary, why is the quality of education so mediocre in many public schools?

A. Local school boards are mainly responsible. The quality of leadership on many city school boards has declined sharply in the last 10 years. There has been a loss of civic responsibility that used to characterize service on local boards.

A school board's first objective should be to set high standards of classroom accomplishment and to make those standards widely known. Too often, that is not being done. The second task is to see that the superintendents and principals and teachers strive to reach those goals. When school superintendents around the country try to implement higher academic standards, they are frequently undercut by school boards that are afraid to back up tougher policies.

That's why I zero in on the school board. It is the chief policymaking body in a school system. I don't think these boards are doing their duty in this country by setting less-than-rigorous standards. Parents and taxpayers have a right to know that students must attain a minimum-competency level, or they will not be able to progress from one grade to the next. If the school boards would set that kind of policy and require it of everyone, I think we'd start to solve this very complex problem.[1]

3. We Must Return Discipline, Authority and Respect to Public Schools The incredible violence in our schools today is a classic testimony to the total failure of the humanist brainchild called permissiveness. It originated in the humanistic mind of Rousseau, who conceived the notion that human nature really was good and if children were left alone, they would naturally choose what was best for themselves. It is incredible that this antibiblical concept came from a "brilliant mind," but far more incredible that gifted educators have adopted the idea. Today one rebellious child can disrupt the teaching environment for thirty others.

We need school boards that will crack down on permissive principals and superintendents. We must have legislators who will change our laws so that children and young people who do not want to learn or do not respect teachers or authorities are transferred to work farms or vocational-training schools or daytime work projects, where they can work off their excess energy until they learn to respect the privilege of an education or learn to work productively.

Parents need to be held accountable for their children's behavior in school. If a child is uncontrollably sassy in class, it should be the parent's job to shut his mouth—not the teacher's. He is there to teach. If the student destroys property or injures other children, the parent should be obliged to make restitution. As long as society accepts the responsibility to rebuild, repurchase, and repair, undisciplined students will keep on burning and destroying. They are going to learn something in school—either how to read and write or how to burn and destroy. In some schools rebellious students are doing a better job of teaching than are the teachers. Unfortunately they are teaching the wrong things.

Returning discipline, authority, and respect to the school is not the classroom teacher's job! The entire community must be engaged in the task. Parents must get involved in elections in order to change state and federal laws, and school-board members who are committed to demanding of their educators a proper learning environment must be elected.

Private schools do not permit these discipline problems and as a result are doing a better job of educating. A minority of students can learn on their own, but the majority need a disciplined and structured environment. Very little learning is accomplished in the absence of discipline.

In April of 1981, Dr. James S. Coleman of the University of Chicago released a survey that hit public educators like a bombshell. He had just studied 58,728 sophomores and seniors from 1,016 high schools. The 1.4 million private pupils notably outperformed the 13.5 million public schoolers.[2]

Historically, private schools have always produced on a higher academic level than public schools. It is therefore in our national interest to encourage them. Our nation's future in the fields of science, technology, space, and economics would be far more secure today if 50 percent of the past generation's youth had attended private rather than public schools. We certainly would not be lagging so far behind Russia, Germany, and Japan if they had.

Instead of looking on Christian and other private schools as a threat, causing them to become targets for persecution by the courts, the IRS, or accreditation boards, our government leaders ought to get off their backs and help them educate the future generation. Such schools are no threat to America, minorities, or the poor. The only people who have cause to fear the Christian schools are the secular humanists, because we refuse to teach their amoral religious doctrines. Interestingly enough, most of the Christian-school persecutors, harassers, and detractors are humanists. Frankly, I don't blame them. If I were a humanist, I would do everything I could to put Christian schools in a bad light. For they constitute a threat to the humanists' total domination of education. Remember, however, that the next time a humanist educrat or IRS bureaucrat or humanist journalist criticizes the Christian school, remember that he reflects two vested interests: his religion and his paycheck.

4. Public Education Needs to Be Made Competitive   If the American dream teaches anything, it is that a free generation thrives on competition. Removing competition from public education has produced a bureaucratic, featherbedding policy that has stifled our once-great school system's learning process. The fastest way to reverse a twenty-year academic decline is to make education competitive, which would instantly get the educrats within the system working for quality education as if their job depended on it—and it would.

Competition in education can be achieved quite simply. We have to get Congress to pass legislation offering parents or grandparents tuition tax credits for sending their children to the school of their choice. No strings attached!

Tuition tax credits may turn out to be the hottest political issue of the eighties. But nothing else would improve the quality of education in a shorter period of time. Suppose, for example, that a parent or grandparent (who may be better able to afford it) could take $1,200 off his income tax for each child whose tuition he paid—provided the child had attended the required number of days in a parent-selected school. He would merely have to show a copy of his cancelled tuition checks or a receipt when he sends in his federal taxes, just as he verifies his religious contributions or other deductions.

This would leave the decision of *where* to send a child to school up to the parent—not some federal or state bureaucrat in Washington, Sacramento, or Lansing. Instantly schools would have to offer the kind of education parents wanted for their children. If the parent is a humanist, fundamentalist, or Mormon, he can choose the kind of education he wishes for his child—just as he now selects his child's doctor, dentist, and minister. Education should be a parent-child responsibility, not a government-child decision.

Surveys indicate that 85 percent of the parents want their children to receive a basic-skills education. Within three years such schools would be flourishing in every neighborhood as a matter of survival.

Don't expect public educators—particularly humanist educrats—to embrace the principle of competition. It will probably strike cold, naked terror in them, but it would work. The incompetent, inept, and inefficient educator who cannot compete in the arena of quality education would go where he belongs—out of the education business.

We buy clothes, groceries, cars, and gasoline where we get the best prices and service. What is wrong with selecting our children's education on the same basis? At present the government autocratically makes all the choices for us. It chooses the school, creates the programs, taxes the constituency, and exercises complete control. Consequently unbelievable inefficiency and waste reign supreme. National statistics show that the average Christian school only costs one-half the dollar amount, per student, to educate as does the public school—and we are doing it better. Why? Because we have to please the consumer: the parent. Public educators are only obliged to please government bureaucrats who seem more interested in schools serving as humanist indoctrination centers than as educational institutions.

In the early days it might be necessary for the government to subsidize the schools by 50 percent of what they are now paying. The other

50 percent would come from the parents, who would be reimbursed by their tax deduction. After three to five years that subsidy could stop, and education would become competitive—and better.

The first result of competition would be efficiency. Payrolls would be cut; unnecessary employees, programs, policies, and courses would be expelled; and unbelievable waste would be eliminated. Our schools would feel the economic pinch and establish new standards of achievement.

Private schools would spring up wherever facilities could be secured, and a purpose for their existence could be justified. Parents and local communities would become more involved in education, and the American dream would again sparkle for every man's child.

What About the Poor?

The chief objection to tuition tax credits relates to the family that pays no income tax and has several children. Such a family could be given an education certificate for every school-age child, redeemable at the school of his choice. This is comparable to food stamps and welfare payments, which are supplied according to need and number. The school, whether public or private, would turn these in and be paid that amount by the government.

Some conservatives may protest that such a program would break the government, which could not afford all those children's education. Nonsense—we are already paying twice as much per child! These payments would come out of the 50 percent *cut* in government education grants. Within three years the other 50 percent would be eliminated, the government would save 50 percent of its present cost of education; and children, including the poor, would receive an education superior to what they are now getting.

The Miracle of Marva Collins

Marva Collins is a black schoolteacher in Chicago who would make both Booker T. Washington and Abraham Lincoln proud.

Five years ago, Marva Collins started the West Side Preparatory School in Chicago's inner-city West Garfield Park neighborhood. After visiting this school, Washington Post columnist William Raspberry reported that Mrs. Collins "has proved wrong all the public school teachers and principals who say poor black children in crowded city neighborhoods can't be expected to learn. Collins dismantled all the excuses for public school failures by taking in 18 children the Chicago public schools had discarded as being retarded, troublesome and truant and bringing them above national test standards in reading and math. And she did it with no public money."

Now, Marva Collins is famous. The television program "60 Minutes" devoted a segment to her story and soon actress Cicely Tyson will play Mrs. Collins in a television special. Her school is no longer on the top floor of her house, but has moved three blocks to an old office building on West Madison Street. The school has grown from one teacher and 18 students to six teachers and 200 children in grades kindergarten through sixth. The walls are covered with the papers of grade "A" students.

Teachers and school administrators from throughout the world have traveled to Chicago to visit Marva Collins' school. Mrs. Collins shakes her head. "It is as though I had some trick or instant soup," she says, "you know, you just add water and it's all there. They have even stolen the papers off the walls as if there were some secret in them. There's no secret to it. I believe in two-by-four teaching: the two covers of the book and the four walls. That and some strong legs to hold me up all day is all I need to stay right on top of these children. Common sense is rare. Men are always astounded by it."

In a seminar concerning "Black Education and the Inner City" sponsored by the Lincoln Institute for Research and Education in Chicago in April, Mrs. Collins told an enthusiastic audience: "The experts got us into this mess. Their answer to our problems has been to dump some more money on them. We say, 'You're going to learn or die.' And we haven't killed one child yet. If we don't make today different, these children will destroy tomorrow for all of us."[3]

Writing in the Chicago *Sun Times,* Marva Collins recalled the many contacts she received from people who wished to observe her teaching methods.

One will perhaps think that I should be proud of this; but, ironically, it makes me very sad. I have no cosmic fairy that waves a magic wand to produce instant results. But I ask readers to think of the stereotyped low achievers, and, of course the incorrigible children who traditionally sit in the back of the room being good only at disrupting the class. And then look at the children in my classes at Cabrini, sent there as problem children. Their faces are enough to make Fort Knox lack lustre. They sit there drinking in knowledge, their eyes holding wonder like a cup.[4]

In a *Human Events* interview she was asked the question:

> Q. Mrs. Collins, you were a teacher in the public schools of Chicago for 14 years. What is it that caused you to leave the public schools and form your own private school?
> A. Basically, I think children are being recruited for failure. I hear such negative attitudes about what children learn and how they learn. I have never been so depressed as when I talk to educators and hear all these negative excuses—the children are underprivileged, they don't get parent support, there's no incentive, they've got learning disabilities—I get really excited about what my staff and I are doing. We all have very positive attitudes, but everything out there is very, very negative. Of course, I don't think it's just public schools alone, it's private schools too and I think the mail I'm getting bears me out. Education is going through a bad period almost everyplace.[5]

Asked about John Dewey's philosophy, she replied, "Well, I'm afraid Dewey's philosophy of education simply does not teach a child to read or to compute or to think. . . ."[6]

Explaining her preference for phonetics as a reading instruction method, she stated:

> When teachers visit us they see a lot of phonetic methods. Children have to know the sound or sounds of each letter and then they have to know the sounds of combinations of letters. They have to recognize vowel patterns and know them cold.
> For instance, there are six ways to spell the "long" A sound in English: the A-silent "e" pattern, AI, AY, EI, EY, and EIGH and those are the only ways you spell that sound. And they need to know that you usually double the consonant after short vowels when you're adding a suffix. They need to learn these spelling rules so they are not always guessing. And that's the way spelling ought to be taught too, but instead the children are given a list of unrelated words to memorize each week and a day after the test they can't remember how to spell them. . . .
> People want to rhetorize and they want to be heard and to be pedantic, but the plain fact is nobody really wants to solve the problem because if they did, they would see to it that teachers were made to

learn phonics in college and told to teach reading that way once they got into teaching positions. To my knowledge there's not a teacher's college in the country that teaches phonics. If our teachers were trained this way, our reading problems could be reversed quickly.[7]

When questioned about goals as a teacher, she responded, ". . . to give those children a chance who might not ordinarily have the inalienable right: the right to an education. . . ."[8]

If Marva Collins can transform 200 "slow learners" into aggressive achievers, if our Christian schools in San Diego can produce 2,500 superior readers, and if thousands of Christian and private schools can give a quality education to millions of students all across this land *without* tuition tax credits, can you imagine what innovative educators could do with them? Currently parents of private-school children must pay twice for education—once (through our taxes) for the wasteful exercise in humanistic futility, as produced by our government-controlled public schools, and once to the private school to which they take their children. This is not merely taxation without representation, but double taxation.

Changing the public schools will not be easy. Our present state of disarray has resulted from 145 years of gradual decline as first the Unitarians and more recently the humanists have gained control of everything from teachers to textbooks. The last 30 years have featured the near-total domination by humanist change agents, more intent on propagating their humanistic religious doctrine than in educating the next generation of Americans. They call what they are doing educating; I call it brainwashing. When enough taxpayers awaken to the fact that they are using our money, but destroying our children, we will experience the kinds of changes education so desperately needs.

Once the turnaround is complete, the moral and intellectual climate of America will improve in less than one generation.

Conclusion

Of the seventeen books I have written, this has easily been the most frustrating because I have really only scratched the surface of our public-school problems. I encountered no difficulty in documenting the many indictments I have made of public education today: in fact there is so much more material available that I could write another book this same size on the subject. Space in this one book would not permit a review of such phenomena as psychodrama, role playing, drug education and abuse on campus, violence, rape, witchcraft and the occult, homosexuality, and other realistic problems parents do not expect their children to confront in our schools. I hope other writers will illuminate these facets of our contemporary educational scene, as well as the new and more dangerous trends that are certain to follow as long as humanists control this nearly 200-billion-dollar-a-year business.

In the meantime, instead of sitting idly by or waiting for others to act, you need to pursue four major courses of action.

1. Protect the minds of your children and those you love by giving them a Christian education.
2. Help elect school-board members who understand how dangerous humanism is. Encourage them to appoint district and school superintendents who will hold classroom teachers accountable to elevate their pupils to grade level in the basics. Consider running for the school board. It's people like you who can return the nation to moral sanity.
3. Help elect local, county, state, and national officers who will stop the misuse of our taxes that now subsidize the religion of humanism—the official doctrine of our public schools.

4. Work for tuition credits so parents can *choose* where they want to send their children to school.

Yes, it will take time, effort, and personal sacrifice, but if enough of us pitch in and use our sphere of influence, we *can* turn this country around. We *can* stop the humanist takeover of our country before the year 2000.

And our nation's 43 million public-school children are worth it!

Source Notes

Chapter 1

1. "School Spending Rises Despite Enrollment Skid," *San Diego Union* (6 September 1981).
2. "Signs of Hope for Our Schools," *U.S. News & World Report,* 91 (7 September 1981), 50.
3. Paul Copperman, *The Literacy Hoax* (New York: William Morrow, 1978), p. 24.
4. Gary Allen, "The Grave National Decline in Education," *American Opinion,* 22 (March 1979), 1, 2, 4.
5. "Signs of Hope for Our Schools," p. 50.
6. Copperman, *Literacy Hoax,* p. 32.
7. *Ibid.,* p. 40.
8. *Ibid.,* p. 41.
9. "Johnny Can't Count—The Dangers for U.S.," *U.S. News & World Report,* 92 (15 February 1982), 45.
10. *Ibid.*
11. *Ibid.*
12. Copperman, *Literacy Hoax,* pp. 47, 48.
13. *Ibid.,* p. 79.
14. *Ibid.,* p. 104.
15. "The Valedictorian," *Newsweek,* 88 (6 September 1976), 52.
16. *Ibid.*
17. Copperman, *Literacy Hoax,* p. 106.
18. Everett S. Ladd, Jr., and Seymour M. Lipset, "The Faculty Mood: Pessimism Is Predominant," *The Chronicle of Higher Education,* 15 (3 October 1977), 14.
19. Copperman, *Literacy Hoax,* p. 114.
20. *Ibid.,* p. 192.
21. "Help, Teacher Can't Teach," *Time,* 115 (16 June 1980), 55.

22. Edward B. Fiske, "Studies Indicate Drop in Teachers' Academic Quality," *San Diego Union* (30 September 1979), p. A-17.
23. "Help, Teacher Can't Teach," p. 58.
24. *Ibid.*

Chapter 2

1. Rudolph Flesch, *Why Johnny Still Can't Read* (New York: Harper & Row, 1981), p. 1.
2. *Ibid.*, p. 2.
3. A University of Chicago sociologist, James S. Coleman, provided a 58,000-student study, reported in *U.S. News & World Report* (20 April 1981).
4. Flesch, *Why Johnny Still Can't Read*, p. 71.
5. *Ibid.*, p. 28.
6. *Ibid.*, pp. 28, 29.
7. *Ibid.*, p. 31.
8. *Ibid.*, p. 39.
9. *Ibid.*, p. 19.
10. *Ibid.*, p. 23.
11. *Ibid.*
12. *Ibid.*, pp. 9, 10.

Chapter 3

1. Rudolph Flesch, *Why Johnny Still Can't Read* (New York: Harper & Row, 1981), p. 23.
2. Paul Copperman, *The Literacy Hoax* (New York: William Morrow, 1978), pp. 135, 136.
3. *Ibid.*, p. 136.

Chapter 4

1. "When Parents Ask: 'Who Needs School?' " *U.S. News & World Report*, 89 (22 September 1980), p. 47.
2. *Ibid.*
3. Christian Liberty Academy Satellite Schools, 203 E. McDonald Rd., Prospect Heights, IL 60070. Telephone: (312) 259-8739.
4. Raymond Moore, "Another Bulletin From Hewitt Research ... Home Grown Kids, a Synopsis" (Berrier Springs, Mich.: Hewitt Research Foundation, n.d.), pp. 1, 2.

Chapter 5

1. Samuel L. Blumenfeld, *Is Public Education Necessary* (Old Greenwich, Conn.: Devin Adair, 1981), p. 11.

2. *Ibid.*, pp. 19, 20.
3. *Ibid.*, p. 27.
4. *Ibid.*, p. 28.
5. *Ibid.*, p. 30.
6. *Ibid.*, pp. 95, 96.
7. *Ibid.*, p. 135.
8. *Ibid.*, p. 159.
9. *Ibid.*, p. 43.
10. *Ibid.*, p. 125.
11. *Ibid.*, p. 166.
12. *Ibid.*, p. 165.
13. *Ibid.*, p. 192, *italics added.*
14. *Ibid.*, p. 247.
15. *Ibid.*, pp. 248, 249.

Chapter 6

1. "Religion," *Webster's New World Dictionary,* 2nd college ed. (Cleveland: World Publishing Co., 1976).
2. Malcolm Lawrence, "Homogenized National Teaching Techniques," *The National Educator,* 8 (June 1976), p. 4.
3. "Buddha, Yes—Jesus, No," *The Barbara M. Morris Report* (September 1981), pp. 8, 9.
4. Mel Gabler, "Humanism" *Educational Research Analysts Handbook No. 1* (March 1981).
5. "Buddha, Yes—Jesus, No."
6. *Ibid.*, p. 58.
7. Paul Copperman, *The Literacy Hoax* (New York: William Morrow, 1978), p. 126.
8. Morris, "Buddha, Yes—Jesus, No," p. 57.
9. *Ibid.*, p. 61.
10. Bill Freeman, "How I Slid Into Education's Permissive Pit and Climbed Out Again," *Christianity Today,* 25 (10 April 1981), pp. 40–42.
11. *Humanist Manifestos I & II* (Buffalo, N.Y.: Prometheus Books, 1973), p. 15.
12. *Ibid.*, p. 13.
13. *Ibid.*, pp. 8–10.

Chapter 7

1. *Teenage Pregnancy: The Problem That Hasn't Gone Away* (New York: Allan Guttmacher Institute, 1981), p. 7.
2. Jacqueline Kasun, *Slaughter on Main Street* (Clovis, Cal.: Valley Christian University Press, n.d.), p. 3.

3. Barbara M. Morris, *Change Agents in the Schools* (Upland, Calif., 1979), pp. 145–147.
4. Sandy McKasson and Karen Davis, *Report on Sex Education Workshop: "Sex Education Teaching Methods in Junior and Senior High Classrooms,"* (Fort Worth: Christian Women's National Concerns, 1981), p. 1.
5. *Ibid.,* pp. 1, 2.
6. *Ibid.,* pp. 3, 4.
7. *Ibid.,* p. 4.
8. *Ibid.,* p. 6.

Chapter 8

1. National Education Association, leaflet no. 051–02066.
2. Dan Smoot, "SIECUS," *Dan Smoot Report,* 15 (17 March 1969), 41, 42.
3. Dan Smoot, "Contributing to the Delinquency of Minors," *Dan Smoot Report,* 15 (31 March 1969), 49.
4. *Ibid.,* pp. 49, 50.
5. *Ibid.,* p. 49.
6. John Kobler, "Sex Invades the Schoolhouse," *Saturday Evening Post,* 241 (29 June 1968), 27, 64.
7. Gary Allen, "Sex Study," *American Opinion,* 12 (March 1969), 3.
8. *Ibid.,* p. 5.
9. *Ibid.,* p. 4.
10. *Ibid.*
11. *Ibid.,* p. 18.
12. Dan Smoot, "The Lust for More in Sex Education," *Dan Smoot Report,* 15 (24 March 1969), 47.
13. Allen, "Sex Study" p. 4.
14. *Ibid.,* p. 3.
15. *Ibid.,* pp. 5, 6.
16. Tim LaHaye "A Christian View of Radical Sex Education," Family Life Seminars.
17. Allen, "Sex Study," p. 5.
18. Leonard Gross, "Sex Education Comes of Age," *Look,* 30 (8 March 1966), 21.
19. Gordon V. Drake, *Is the School House the Proper Place to Teach Raw Sex?* (Tulsa: Christian Crusade Publications, 1968), pp. 6–8.
20. *Ibid.,* pp. 8, 9.
21. John Steinbacher, "School and Family," *Anaheim Bulletin* (3 March 1969).
22. V. Meves, "Sol Gordon Comes to Wisconsin—Parents Object," *Wisconsin Report,* 6 (3 December 1981), 2, 8.
23. Smoot, "Contributing to the Delinquency of Minors," p. 51.

24. Suzanne B. Glasgow and Richard D. Glasgow, *An Expose on Planned Parenthood's Three-Lane Road to the Brave New World* (Altoona, Pa.: Human Life Education Fund, 1979), p. 1.

Chapter 9

1. "The Sex Education Scandal: What Are They Teaching Your Children?" *New Solidarity,* 11 (25 April 1980), p. 1.
2. Kitty Schmidt, "School Movie Leaves Nothing to Imagination," *National Educator,* 13 (June 1981), p. 12.
3. Spencer Rich, "Sexual Activity Up Sharply for Teen-Aged Girls," *The Washington Post* (17 October 1980), p. A1.
4. *Ibid.,* p. A28.
5. Max Rafferty, " 'Educators' Uphold Immorality," *Human Events* (15 March 1980), p. 9.
6. *Sex Education: the Assault on Christian Morals,* Special Report No. 6 of the Christian Defense League, Baton Rouge, La. (1979), p. 5.
7. Robert J. Braun, "Sex 'Book' Author Stirs Controversy with Position on State Board Panel," *Sunday Newark Star Ledger,* (11 May 1980), p. 1.
8. Douglas Kirby, Judith Alter, Peter Scales, *An Analysis of U.S. Sex Education Programs and Evaluation Methods.* (Bethesda, Md.: Mathtech, Inc., 1979).

Chapter 10

1. Barbara Morris, *Change Agents in the Schools* (Upland, Calif.: Barbara M. Morris Report, 1979), p. 144, *italics added.*
2. *The Wall Street Journal* (19 September 1967).
3. Gary Allen, "Problems, Propaganda, and Pornography," *American Opinion,* 12 (March 1969), 6.
4. *Western Voice,* vol. 34 (6 March 1969).
5. Allen, p. 12.
6. Dan Smoot, "The Lust for More in Sex Education," *Dan Smoot Report,* 15 (24 March 1969), 47.
7. Jo Hindman, "School House Pornography: Road to Pre-Marital Sex," *The Eagle* (Yakima, Washington), 27 February 1969.
8. Allen, "Problems, Propaganda, and Pornography," p. 12.
9. *Anaheim Bulletin* (3 March 1969).

Chapter 11

1. "Sex-ed: the Social Disease That Won't Go Away," *The Barbara M. Morris Report,* 8 (June 1981), p. 2.
2. " 'Super Gonorrhea' Strains Resist Antibiotics," *San Diego Union* (5 April 1980).

3. "Sex-ed: the Social Disease That Won't Go Away," p. 2.
4. *Ibid.,* pp. 2, 3.
5. " 'A Change of Direction,' " *Time,* 118 (9 Feburary 1981), 22.
6. "Departments of Labor, Health and Human Services, and Education, and Related Agencies Appropriations, 1981," *Congressional Record,* 126 (27 August 1980), H 7941.
7. "Black and White, Unwed All Over," *Time,* 118 (9 November 1981), 67.
8. *Ibid.*
9. Mel Gabler, "Sex Education" *Educational Research Analysts Handbook No. 3* (March 1981).
10. Eleanor Howe, "Even Teachers Turn Against Sex Instruction," *The National Educator* (13 September 1981), 1, 13.
11. "Michigan State Tells Sex Ed Teachers: 'Classes Will Not Lower VD, Illegitimacy,' " *Sex Education & Mental Health Report,* 10 (Winter 1980), 1.
12. "Sex Education Called a Charade," *San Diego Union* (27 April 1981), p. A–15.
13. Southwest Allen Update, "The Result of Sex Education Programs," *Family Review* (Spring 1981), pp. 18, 19.

Chapter 12

1. Peter L. Benson, "God Is Alive in the U.S. Congress, but Not Always Voting Against Civil Liberties and for Military Spending," *Psychology Today,* 15 (December 1981), 52.

Chapter 13

1. Mel Gabler, "Values Clarification," *Educational Research Analysts Handbook No. 2.* (March 1981).
2. Dr. O. M. Wellman, "Values Clarification," *Educational Research Analysts Handbook No. 2* (March 1981).
3. *Ibid.*
4. Gabler, "Values Clarification" (Originally published in Sidney B. Simon et al., *Values Clarification: A Handbook of Practical Strategies for Teachers and Students,* rev. ed. [New York: A & W Pubs., 1972, 1978]).
5. *Ibid.*
6. *Ibid.*
7. *Ibid.,* italics added.
8. Barbara Morris, *Change Agents in the Schools* (Upland, Calif.: Barbara M. Morris Report, 1979), p. 84.
9. *Ibid.,* pp 64–70.
10. "Psychologist Explains How Social Studies Books Attack Family," *Sex Education and Mental Health Report,* 10 (Winter 1980), 6.

11. "Baton Rouge Parents End Values Clarification," *Sex Education and Mental Health Report,* 10 (Winter 1980), 7.

12. "New York Parents Halt Values Clarification," *Sex Education and Mental Health,* 10 (Winter 1980), 2.

13. "Senator Hayakawa Says Schools Teaching 'Heresy,' " *Sex Education and Mental Health Report,* 10 (Winter 1980), 5.

14. "More Schools Dump Values Clarification," *Sex Education and Mental Health Report,* 10 (Winter 1980), 5.

15. "MACOS—Study in Adultery, Suicide, and Murder," *Sex Education and Mental Health Report,* 10 (Winter 1980), 10.

16. "Teacher Tells Why She Quit, Rather Than Teach MACOS," *Sex Education and Mental Health Report,* 10 (Winter 1980), 10.

17. Jo-Ann K. Abrigg, *Values Changing—Whose Values?* (Longview, Tex.: Educational Research Analysts, 1977), p. 7.

18. *Humanist Manifestos I & II* (Buffalo, N.Y.: Prometheus Books, 1973), pp. 9, 10.

19. *Ibid.,* pp. 15, 16.

Chapter 14

1. *Humanist Manifesto II* (Buffalo, N.Y.: Prometheus Books, 1973), pp. 16, 17, 19.

2. "Death Education—Emotional Manipulation," in Mel and Norma Gabler, *Death Education: Handbook No. 8* (Longview, Tex.: Educational Research Analysts, 1981), p. 2.

3. *Ibid.*

4. Casey Banas, "Dying Is No Longer Dead Subject in School Curriculums," in Gabler, p. 3.

5. *Ibid.*

6. Kris McGough, "Don't Make It Compulsory," in Gabler.

7. Dan Chiszar, "Field Trip Gives 6th–7th Graders Facts on Death," in Gabler.

8. Barbara Morris, *Change Agents in the Schools* (Upland, Calif.: Barbara M. Morris Report, 1969), p. 176.

9. Margaret Walker, "Death Education," in Gabler.

10. "Humanist Trend in Education Curriculum Dwelling on Death, Dying, Suicide & Choosing Who Lives or Dies," in Gabler.

11. Morris, *Change Agents,* p. 173.

12. *Ibid.,* p. 174.

13. *Ibid.,* pp. 168, 169, *italics added.*

14. *Ibid.,* pp. 172, 173.

15. Frances Schaeffer, *How Should We Then Live?* Frances Schaeffer and C. Everett Koop, *Whatever Happened to the Human Race?* Francis Schaeffer, *The Christian Manifesto.*

16. "Humanist Trend in Education Curriculum . . . ," in Gabler.
17. *Ibid.*
18. *Ibid.*
19. Francis A. Schaeffer and C. Everett Koop, *Whatever Happened to the Human Race?* (Old Tappan, N.J.: Fleming H. Revell Company, 1979), pp. 102, 103.
20. *Ibid.,* p. 103.
21. *Ibid.*
22. *Ibid.,* p. 107.
23. *Ibid.,* p. 100.
24. *Ibid.,* pp. 100, 101.

Chapter 15

1. Myron C. Fagan, *UNESCO: No. 1 Enemy of American Youth!* November-December, 1961 News-Bulletin, p. 15.
2. William G. Carr, "On the Waging of Peace," *NEA Journal,* 7 (October 1947), 497.
3. *Ibid.*
4. *Ibid.,* p. 495.
5. *Ibid.,* p. 496.
6. *Ibid.,* p. 495.
7. *Ibid.,* p. 497.
8. Barbara Morris, *Change Agents in the Schools* (Upland, Calif.: Barbara M. Morris Report, 1979), pp. 208, 209.
9. Mel Gabler, "Humanism" (Longview, Tex.: Educational Research Analysts).
10. James C. Hefley, *Are Textbooks Harming Your Children?* (Milford, Mich.: Mott Media, 1979), p. 205.
11. Dan Mantooth, "Defend Americanism: Stop Negley's 'World' Program!" *The Mantooth Report,* 3 (15 August 1981), 1, 2.
12. Donald M. Johnson, "A Critical Appraisal of: National School Boards Association Convention—San Francisco Civic Center . . . Monday, April 21, 1980," pp. 1, 2.
13. *Ibid.,* pp. 2, 3.

Chapter 17

1. "How to Improve Our Public Schools," *U.S. News & World Report,* 90 (8 June 1981), 61.
2. "Can Public Learn from Private?" *Time,* 117 (20 April 1981), 50.
3. "An Interview With Marva Collins," *Human Events,* 41 (12 September 1981), 12.

4. "All Good Things ...," *Let's Improve Today's Education* (September 1981), p. 685.
5. "An Interview With Marva Collins," p. 12.
6. *Ibid.*
7. *Ibid.,* pp. 12, 13.
8. "All Good Things," p. 685.

Bibliography

Barton, John, and Whitehead, John. *Schools on Fire.* Wheaton, Ill.: Tyndale House, 1980.

Blumenfeld, Samuel L. *Is Public Education Necessary?* Old Greenwich, Conn.: Devin Adair, 1981.

The Boston Women's Health Book Collective, Inc. *Our Bodies, Ourselves.* rev. 2nd ed. New York: Simon and Schuster, 1976.

Carle, Erica. *The Hate Factory.* Milwaukee: Erica Carle Foundation, 1974.

Chambers, Claire. *The Siecus Circle: A Humanist Revolution.* Belmont, Md.: Western Islands, 1977.

Conn, Harry. *Four Trojan Horses.* Nyack, N.Y.: Parson Publishing, 1978.

Copperman, Paul. *The Literacy Hoax.* New York: William Morrow, 1978.

Dobbert, John. *How To Improve Your Child's Education.* Eugene, Ore.: Harvest House, 1980.

Duncan, Homer. *Humanism in the Light of the Holy Scripture.* Lubbock, Tex.: Missionary Crusader, 1981.

Flesch, Rudolf. *Why Johnny Can't Read and What You Can Do About It.* New York: Harper & Row, 1966.

Flesch, Rudolf. *Why Johnny Still Can't Read: A New Look at the Scandal of Our Schools.* New York: Harper & Row, 1981.

Fortkamp, Frank E. *The Case Against Government Schools.* Westlake Village, Calif.: American Media, 1979.

Hall, Robert T., and Davis, John U. *Moral Education in Theory and Practice.* Buffalo: Prometheus Books, 1975.

Hefley, James C. *Are Textbooks Harming Your Children?* Milford, Mich.: Mott Media, 1979.

Hefley, James C. *Textbooks on Trial.* Wheaton, Ill.: Victor Books, 1977.

Herron, Orley. *Who Controls Your Child?* Nashville: Thomas Nelson, 1980.

Hill, Robert Allen. *Your Children: The Victims of Public Education.* Medford, Ore.: Omega Publications, 1978.

Hinmon, Nelson E. *Answer to Humanistic Psychology.* Eugene, Ore.: Harvest House, 1980.

Howard, Donald R. *Rebirth of Our Nation.* Lewisville, Texas: Accelerated Christian Education, 1979.

Johnson, Ronald E. *Hugs, Hurdles, and Happiness.* Lewisville, Texas: Accelerated Christian Education, 1976.

Kaub, Verne P. *Communist Socialist Propaganda in American Schools.* Pittsburgh: Pittsburgh Laymen's Commission of the American Council of Christian Churches, 1967.

Kienel, Paul, ed. *The Philosophy of Christian School Education.* Whittier, Calif.: Western Association of Christian Schools, 1977.

Lamont, Corliss, ed. *Dialogue on John Dewey.* New York: Horizon Press, 1959.

Lamont, Corliss. *The Philosophy of Humanism.* New York: Frederick Ungar, 1965.

LeBoutillier, John. *Harvard Hates America.* Chicago, Ill.: Regnery Gateway Inc., 1978.

Leonard, George B. *Education and Ecstasy.* New York: Dell, 1968.

Lockerbie, D. Bruce. *Who Educates Your Child?* Grand Rapids: Zondervan, 1981.

Marr, Ron. *Education Time Bomb.* Rochester: Family Freedom Foundation, n.d.

Marshner, Connaught Coyne. *Blackboard Tyranny.* New Rochelle, N.Y.: Arlington House, 1978.

Marx, Karl. *The Communist Manifesto.* Belmont, Mass.: American Opinion, 1974.

Moore, Raymond S., and Moore, Dorothy N. *Better Late Than Early: A New Approach to Your Child's Education.* New York: Reader's Digest Press, 1977.

Moore, Raymond S. and Moore, Dorothy N. *Home Grown Kids.* Waco, Tex.: Word Books, 1981.

Morris, Barbara M. *Change Agents in the School.* Upland, Calif.: Barbara M. Morris Report, 1979.

Morris, Barbara M. *Why Are You Losing Your Children?* Upland, Calif.: Barbara M. Morris Report, 1976.

Morris, Henry M. *Education for the Real World.* San Diego: Creation-Life Publishers, 1977.

Ravitch, Diane. *The Great School Wars.* New York: Basic Books, Inc., 1975.

Read, Donald A. and Simon, Sidney B., eds. *Humanistic Education Sourcebook.* Englewood Cliffs, N.J.: Prentice-Hall, 1975.

Roche, George Charles III. *Education in America.* Irving-on-Hudson, N.Y.: Foundation for Economic Education, Inc., 1977.

Root, Merrill E. *Brain Washing in the High Schools.* Old Greenwich, Conn.: Devin Adair, 1959.

Root, Merrill E. *Collectivism on the Campus.* Old Greenwich, Conn.: Devin Adair, 1956.

Rosenfeld, Jeffrey P. *Relationships: The Marriage and Family Reader.* Glenview, Ill.: Scott, Foresman and Co., 1981.

Rushdoony, Rousas John. *The Messianic Character of American Education.* Nutley, N.J.: Craig Press, 1979.

Rushdoony, Rousas John. *The Nature of the American System.* Fairfax, Va.: Thoburn Press, 1978.

Steinbacher, John. *Bitter Harvest.* Fullerton, Calif.: Educator Publications, 1970.

Stonehouse, Catherine M. *Patterns in Moral Development.* Waco, Tex.: Word Books, 1980.